puṣpikā

A puṣpikā ('little flower') is the scribes' way of marking the end of the main text and the beginning of the colophon. The present logo is an artistic impression by Shubhani Sarkar based on such a scribal flourish seen on a Nepalese manuscript.

Puṣpikā

Tracing Ancient India, through Texts and Traditions

Contributions to Current Research in Indology

Volume 5

Proceedings of the Seventh International Indology Graduate Research Symposium
(September 2017, Ghent)

Edited by

Heleen De Jonckheere
Marie-Hélène Gorisse
Agnieszka Rostalska

OXBOW | books
Oxford & Philadelphia

Published in the United Kingdom in 2020 by
OXBOW BOOKS
The Old Music Hall, 106–108 Cowley Road, Oxford OX4 1JE

and in the United States by
OXBOW BOOKS
1950 Lawrence Road, Havertown, PA 19083

Paperback Edition: ISBN 978-1-78925-282-8
Digital Edition: ISBN 978-1-78925-283-5 (epub)

A CIP record for this book is available from the British Library

Typeset in India for Casemate Publishing Services. www.casematepublishingservices.com

For a complete list of Oxbow titles, please contact:

UNITED KINGDOM
Oxbow Books
Telephone (01865) 241249
Email: oxbow@oxbowbooks.com
www.oxbowbooks.com

UNITED STATES OF AMERICA
Oxbow Books
Telephone (610) 853-9131, Fax (610) 853-9146
Email: queries@casemateacademic.com
www.casemateacademic.com/oxbow

Oxbow Books is part of the Casemate Group

Contents

Preface

Heleen De Jonckheere, Marie-Hélène Gorisse & Agnieszka Rostalska

This volume is the result of the ninth International Indological Graduate Research Symposium (IIGRS 9), held at the Department of Languages and Culture, Ghent University, on 22 and 23 September 2017. Like previous *Puṣpikā* volumes, it presents original research by young scholars working with primary sources written in South Asian languages: Sanskrit, Prakrit, Pali and various regional dialects, on topics related to linguistics, literatures and philosophies, as well as religious traditions, of South Asia.

The aim of IIGRS 9, and of this volume, is to shine a spotlight on Jainism, and three out of the nine articles are situated within Jaina studies. This choice was made so as to reflect the strong tradition of Jaina studies at Ghent University. Initiated by Jozef Deleu, who defended his doctoral thesis on Jaina narrative literature in 1957 and studied Jaina Prakrit literature with Walther Schubring and Ludwig Alsdorf, this tradition continued with Frank Van Den Bossche's research on Jaina metaphysics and Jaina Prakrit grammar. Today, Eva De Clercq has stimulated further research thanks to her own studies on Jaina epics and *Purāṇas* and by coordinating the South Asia Network Ghent (SANGH), a dynamic hub of Indological scholarship, with a particular focus on Jaina studies and on associated vernacular languages, that offers attractive opportunities to doctoral and postdoctoral scholars.

The articles in the present volume that express this focus on Jaina studies also show the diversity of textual research within this field. Chapter 2, Adrian Plau's investigation of a mid-17th-century Jaina version of the *Rāmayāṇa* encourages us to rethink not only what a Jaina *Rāmāyaṇa* or *Purāṇa* is, but also how to conceptualise *Rāmāyaṇas, Purāṇas* and narrative traditions in India in general. In Chapter 3, Heleen De Jonckheere takes another perspective on Jaina narratives in dialogue, when she assesses the representation of other traditions – here Buddhism – through her examination of the satirical genre of *Dharmaparīkṣā*. In Chapter 4, Samani Pratibha Pragya further examines the blurred line between scriptural study and spiritual practice, as she draws the history of the meditative practices developed by the Jain scholar monk Jayācārya (1803–81).

The IIGRS 9 not only welcomed promising scholars working on Jaina studies, but also on a diversity of Indological topics. In this volume, the study of Indian poetry is represented in Chapter 5, by Chiara Livio's paper, which analyses the *Śrīkaṇṭhacarita*, the deeds of Śrīkaṇṭha (Śiva), a poem in 25 cantos composed by Maṅkha in 12th-century Kashmir on the mythological episode of the destruction of Tripura. Livio demonstrates that the descriptions of the Himalayan mountain Kailāsa serve the purpose of characterising the ideal poet. Another aspect of ritual literature is explored in Chapter 6, Amandine Wattelier-Bricout's paper which, comparing several texts of the *Dharmanibandha* tradition, questions the history, specificities, outcomes and legacy of a particular ritual in which a tree can be adopted as a son. Next to these papers on literary traditions, primary sources of Indian grammar are scrutinised. In Chapter 7, Yuto Kawamura shows that the interpretation of compounds of the type x-*bhūta* developed by the grammarian Bhartṛhari implies a historical link between this type of compound and the Vedic *idáṃ bhū*-construction. In the following paper, Chapter 8, Yiming Shen explores the metalinguistic rules (*paribhāṣā*) of the Pāṇinian system that introduces augments, those meaningless sounds added to a stem or suffix in order to give an account to the construction of declined and conjugated forms from root forms. The interpretation of this widely commented metalinguistic rule is still problematic, and Shen contributes to our understanding of it by his investigation of Nīlakaṇṭha Dīkṣita's 17th-century *Paribhāṣāvṛtti*. The final paper of this volume, Chapter 9, by Karl-Stéphan Bouthillette, is a contribution to discussions on the dating and authorship of an important doxographic philosophical work, the *Sarva-siddhānta-saṅgraha*. It analyses the different layers of the text and assesses relevant features of the doxographic genre and of Śaṅkara's pedagogical strategies.

In order to frame this volume within the context of the location of IIGRS 9, the opening chapter by Winand M. Callewaert draws a picture of the Indological tradition in Belgium, proving it to be as internationally orientated, as flourishing and as full of promising Indological research as the IIGRS 9 itself.

Finally but not least, we wish to thank the FWO, Research Foundation – Flanders, for its steady financial support for both the organisation of the colloquium and the editing process of this volume.

Contributors

Winand Callewaert is an emeritus professor who teaches Sanskrit at the university of Leuven. He holds degrees from Ranchi University, the Sanskrit University of Benares, Pune University and KULeuven. He works on devotional literature.

Adrian Plau has just finished his doctoral work on Jain literature in Brajbhāṣā at SOAS, University of London. He currently leads a Wellcome Trust-funded research project on health, medicine and treatment in early modern North India based at the Wellcome Library.

Heleen De Jonckheere is a PhD candidate at the Department of Languages and Cultures of Ghent University in Belgium. Her research deals with Jain narratives, inter-religious, literary dialogues and practices of translation in medieval India focusing on the textual tradition of *Dharmaparīkṣā*.

Samani Pratibha Pragya is a scholar of Jain studies specialised on the Terāpanth lineage, to which she belongs as a Samani (saint). Her current research centres on the history and methods of modern Jain meditation and yoga. She is working as a Research Assistant at SOAS with Peter Flügel on his Jaina-Prosopography project.

Chiara Livio is currently a PhD student at Sapienza University of Rome, under the supervision of Prof. Raffaele Torella and Dr Daniele Cuneo. Her research interests include Classical Indian Poetry (*kāvya* and *mahākāvya*), *kāvya* commentaries, history and literature of medieval Kashmir and textual criticism.

Amandine Wattelier-Bricout is a PhD student at Sorbonne Nouvelle University (Paris III). Her research focuses on the representations of motherhood in the *Skandapurāṇa* in its different recensions and in relation to other period sources. She studies myths concerning maternity and seeks to establish the evolution of the ritual prescriptions for women as reflected in the *Skandapurāṇa* and period literature, notably through *Dharmanibandha* literature.

Yūto Kawamura is a JSPS overseas research fellow at the Faculty of Oriental Studies, University of Oxford. His current research centres on 1) Vedic (and therefore Indo-European) linguistics and mythology; 2) the traditional Sanskrit etymology and grammar (*nirvacana* and *vyākaraṇa*); and 3) the traditional Vedic hermeneutics (*mīmāṁsā*).

Yiming Shen is currently a doctoral student at the Faculty of Oriental Studies, University of Oxford. His main research interest is the Sanskrit grammatical tradition (*vyākaraṇa*).

Karl-Stéphan Bouthillette obtained his PhD in Indian Philosophies from the Institute for Indology and Tibetology of the Ludwig-Maximilians-Universität in Munich. He received his first master's degree in Sciences of Religions at Laval University in Quebec City, and his second master's degree in Sanskrit Studies at Jawaharlal Nehru University in Delhi. His current areas of research focus upon early developments in Indian philosophical doxography and the Indian formulation of an Intellectual approach to spirituality and contemplation.

Figure 1: Group Picture of the Ninth IIGRS at Ghent University 22–23 September 2017.

Indology Studies in Belgium

Armchair Scholars and Travellers[1]

Winand M. Callewaert

Indological studies – studies of mainly ancient Indian languages and texts – in Europe are a spin-off of imperial colonialism. The exploration and conquest of India brought about a growing fascination with the ancient history and very rich culture of the subcontinent. It was also soon evident that knowledge gave power, and this was definitely one of the reasons why the study of Sanskrit (and later of vernacular languages) became popular with the East India Company in London and India, and later on the European continent. Sanskrit also appeared to be the most ancient Indo-European language, used for the creation of an immense literature and 'spoken' by traditional *pandit*s even up to the present day.

The first European Indologists were missionaries who wanted to understand the ancient texts known only to Brahmins. They also wanted to become familiar with the vernacular languages in order to preach and convert. In 2010, in the library of an Italian monastery near Rome, Dr Toon Van Hal, a linguist at the Leuven University (now in charge of the Sanskrit course), discovered a manuscript thought to be lost, of a Sanskrit grammar: *Grammatica Grandonica*, written by the German Jesuit Johann Ernst Hanxleden (1681–1732).[2] This was not the very first Sanskrit grammar by a European. That honour goes to another Jesuit, Heinrich Roth (1620–68), but Hanxleden's grammar is the direct source of Paulinus a Sancto Bartholomaeo's own Sanskrit grammar, the first one to be printed in Europe, in 1790.

As the British East India Company consolidated its power in India – from around 1750 onwards – the need for 'Indologists' became very urgent. The Company agents not only wanted plenty of trade and a little culture, they also needed an insight into the jurisprudence and the political organisation of the (mainly Hindu) Mahārājā territories. To the East India Company, the Persian language of the Mogul empire in India was more easily accessible.

1 This article is a revised version of my article in Dutch (see Callewaert 2013). I thank my colleague Prof. Dr Christophe Vielle (UCLouvain, see p. 10), who gave me important information and valuable suggestions about Indology studies in the 19th and early 20th centuries.

2 See Van Hal and Vielle 2013.

Charles Wilkins (1749–1836), an agent of the Company in Calcutta, was the first Briton to study Sanskrit thoroughly. In 1785 he completed the first English translation of the *Bhagavadgītā*. This small gem of *c.* 200 BCE is now, after the Bible, the most translated text in religious literature of the world. The Sanskrit grammar of Wilkins, published in 1808, became the basis for all other grammars published by later Europeans. Indological research at that time was very much promoted by the *Asiatick Society*, founded in Calcutta by the British scholar William Jones (1746–94).

The French, too, had 'invaded' India, but lost their position as a result of the Seven Years' War in Europe (1756–63) and military defeats in India. They tried in vain to regain access under Napoleon, but their contribution to Indological studies should not be underestimated. Part of their colonial loot was a selection of manuscripts that found their way into the Bibliothèque nationale in Paris. Alexander Hamilton (1762–1824) had, in India, gained great proficiency in Sanskrit, and on his way back to England he wanted to consult these manuscripts in Paris. The French arrested him as a spy! His house arrest in Paris was a boon for later Sanskrit studies in Europe, because Hamilton became the guru of enthusiastic students from France and Germany. That was the end of the period when Europeans had access to ancient Indian texts and philosophy only through French or German translations of English translations – now the study of Sanskrit itself had begun.

This was the beginning of a glorious tradition that had its impact in Belgium, too. Sanskrit is taught in four universities today: UGent, ULiège, UCLouvain and KULeuven.[3] In this chapter I should like to introduce the most important Belgian Indologists, from the beginning in the 19th century. This is not an exhaustive survey, but an introduction to famous scholars and important areas of research, as well as some interesting trends.

The Pioneers

Eugène Jacquet (1811–38) from Brussels claimed he was the very first 'Belgian' Indologist; sadly, he died at the age of 27, after having spent all his life in Paris working at the Société Asiatique. In the obituary in the *Asiatic Journal* we read:

> [Jacquet] had made extraordinary advances in oriental learning. He had devoted himself especially to the study of Sanscrit and Chinese, and, young as he was, he could not only read the former [Sanskrit] with great ease, but had followed it into the languages derived from it.

3 'Louvain' is the French and English name for the city of Leuven, where in 1425 a university was established. In the bilingual context of Belgium, this university was in 1968 divided on a linguistic basis. Leuven (Louvain) remained the place of the Flemish/Dutch Katholieke Universiteit Leuven (KU-Leuven, with *c.* 50,000 students in 2016), while on a new campus ('Louvain-la-Neuve') 25 km to the south the French-speaking Université Catholique de Louvain (UCLouvain, with *c.* 30,000 students in 2016) was established.

In the field of Sanskrit palaeography 'he was supposed to know more than any other continental scholar'.[4]

Sanskrit was taught for the first time in a Belgian university in 1841, the University of Louvain, by Félix Nève, then 25 years old. Like several Sanskrit scholars after him, Nève was allowed to teach the language as an optional course, in addition to his regular classes of Latin and Greek. One year after his appointment as Professor of Sanskrit in Louvain, Nève published his first book, *Études sur les hymnes du Rig-Véda avec un choix d'hymnes traduits pour la première fois en français* (1842). In this study he thought he could discover traces of monotheism in pre-Vedic times. This ambition would remain in all his later research. The defence of his Christian faith was the foundation for Nève's Indological studies. He was convinced that an 'Eastern renaissance' could enrich European civilisation without harming Christianity. It must be noted that this was a common trend in Nève's days.

His second book was a state-of-the-art Indological product, published in Paris in 1847: *Essai sur le mythe des Ribhavas, premier vestige de l'apothéose dans le Véda, avec le texte sanscrit et la traduction française des hymnes adressés à ces divinités*, a text edition based on manuscripts found in France, Berlin and London, along with a French translation. Even Max Müller was impressed; he wrote that he did not know anyone who so successfully 'combined the French and the German spirit', whatever he may have meant by that. Later on, Nève published a dozen articles about Buddhism and two articles about the (mythological) flood. He claimed that the origin of the myth was to be found in the Bible, while others maintained that it originally developed from India. Nève's thesis illustrates the Christian attitude with which Indologists in his day conducted their research. Nève's career spanned 50 years. In 1877 he retired from his academic duties and died in Leuven in 1893.[5]

I should mention here that in 1845 Léopold van Alstein (1791–1862) was appointed to teach at Ghent University (UGent) and became the pioneer of Oriental studies there. He was 54 years of age then, and is in fact more remembered for his unique library than for his research. Born into an aristocratic family in Ghent, he did not need to take up paid employment and could devote his time and money to book collecting and the study of languages. He may have been a self-taught scholar, but he was highly esteemed by professionals and he corresponded with well-known Indologists and linguists of his time. He spent much time alone in his room and was extremely shy and modest, but very helpful to anyone who wanted access to his vast library. He had a personal supplier of books in Paris and he also went to many auctions. When eventually his own library was auctioned, there were 13,513 entries in the catalogue: including a vast collection of Bibles, dictionaries and grammars of all kinds of languages and dialects, a set of volumes printed in China, more than 100

4 See *The Asiatic Journal and Monthly Register for British and Foreign India, China and Australasia. New Series*, 28 (London, January–April 1839), Asiatic Intelligence, 164. See also Nève 1856.

5 For an evaluation of the work of Nève, refer to Isebaert 1995.

oriental manuscripts in Persian, Arabic and Sanskrit, as well as a large collection of medieval manuscripts.[6]

One of Nève's students, the classicist Charles Michel (1853–1929) started teaching Sanskrit at the University of Liège in 1880, and in 1885 at Ghent University (returning to Liège in 1892). One of his first students in Liège was the lawyer Eugène Monseur (1860–1912), who himself compiled (according to L. Sternbach) a good, pioneering edition of the *Cāṇakya*(*nīti*) (1887) and started a Sanskrit course at the University of Brussels in 1888.[7]

It was not only academics and scholars who were attracted to Indology. The remarkable Philippe Van der Haeghen (1825–86) was a contemporary of Félix Nève. He was a typical product of the enthusiasm for Sanskrit studies in European fashionable circles in the 19th century. Initially, he was an employee and then librarian for a nobleman; a staunch Catholic, he was an amateur who endeavoured to study a great variety of research areas. He published about works on education in Belgium (a work honoured by the Belgian Academy in 1850), the history of the (French) Languedoc region, a French translation of a German article about German elements in the French language, a Dutch translation of a Swedish tale, a translation of an Italian text and an anti-British pamphlet about the Anglican Church and torture in India, and so on!

His main contribution to Indology was in the field of Dravidian languages (South India), especially Tamil. At the age of 30, in 1855, he contributed his first article in the *Bulletin* of the Belgian Royal Academy ('De l'étude du Tamoul'). For the printing of this publication a Tamil font had to be ordered from Leipzig (Germany). In 1858 Van der Haeghen published a review of 100 Tamil proverbs and in 1863 he acquired the original manuscript of the Tamil-French Dictionary by Constanzo Beschi, written in 1744. He also compiled a list of Tamil grammars and translations by Europeans since the end of the 17th century.

Van der Haeghen may have been less thorough than an academic Indologist, but he did draw the attention of scholars to a vast and at that time less researched area in India (Tamil). He did not really succeed in this: in 1874 he gave another article to the Academy, but Nève rejected it, stating that Tamil was an inferior language when compared to Sanskrit. That was, unfortunately, also the last linguistic contribution by Van der Haeghen.[8]

---

6 See *Catalogue des livres et manuscrits formant la bibliothèque de feu Mr P. Léopold Van Alstein, Professeur agrégé à l'université de Gand, dont la vente aura lieu le Mardi 26 Mai 1863 et jours suivants …*, Anonymous, 1863, 'notice', ix–xii. Also Auguste Voisin, 1837, *Bibliotheca Hulthemiana*, vol. 6, xxxviii n.

7 Later, Paul-Émile Dumont (1879–1968; see below) started to study Sanskrit with Eugène Monseur.

8 My brief note on Van der Haeghen is based on the detailed and very well-informed publication of Christophe Vielle (2012).

Another less known non-academic Indologist of that time is the abbot A. Girard, who perhaps studied with Nève and died in Liège in 1887. We have only his preliminary study on *Le Rig-Véda et ses derniers exégètes* (1886), but we know through Charles Michel that he had completed a French translation of the whole Rigveda (unfortunately lost).

The Giants: de Harlez, de La Vallée Poussin, Lamotte

If Nève has the honour of introducing Indological studies in Belgium, we may speak of the founding of an Indological school when the knighted Monseigneur Charles de Harlez (de Deulin) (1832–99) was appointed in Louvain in 1871. His career can be divided into two periods: one of Iranian studies (1871–83), and one of Chinese studies (until 1899). In both fields of research he made pioneering contributions cited even today. His weak health forced the young de Harlez to stay in his room when his peers in high school were outside, engaged in sports. At the age of 23 he was already promoted as Doctor in Law. He decided to break with the political tradition of his family and joined the Catholic seminary, to be ordained a priest three years later. Before he was 30 years old he was appointed on the Chair of Oriental Languages in Louvain. For each language he studied, he composed his own grammar: *Grammaire pratique de la langue sanscrite* (1878, second edition 1885), *Manuel de la langue de l'Avesta* (1879) and *Manuel du Pehlvi* (1880).

His *magnum opus* is the translation into French of the *Avesta*, the collection of religious texts attributed to Zarathustra. A further translation into Gujarati (1887) made de Harlez very popular with the Parsi community in Bombay/Mumbai, who claimed to be the descendants of the Zoroastrian Persians who had fled the invading Muslims in Persia/Iran in the 7th century and migrated to the western part of India. We should remember that the statements of de Harlez regarding the Avesta were not accepted by all of his contemporaries. In 1883 he left that area of research and started to study Chinese, at the age of 51. In 1882, he started *Le Muséon*, the still famous Belgian journal of Oriental studies.[9]

De Harlez was the first real expert in Louvain and Louis de La Vallée Poussin (1869–1938), disciple of de Harlez, as he declared himself, was the first at Ghent University – which was inaugurated in 1817 (Dutch became the official language in Ghent only in 1930), where he was appointed in 1892 for Sanskrit and comparative grammar of Greek and Latin, as a successor to Charles Michel (who had gone back to Liège). Besides these, he studied other languages as well and was, in 1965, called 'le plus grand indianiste belge' by his own disciple, the great scholar Mgr Étienne Lamotte (see below).[10]

9 See Étienne Lamotte's Notice on de Harlez (1953).

10 See Lamotte 1965.

With Louis de La Vallée Poussin of Ghent we remain in the world of nobility and aristocrats in Belgium in the 19th century. In 1832 his French grandfather had been invited by the first Belgian king, Leopold I, to assist in the organisation of the (nascent) Belgian army. Louis had lost his mother when he was seven and was raised in the home of his grandparents. He was inspired by Oriental studies in France and, after studying classical languages in Liège, he went to Louvain to study Sanskrit, Pali, Avestan and comparative linguistics with Professors Charles de Harlez and his successor, Philémon Colinet. De La Vallée Poussin completed his PhD in Oriental studies in Louvain in 1891. He continued his studies in Paris (1893–1903) and Leiden (1904) with the famous Professor Kern. During the Great War he emigrated to Cambridge, and eventually studied and lectured in London and Oxford. He self-studied Tibetan and, at the age of fifty, also started to study Chinese. A knowledge of all these languages was a must for Buddhism, his chosen field of research. It is amazing that at that time only a few books were available to him: *Petit dictionnaire chinois-français* by A. Debesse and *Vocabulary of Chinese Buddhist Terms and Names* by O. Rosenberg. Eventually, de La Vallée Poussin became an authority on Chinese Buddhism.

In 1898 (at the age of 29) he published an important work, *Buddhisme: Études et Matériaux*. In academic circles the book was not received enthusiastically, however, because of its main topic, Tantric Buddhism. De La Vallée Poussin then applied his immense scholarship to the study of other forms of Buddhism and eventually reached the highest levels of recognition. In 1956, the 2,500th anniversary of the Buddha's birthday was celebrated, and in Japan golden medals were given to the eight most outstanding scholars. The only European to get one was de La Vallée Poussin. He certainly deserved it; his list of published works comprised 324 titles, of which 20 were extensive works. He published his translation of the *Abhidharmakośa* of Vasubandhu, the Indian monk (4th century CE) who is considered the most important personality in the history of early Buddhism, in five volumes. With this publication de La Vallée Poussin paved the way to the discovery of classical Buddhism.

Like the Catholic University of Louvain, founded in 1425, Ghent University was initially French-speaking. In 1929 it became more and more obvious that the university (situated in Flanders) would become Flemish-/Dutch-speaking, and (French-speaking) de La Vallée Poussin (then 60 years of age) asked to be released from his academic duties. The famous scholar Mgr Étienne Lamotte at the (then completely French-speaking) Catholic University of Louvain (until 1968) tried in vain to invite him to Leuven. De La Vallée Poussin preferred to retire. He died in 1938.

Monseigneur Étienne Lamotte (1903–83) is the third renowned expert among the Belgian Indologists. After his studies at the seminary in Malines/Mechelen and also in Rome, he gained his PhD in Oriental languages in 1929 (at the age of 26), with a dissertation about the *Bhagavadgītā*. He then went to Paris to study Chinese,

Tibetan and Pali. For this selection of languages he followed the advice of de La Vallée Poussin, who gave the young man the privilege of meeting him at his home, twice a week, to study and discuss Sanskrit and Tibetan texts. In 1934 Lamotte started to teach these languages at the Catholic University of Louvain.

The beginning of the Second World War was disastrous for this university and its Indological studies: in 1940 a fire broke out in the central library and the complete collection of de La Vallée Poussin, which Lamotte had managed to bring there, was destroyed. Several important books that were essential for Lamotte's research were also destroyed. Lamotte himself had a narrow escape four years later when the allied armies bombed the city. All this forced Lamotte to shift his interest to Chinese studies and specifically to a huge Chinese text (printed in Japan), attributed to the famous Indian Buddhist philosopher Nāgārjuna (*c.* 150–250 CE). For nearly 36 years Lamotte worked on this text and eventually published the resulting work in five volumes: *Traité de la Grande Vertu de Sagesse* (2,600 pages).

Besides the numerous articles and books, worth mentioning is Lamotte's standard *Histoire du bouddhisme indien* (862 pages), which appeared in 1958 (and was translated in English in 1988). Lamotte told me that he sent a handwritten manuscript to the press (in several alphabets).

Lamotte has been greatly respected and honoured as Doctor honoris causa at Ghent University and several foreign universities. In 1964, and later, he was special advisor for non-Christian religions at the Second Vatican Council in Rome. In 1968 (543 years after its foundation in 1425) the Catholic University of Leuven/ Louvain was divided into two universities, one Flemish-/Dutch-speaking, one French-speaking (see above, fn. 3). Lamotte had been teaching and publishing only in French, and he moved to the French-speaking university. The division of the university on two different sites (along with half the library) was a very difficult process. Lamotte continued to teach until his retirement in 1974, at the age of 70.

In 1977, for the first time in his life, he undertook an adventurous journey to the Buddhist country of Japan. In great triumph he travelled there and was honoured for his immense contribution to Buddhist studies. In his Notice on Lamotte, Professor Ryckmans could not help remarking: 'En dépit de sa magistrale compréhension de la doctrine bouddhique. il m'a confié un jour qu'il n'en avait pas vraiment subi la séduction' ('With all his impressive knowledge of Buddhism, Lamotte told me one day that he never gave in to the temptation to be seduced by it').[11]

In 1980 Lamotte was given the traditional Festschrift, with articles by scholars from all over the world. In it, we find a splendid photograph of Etienne Lamotte, in a solemn cassock and the broad sash of a Catholic Monseigneur. I had the opportunity of meeting him in that impressive attire in 1971, when I had just returned after seven years in India. Full of admiration for my years of study at different universities in

11 Ryckmans 1987; on Lamotte, see also Daniel Donnet (1980) and the long article by Lamotte's disciple, Hubert Durt (1985).

India, he told me that he had never dared to travel to India because he was afraid of snakes. Several years after his death a young Buddhist monk from Sri Lanka came to see me, trying to visit the (sacred) places where Lamotte had lived.

I am still wondering how scholars like Lamotte and his predecessors managed to master all these languages with so little basic material at their disposal. Equally impressive is the fact that they produced their lengthy volumes with a handwritten final copy sent to the press, giving (in the original script) quotations in Sanskrit, Pali, Tibetan and Chinese.

Indology in Louvain/Leuven

In Leuven, there were quite a few renowned Indologists between de Harlez and Lamotte. Some concentrated on Sanskrit, while others focused on comparative studies of Indo-European languages. Philémon Colinet (1853–1917), the disciple and successor of de Harlez, devoted his PhD research to the *Bhagavadgītā*, and after that specialised in comparative grammar and linguistics. His work was continued by Albert Carnoy (1879–1961), author of *Grammaire élémentaire de la langue sanscrite comparée avec celle des langues indo-européennes* (1925, second edition 1937). Carnoy began teaching Iranian languages in 1904 and taught Vedic Sanskrit until his retirement in 1951. He was also minister of Interior Affairs in the Belgian government from 1927 to 1929.

I should like to mention here several outstanding scholars who were Belgian Jesuits in India involved in various fields of Indology: Vedānta studies with Georges Dandoy (1882–1962), Pierre Johanns (from Luxemburg, 1882–1955), Michel Ledrus and Richard De Smet (1916–97); Hindi, Sanskrit or Bengali studies with Camille Bulcke (1909–82), Robert Antoine (1914–81) and Paul Detienne (1924–2016). Between 1935 and 1971 an Indological course (including Sanskrit) was organised for the Belgian Jesuit missionaries at the 'Juvénat indien' of the Institut Saint-Robert-Bellarmin, at La Pairelle (Wépion), affiliated to the Jesuit University College of Namur.

The main focus for Carnoy in Louvain was on Indo-European languages and philology. A number of scholars, mentioned below, studied for their PhDs with him: Jacques Duchesne-Guillemin, Walter Couvreur, Adriaan Scharpé and Albert Joris Van Windekens.

Tocharian languages became the special field of Albert Van Windekens, who was born in England (during the Great War) but returned to Belgium with his parents after the war and became the disciple of Professor Carnoy. From him he gained an enthusiasm for Tocharian and for comparative grammar. After graduating in classical studies, Van Windekens went to Paris where he studied under the guidance of Jean Filliozat, resulting in a PhD (in 1939) on the shifts in the Indo-European sounds in Tocharian A and B. A second PhD two years later in Louvain, on Oriental languages, produced an etymological lexicon of the two languages. From 1946 onwards until 1965, he taught Sanskrit in Louvain (following Carnoy, Vedic and also elementary Sanskrit for the Dutch-speaking students; the main courses of Sanskrit being taught by Lamotte) and comparative grammar. He edited six volumes and wrote eight books and nearly 300 articles.[12]

At the time of Lamotte and Van Windekens, there were also in Louvain, as occasional teachers in Indology, two students of Lamotte: Marcel Hofinger (1913–97), whose PhD in 1946 was an *Étude sur le Concile de Vaiśālī* (later he published two volumes of *Le Congrès du lac Anavatapta*, relying on Tibetan sources) for the course on the history of Asia (his main academic subject was in classics), and Joseph Masson (Society of Jesus, 1908–98), whose PhD in 1942 was on *La religion populaire dans le canon bouddhique pali*, for the Satsuma chair.

Pierre H.L. Eggermont (1914–95), of Dutch parents but born in Indonesia, joined the KULeuven in 1968 after the division into the Flemish-/Dutch- and the French-speaking universities. Until 1984, he taught Indian art and history as well as Pali, focusing his research on Alexander the Great and Emperor Ashoka. His publications made him an authority in this field.

In the same period Gilbert Pollet (1930–2014) taught Hindi and Sanskrit and focused his research on the languages of the Bhakti period in North India (his PhD at SOAS, London, in 1963, was on the *Bhaktamāla* of Nābhādās). He wrote several articles about this and edited three books. With Eggermont and Greta Van Damme (PhD in 1990 on Pañcatanta literature) he published one volume of the *Corpus Topographicum Indiae Antiquae*, a joint project with Ghent University. At his retirement in 1995, the full course in Indology was discontinued at the KULeuven, where now only an introductory course of Sanskrit is taught.

However, the rigid discipline of textual studies was continued in Leuven by Winand M. Callewaert (1943–) who went to India in 1965 and studied Hindi, Sanskrit and philosophy at the universities of Ranchi, Benares/Varanasi and Pune. After his PhD (1975) and DLitt (1993) in Leuven, he continued to travel to India (more than 60 times), mainly in search of manuscripts. During a year of study at the Sorbonne, Paris, in 1971, he was inspired by Professor Charlotte Vaudeville to enter the field of Bhakti studies in northern India. This research focused on a rather neglected area in Indological studies: the Bhakti poets who from 1500 onwards sang their inspiring songs no longer in Sanskrit, but in the vernaculars of each region. Until the 1960s, most Bhakti songs were preserved only in manuscripts and very little was published (now this field is represented in most international conferences on Indian studies).

Callewaert travelled all over northern India and visited temples, libraries and private collections, looking for manuscripts dated 1600 CE onwards. Eventually, he

12 See the bibliography of Van Windekens with 91 titles in the Liber Amicorum, in: G. Pollet, ed., *India and the Ancient World. History, Trade and Culture before A.D. 650*, Orientalia Lovaniensia Analecta, 25 (1987), ix–xii.

copied about 15,000 folios, creating on film the most extensive databank on Bhakti literature (now preserved in Heidelberg University Library). He also prepared a scanned version of 30 text editions (now preserved in the Lausanne University databank of Bhakti literature).

Between 1974 and 2019 Callewaert published 38 books and 139 articles in English, Hindi and Dutch. His *magnum opus*, *Dictionary of Bhakti: North-Indian Bhakti Texts into Kharī Bolī Hindī and English*, appeared in New Delhi in 2009: 2,187 pages in three volumes, giving about 40,000 entries with context references and Hindi and English translation. After Pollet's retirement in 1995, Callewaert also taught Sanskrit until 2018 (in addition to a course on Hinduism and Buddhism).

Two former students from the KULeuven have also continued careers in the field: Heidi Pauwels at the University of Washington (Seattle; PhD in 1994), with research in medieval and modern Hindi literature. As a free-lance author, Koenraad Elst focused on *hindutva* and published several books about this topic.

In the French-speaking Université Catholique de Louvain, the tradition of Mgr Lamotte was interrupted after his retirement in 1974, although some of his final students continued to publish: Hubert Durt (1936–2018; PhD in 1970 on *La version chinoise de l'Introduction historique de la Samantapāsādikā*), José Van den Broeck (PhD in 1976–77 on *La version chinoise de l'Amṛtarasa de Ghoṣaka*), Marcel Van Velthem (PhD in 1976–77 on the *Abhidharmāvatāra-śāstra*) and Jean Dantinne (PhD in 1982–83 on the *Akṣobhyavyūha*).

At the Oriental Institute on the new campus of Louvain-la-Neuve, the teaching of Sanskrit was continued, first (after an interim by the French scholar Bruno Dagens) by the classicist Daniel Donnet (1938) and Dominique Forthomme (1957; PhD in Paris on the *Dhātukāvya* of Nārāyaṇabhaṭṭa), and from 1996 onwards (until today) by Christophe Vielle (1967–). Vielle started with Indo-European studies (his PhD dissertation, in 1996, was a comparative study of the Greek and Sanskrit epics). Then, after a postdoctoral position in Oxford, he specialised in *kāvya* and *śāstra* philology, in the historiography and epistemology of Western (pre-)Indology, and in the cultural history and anthropology of pre-modern Kerala (based on Sanskrit, Malayalam and Western sources). Kerala is a South Indian state where Veille has travelled extensively since 2000. His DLitt (2007) was an edition of the hitherto unpublished *Jaiminīyasaṃhitā* of the *Brahmāṇḍapurāṇa*, on the basis of Malayalam-script manuscripts. His student, Emmanuel Francis (PhD in 2009 on the history of the Pallava dynasty), is now a researcher at the CNRS (Paris), specialising in Tamil epigraphy and manuscripts.

At the Université Catholique de Louvain, the Jesuit Jacques Scheuer (1942–; PhD in Paris with Madeleine Biardeau) taught Buddhism and Hinduism and their relation with Christian traditions. Scheuer retired in 2008. Robert Deliège (1953–; PhD from Oxford)) taught social and cultural anthropology, focusing on tribal cultures, the Gandhian legacy, the caste system and untouchables. He retired in

2018. Lambert Isebaert (1955–) taught Pali and Tocharian until his retirement in 2019.

Indology in Ghent

The Rijksuniversiteit Gent (RUG), now Ghent University (UGent), is the only Belgian university with a complete course in Indology. The study of Sanskrit and of Tocharian has continued and at the same time new areas and languages have been introduced, specifically Jaina literature and its affiliated languages.

After the Second World War, in 1944, Adriaan Scharpé (1913–86) was appointed. Scharpé wrote his PhD dissertation in Leuven on *The Classical Sanskrit Romance* and his DLitt in Utrecht (with Jan Gonda) on *Bāṇa's Kādambarī*. He taught Sanskrit and comparative Indo-European grammar. In three (small) volumes he wrote a (Dutch) Sanskrit grammar, in which he printed the Sanskrit words in Roman script, convinced that for students it was a sheer waste of time to learn the Devanāgarī alphabet. His main contribution to Indology is in the study of Kālidāsa and, with his interest in Indian topography, he supervised the publication of two volumes of the *Corpus Topographicum Indiae Antiquae* (1965 and 1966).

Walter Couvreur (1914–96) initially also taught comparative grammar of the Indo-European languages, but specialised in Hittite and Tocharian languages. This tradition in Ghent was continued by Eddy Moerloose (1945–), who lectured from 1991 to 2010 (Sanskrit, Tocharian and history and literature of Central and South Asia). His publications are in the field of Tocharian Buddhists texts.

The most famous student of Scharpé was Ludo Rocher (1926–2016), a giant in the field of ancient Indian law. Doctor in Law in 1950, his PhD in 1952 was on the *Daṇḍaviveka* of Vardhamāna, to which he added a DLitt in 1956 on the *Vyavahāracintāmaṇi* of Vācaspati Miśra. He taught Sanskrit at the University of Brussels from 1956 to 1967, where he met his future wife, Rosane Rocher (born Debels; PhD in 1965; *La théorie des voix du verbe dans l'école pāṇinéenne*, published in 1968), until his departure to the USA where he became Professor at the University of Pennsylvania in 1966. The American scholars Richard Salomon and Patrick Olivelle are among his students.

As a student of Scharpé and Couvreur, Jozef Deleu (1925–94) started, in Ghent, the new research area of Jaina literature. With Scharpé as supervisor he prepared his PhD dissertation on Rājaśekhara's *Prabandhakośa* (1957). This Middle Indian text brought Deleu to Jaina studies, with main publications *Chapters I–III of the Mahānisīha, Critically Edited* (1963), *Viyāhapannatti* (*Bhagavaī*) and *The Fifth Anga of the Jaina Canon* (1970). In 1971 he travelled for the first time to India to improve his spoken Hindi.

Frank Van Den Bossche (1955–) continued the Jaina studies with his dissertation *Zijn en Niet- zijn in de Anekāntajayapatākā van Haribhadra Sūri* (of the 8th century CE). He taught from 1986 until 2013, and thus became the guru of numerous students in a great variety of Indological disciplines. He also published a *Basic Manual of Middle Prākrit Grammar.*

Eva De Clercq (1976–; PhD in 2003) is now in charge of the Indian studies programme at Ghent University, working mainly on Jaina studies (with a study of a Jaina *Rāmāyaṇa*) and specialising in Apabhraṃśa. She teaches both Sanskrit and Hindi.

In Ghent University, there is also the Ghent Centre of Buddhist Studies (since 2007), which, in the footsteps of Louis de La Vallée Poussin, the great precursor, brings together scholars of Chinese, Indian and Japanese Buddhist studies. Its leaders are the Sinologists Bart Dessein (specialist in the *Abhidharma*) and Ann Heirman (specialist in the *Vinaya*), both students of Charles Willemen (whose PhD in 1971 was on the Chinese *Udanavarga*; his DLitt in 1975 was on the *Abhidharmahṛdaya*).

Several students of Ghent University have continued a career outside the academic arena. Jan Van Alphen (1953) worked in museums in Brussels and Antwerp, and the Rubin Museum of Art in New York. Rembert Lutjeharms is a specialist of Gauda Vaiṣṇava Sanskrit poetry and poetics and is member of the Oxford Centre for Hindu Studies.

Indology in Liège and Brussels

After Charles Michel (1853–1929; see above), Sanskrit was taught at the University of Liège by scholars of classical Greek and Latin: Joseph Mansion (1877–1937), René Fohalle (1899–1984) and Louis Deroy (1921–2003). After the retirement of the Iranologist Jacques Duchesne-Guillemin (1910–2012) in 1980, the Chair of 'Indo-Iranian philology' was started, with the scholars Jean Kellens (1944–), Eric Pirart (1950–) and now Philippe Swennen (1968–), focusing, for the Indian side, on Vedic philology and religion. I should also mention Jean-Marie Verpoorten (1938–; PhD in 1974), who specialised in *Mīmāṃsā* philosophy and published important studies in the field.

At the University of Brussels, after Eugène Monseur, the Veda scholar Paul-Émile Dumont (1879–1969)[13] taught Sanskrit between the two wars, before leaving for the John Hopkins University in Baltimore, where he was appointed professor in 1929. Between 1945 and 1954, Sanskrit was taught by his student, the classicist Roger Goossens (1903–54).[14] After him, Ludo Rocher (see above) was in charge of the course.

13 See above, fn. 7.

14 See Lamotte 1954.

After an interim by the French scholar Jean Naudou (1921–2018) between 1967 and 1976, Sanskrit was taught by Francine Mawet (1948; a student of Maurice Leroy) until 2008. She published a useful *Grammaire sanskrite à l'usage des étudiants hellénistes et latinistes* in 2012. A course in the history of Indian art was given by Claudine Picron-Bautze (1952–) from 1992 to 2017. Now there remains only an introductory course of Sanskrit given by the historian of Indian mathematics **Jean-Michel Delire** (1956–; PhD in 2002 on the *Baudhāyana Śulbasūtra*) at the Institut des Hautes Études de Belgique.

Conclusion

Indological studies in Belgium have an impressive history, with outstanding scholarly publications. The studies originated in a Christian interest for other religions, and that religious accent remained in the specialisation of many scholars: Buddhism in de La Vallée Poussin and Lamotte, and the mysticism of *bhakti* in Callewaert. The main interest, however, remained philological, focusing on ancient languages and texts. Many scholars started with Greek and Latin and eventually turned to Sanskrit, at the same time studying other languages: Avestan, Pali, Tocharian, Brajbhasha, Apabhramsha, Chinese and Tibetan.

It keeps amazing us that scholars in the early period managed to become so proficient in old languages with so little material available. Often they wrote their own grammars. Some were very young doing this: de La Vallée Poussin received his PhD degree at the age of 19. At the same time, until the second half of the 20th century, most scholars never went to the countries that were the object of their studies. Adriaan Scharpé, who taught Sanskrit in Ghent until 1980, even continued to use the Roman alphabet, not the Devanāgarī script. Lamotte wrote his immense works with a pen, giving citations in Chinese, Sanskrit, Tibetan and Pali.

References

Anonymous (1839) 'Obituary for Eugène Jacquet'. *The Asiatic Journal and Monthly Register for British and Foreign, India, China and Australasia* 28, London, W.H. Allen & co, January–April 1839, 164.

Anonymous (1863) *Catalogue des livres et manuscrits formant la bibliothèque de feu Mr P. Léopold Van Alstein, Professeur agrégé à l'université de Gand,* vol.1, Ghent, Imprimerie et lithographie de C. Annoot-Braeckman.

Callewaert, W.M. (2013) Van kamergeleerden tot reizigers: Indologie in België. In Goddeeris, I. (ed.), *Het Wiel van Ashoka. Belgisch-Indiase contacten in historisch perspectief,* 139–154. Leuven: Leuven University Press.

DONNET, D. (1980) L'œuvre de Mgr. Étienne Lamotte. *Indianisme et Bouddhisme: Mélanges offerts à Mgr Étienne Lamotte*, Publications de l'Institut Orientaliste de Louvain 23, VII–XVI.

DURT, H. (1985) Étienne Lamotte (1903–1983). *Bulletin de l'École Française d'Extrême-Orient* 74, 1–28.

ISEBAERT, L. (1995) Félix Nève and the beginnings of Sanskrit teaching in Louvain (1841). In Pollet, G. (ed.), *Indian Epic Values: Rāmāyaṇa and its Impact*, Orientalia Lovaniensia Analecta 66, 101–113.

LAMOTTE, É. (1953) Notice sur le Chevalier Charles de Harlez de Deulin. *Annuaire de l'Académie royale de Belgique* 119, 415–440.

LAMOTTE, É. (1954) L'œuvre indianiste de Roger Goossens. *Le Flambeau* 37, 295–302.

LAMOTTE, É. (1965) Notice sur Louis de La Vallée Poussin. *Annuaire de l'Académie royale de Belgique* 131, 145–168.

NÈVE, F. (1856) *Mémoire sur la vie d'Eugène Jacquet, de Bruxelles et sur ses travaux relatifs à l'histoire et aux langues de l'Orient, suivi de quelques fragments inédits.* Bruxelles: Académie royale de Belgique.

RYCKMANS, J. (1987) Notice sur Étienne Lamotte. *Annuaire de l'Académie royale de Belgique* 153, 191–218.

VAN HAL, T. AND VIELLE, C. (2013) *Grammatica Grandonica: The Sanskrit Grammar of Johann Ernst Hanxleden S.J. (1681–1732).* Potsdam, University of Potsdam. Retrieved from http://opus.kobv.de/ubp/volltexte/2013/6321/.

VIELLE, C. (2012) Les débuts de l'Indianisme au XIXe siècle en Belgique. Note sur le Bruxellois Philippe Van der Haeghen (1825–1886), précurseur oublié des études tamoules. *Acta Orientalia Belgica* 25, 111–126.

Voisin, A. (1837) *Bibliotheca Hulthemiana ou Catalogue méthodique de la riche et précieuse collection de livres et de manuscrits délaissés par M.Ch. Van Hulthem*, vol. 6, Ghent, Imprimerie de Joël Poelman.

'There Was a City Called Mithilā'

Are All Jain Rāmāyaṇas Really Purāṇas?

Adrian Plau

In his survey of the Jain *Rāmāyaṇas*, Kulkarni (1990) famously declared that these texts 'are essentially Purāṇas', and not to be compared with *kāvya* literature. Yet Kulkarni's survey does not include later versions that shorten or entirely omit the cosmological framework that distinguishes Purāṇic literature. Does this mean that these other Jain *Rāmāyaṇas* are not *Purāṇas*? Or does it mean that we should broaden our concepts of what a Jain *Purāṇa* can be? Taking up these questions allows us to reflect critically on the Jain *Rāmāyaṇa* tradition as a whole, and to discuss how vernacular Jain literature relates to its earlier precedents. I will in this paper first survey the various positions on the Jain *Purāṇas* as a distinct category of literature, and highlight Purāṇic features in foundational Jain *Rāmāyaṇas* such as Vimalasūri's *Pauma-Cariya*. I will then analyse the narrative structures of hitherto under-studied Jain *Rāmāyaṇas* that emphasise Sītā's character, such as the anonymous Sanskrit *mahākāvya Sītācaritra* and Samaysundar's early Gujarātī *Sītārāmcopāī*, focusing especially on the mid-17th-century Brajbhāṣa *Sītācarit* by Rāmcand Bālak. Through this approach, I aim to present a comparative range that allows us to engage in a wider discussion on how we conceptualise the Jain *Purāṇas*, the Jain *Rāmāyaṇa* tradition and, by extension, Jain narrative literature in general.

Introduction

This paper raises more questions than it answers. Alongside my own patchy understanding, the paper owes this confusion to the nature of what it seeks to do: bringing some of the less studied (some of them even completely neglected) Jain *Rāmāyaṇas* in conversation with their older, canonical relatives and the discussions that follow in their wake. More specifically, I want to enquire more closely into the question of whether Kulkarni (1990: 248) was right when he said that the Jain *Rāmāyaṇas* can all really be said to be *Purāṇas.* It is, of course, possible that they can, but in my work with the *Sītācarit,* a mid-17th century-composition in Brajbhāṣā, and other texts like it, I frequently note tendencies that go beyond what I believe is typically deemed to be Purāṇic in a Jain context. And so the present paper is my attempt at sorting these thoughts into debatable questions – let us see where they take us.

But let me first briefly touch on what is perhaps the most striking question of all: is this inquiry just about minor technical details or the semantics of genre? What does it matter whether all Jain *Rāmāyaṇas* are *Purāṇas* or not?

I see two reasons why it matters. Firstly, following Ramanujan's (1991) seminal essay on the historical diversity of the South Asian *Rāmāyaṇa* tradition, we have an academic consensus that emphasises this very mutability, perhaps best expressed by Richman's (1991) phrase, 'many *Rāmāyaṇas*'. While I wholeheartedly agree with this consensus, I also am concerned by the general tendency to see the Jain *Rāmāyaṇa* tradition as a monolith – 'the Jain *Rāmāyaṇa*' – that primarily serves as a rhetorical example of variation when one wishes to demonstrate the mutability of the 'many *Rāmāyaṇas*' tradition. Did Jains compose *Rāmāyaṇas* for nearly 2,000 years and across a variety of languages and localities without giving rise to any major variations? Raising the question of whether the Jain *Rāmāyaṇas* all fit within a single historical genre allows us to engage with this concern and potentially discover that the 'many *Rāmāyaṇas*' tradition is even more dynamic than we thought.

The second reason springs from a commonly held assumption, also expressed by Kulkarni (I discuss this in more detail later), that it is the canonical iterations of the Jain *Rāmāyaṇa* tradition that really matters – that is, those that were composed in Prakrit, Sanskrit or Apabhraṃśa. Later versions in the various vernaculars of North India, such as Maru-Gurjar (which encompasses early Gujarātī and Rājasthānī) and Brajbhāṣā, are less significant translations or watered-down retellings of the original mould-breakers. On the other hand, Jains of late medieval and early modern North India produced a great amount of material that remained broadly popular in the preceding centuries. Moreover, this body of Jain literature was contemporary with the wider socio-religious changes that marked early modern North India, such as the rise of *bhakti* devotionalism, the emergence of transregional vernaculars and the increased influence of the Persianate cultural world. Can we really assume that the early modern Jain *Rāmāyaṇas* did not engage with or reflect these shifts in ways that resulted in genuinely original works – perhaps even going beyond the Purāṇic genre?

The Jain *Rāmāyaṇas* as *Purāṇas* – But What is a Jain Purāṇā?

Towards the end of his encyclopedic survey of the Jain *Rāmāyaṇas,* Kulkarni (1990: 248) makes the following observation:

> On the whole, we may conclude that the Jain Rāmāyaṇas, as a rule, are essentially Purāṇas. They are written not as Kāvyas pure and simple but to glorify the Dharma of the Jinas and teach the people Jain doctrines and criticise the Brahmanical Dharma.

The first and defining Jain *Rāmāyaṇa*, Vimalasūri's *c.* 3rd-century Prakrit *Paüma Cariya*, Kulkarni (1990: 16) notes, even refers to itself as a *Purāṇa*. All this gives rise to the question of what specifically constitutes a Jain *Purāṇa*. However, let me first note that while Kulkarni's sample of Jain *Rāmāyaṇas* covers the foundational texts, such as the aforementioned *Pauma Cariya* and the Sanskrit versions *Padma Purāṇa* and *Triṣaṣṭiśalākāpuruṣacarita*, it effectively stops with Hemacandra in the 12th century. Later versions, such as a 17th-century *Laghu-Triṣaṣṭi* by Meghavijaya, are summarily dispensed with or mentioned in passing as being either insignificant abridgements or simply unavailable. Some of the Sītā-oriented texts that I will discuss here are given in a list drawn from the *Jinaratnakośa*, but Kulkarni (1990: 14) notes that the total list of 30 titles 'probably do not contain any new remarkable features but repeat in their own language what the older Jain writers have already said'. I think Kulkarni is, in part, correct, in that the material I present here indeed mostly does contain things that have been said before. But he is also, in part, incorrect, because this material can be seen to say old things in new ways. This makes it innovative, which again has implications for what we make of the Jain *Rāmāyaṇa* tradition as a whole.

We should first turn to the question of which exact particularities mark out the Jain *Purāṇas* as *Purāṇas*. We have seen some of what Kulkarni thinks on the subject: in the above quote he underlined the quality of didacticism, to the extent that the Jain *Rāmāyaṇas* should not be assessed with the same stringent aesthetic expectations we would bring to *kāvya* literature. In the same volume, Kulkarni notes that the Jain Purāṇas have a variety of subjects in common with the Hindu *Purāṇas*. These include the history of the universe from origin through dissolution to recreation, the histories of the ancient royal dynasties and their important individuals, including Rāma and Kṛṣṇa, and religious instruction on the four aims of man (the *puruṣārtha*: *dharma*, *artha*, kāma, *mokṣa*). Interwoven with these story elements come a vast number of teachings on points of learning, religion and many other topics, to the point that Kulkarni (1990: 10) sees both Hindu and Jain *Purāṇas* as 'popular encyclopedia' of their respective religious cultures. Moreover, *Purāṇas* are typically modelled as narratives or expositions told by a person of authority to one or more listeners. For instance, the *Pauma Cariya* is framed as told by Mahavīra's prime disciple Gautama to the pious king Śreṇika, similarly to how the storyteller Ugraśravas tells the Hindu *Bhāgavata Purāṇa* to an assembly of *munis*.

What makes the Jain *Purāṇas* specifically Jain is, to Kulkarni, their emphasis on the 63 Great Men (*śalākāpuruṣa*) of Jain mythology. These are divided into the 24 *tīrthaṅkaras*, establishers of the Jain order; 12 *cakravartins*, universal rulers;

nine *baladevas*, rulers of one third of the world; nine *vāsudevas*, brothers of the *baladevas*; and, finally, nine *prativāsudevas*, the *vāsudevas*' natural enemies. The three latter categories appear in nine interlinked triplets. Rāma (*baladeva*), Lakṣmaṇa (*vāsudeva*) and Rāvaṇa (*prativāsudeva*) make up one such triplet; Balarāma, Kṛṣṇa and Jarāsandha another.

Here it gets a bit murky. Kulkarni records that the 8th-century Jinasena speaks of his *Ādipurāṇa* as a '*mahāpurāṇa*', since it speaks of great beings, is narrated by great beings and generally teaches great things. Yet, since it contains many stories, Jinasena says it is an *itihāsa*, too, and so the two concepts appear synonymous. A commentary on Puṣpadanta's *Mahāpurāṇa*, however, sees *itihāsas* as compositions that only deal with a single individual, whereas *Purāṇas* take up all of the 63 Great Men. In other words, things are not settled. But we now understand that, when Kulkarni speaks of the 'essentially' Purāṇic nature of the Jain *Rāmāyaṇas*, we may expect them to frame the story of Rāma within the universal history of the 63 Great Men, and to do so in a way that explicates fundamental Jain teachings. In other words, both structure and intent are giveaways.

So far, so good. Cort (1993) looks at a broader range of sources discussing the nature of Jain *Purāṇas*, including both modern scholarly work and the Jain compositions themselves. He notes that the term *caritra* ('deeds, acts'; *i.e.* 'biography') has an almost equal currency to '*purāṇa*' amongst the Jains (Śvetāmbaras generally favouring it for their biographical works), and that this state of things indicates a fundamentally biographical concern in the Jain *Purāṇas*. Consequently, Cort (1993: 187) finds that a broad definition of the Jain *Purāṇa* may be 'postcanonical biographical *kāvya*'. In this, Cort emphasises the Jain storytelling (*kathā*) tradition that is so popular and well attested, and this is presumably why Cort's initial definition of the Jain *Purāṇas* identifies them as *kāvyas* ('ornate poetry') – the very thing Kulkarni warned us against comparing the 'essentially' Purāṇic Jain *Rāmāyaṇas* to! But Kulkarni, too, included the *kathā* tradition when he talked of the Jain *Purāṇas* as encyclopaedic. I will let this matter rest here, so as not to go into the endless debate of what exactly *kāvya* is and what it does, but it is interesting to note the disagreement.[1]

Cort rejects attempts by both Jain authors such as Jinasena and modern scholars to root the characteristics of Jain *Purāṇas* in definite topics, such as the practices of asceticism and gifting, the natural order, lineages and the various epochs and kingdoms. All of these topics appear in other Jain texts, Cort notes, that do not claim to be *Purāṇas* at all. It is rather the 63 Great Men that defines them, by providing the universal history in which the individual *Purāṇa* is set. Cort divides the Jain *Purāṇas* into three categories, based on their different contents. The first category comprises the *Jinacaritras*, which tell of the 24 *tīrthaṅkaras*; the second the Jain

1 An essential read for the discussion on *kāvya* and its ramifications in South Asian literary and cultural history is, of course, Pollock 2006.

Rāmāyaṇas; and the third the Jain *Mahābhārata*, including the story of Kṛṣṇa. The *Mahāpurāṇas*, then, cover all of these and, in so doing, give us a fourth category that includes complete accounts of all 63 Great Men. So when the *Pauma Cariya* sets its story of Rāma within the framework of these Great Men, it is significant. Cort quotes Warder on the matter, who states that the setting up of such a framework 'is not simply an introduction [...]: it is an essential part of the narrative' (Warder in Cort 1993: 201). This is significant in that it shows that, even as the individual *Purāṇa* takes up the story of a single Great Man, it does so as a 'zoom in' effect from the bird's-eye perspective of the universal history of all 63 Great Men, and it is within this context that the resulting narrative makes sense. A reiteration of Cort's definition is that a Jain *Purāṇa* is a '*kāvya* that narrates the biography of one or more of the sixty-three Great Heroes of the Jaina universal history' (Cort 1993: 205).

So here we see that Kulkarni and Cort are in perfect agreement on what a Jain *Purāṇa* is, excepting the bit about *kāvyas*. They also agree that the Jain *Purāṇas*, by recounting the lives and deeds of important persons who succeeded on the path to *mokṣa*, have an important didactic significance to Jains who read, hear or see the *Purāṇas* performed. So what is my problem with expanding this explanation of the Jain *Purāṇa* genre to include the Jain *Rāmāyaṇas*?

I have already noted that Kulkarni's survey of Jain *Rāmāyaṇas* more or less ends before the early modern period. While there is much variation to trace between the pre-modern versions, they seem to share the basic narrative structure. For instance, De Clercq (2005) has very clearly shown how the *Pauma Cariya*, the *Padma Purāṇa* and the 9th- or 10th-century Apabhraṃśa *Paümacariu* all share the same introductory structure, going from the formal benedictions via the establishing of the narrative frame of Gautama answering Śreṇika's questions to a description of the universe that at last narrows down to the story of Rāvaṇa's lineages and former births. This is the significant beginning that we saw Warder emphasise so heartily. But what, then, about Jain *Rāmāyaṇas* that stray from this mould or even break it completely?

Beginnings and Relations

Of the beginning of any work, Said (1975: 3) writes that it 'immediately establishes relationships with works already existing, relationships of either continuity or antagonism or some mixture of both'. This is precisely what I will be looking for here: relationships of either continuation or departure, or a bit of both, in the beginnings of Jain *Rāṃāyaṇas*. So how do we talk about such relationships? How to compare them? One way is to do what I will do here, and that is to pick from the toolbox of conceptual tools for analysing narratives and intertextual relationships provided by Genette (1980: 1997).

To begin with the narrative: Genette (1980) differentiates between the 'story' or 'diegesis', which simply is the narrative and its contents; the 'narrative', which is the 'story' as it is told in any given work; and the 'narrating', the act of producing such a 'narrative'. In the context of our questions concerning the Jain *Rāmāyaṇas* and their Purāṇic character, this subtle delineation allows us to separate between the universal story of the 63 Great Men, the 'story' and the way that any given Jain *Rāmāyaṇa* as a 'narrative' does its individual 'narrating'. Of course, we have already seen that the quality that makes the Jain *Rāmāyaṇas* 'essentially' *Purāṇas* is in part their similarities as narratives framed within the story of those Great Men. So how to describe the potential differences between 'narratives'?

Describing a base text as the hypotext (*e.g.* Homer's *Odyssey*) and any text that follows it in some way or the other as the hypertext (*e.g.* Joyce's *Ulysses*), Genette (1997) coins the concept of hypertextuality. Genette also describes a wealth of ways or 'operations' in which a text may transform from hypotext to hypertext. Especially useful here is the group of operations that Genette (somewhat forbiddingly) styles 'intramodal transmodalizations'. These are the operations that change the 'mode' of a work, by altering the chronology of a narrative ('temporal order'), its pace ('duration and frequency'), the relation of the narrator to narrative ('distance') or, most importantly, its focus ('perspective'). This latter operation represents a transfocalisation; the classic example is Stoppard's *Rozenkrantz and Guildernstern are Dead*, which makes leading men out of two supporting parts from Shakespeare's *Hamlet.* All of these 'transpositions' have repercussions for the theme of the hypertext. Genette (1997: 294) notes: 'there is no such thing as an *innocent* transposition; *i.e.* one that does not in one way or another alter the meaning of its hypotext' (original emphasis). They may, for instance, lead to the re-evaluation of one or more of a narrative's characters. So in the following I would like to study how the beginnings of my Jain *Rāmāyaṇa* samples establish their narratives, and what, if any, operations they perform on the way from hypotext to hypertext. These samples all have one thing in common: they focus on a character intrinsic to the *Rāmāyaṇa* story, but not one of the 63 Great Men. This, of course, is Sītā.

Sītā and the Great Men – *Kāvya*, *Caupāī*, *Carita* and a Song

The compositions I will deal with here are from several different centuries, and some of them are undated. They are in different languages and represent different genres. Sītā is their common denominator, as they all tell the story of Sītā's life and actions, and so establish her as an ideal Jain lay woman whose path is crowned with renunciation and *mokṣa*. In this, these *Rāmāyaṇas* are related to the popular *satī* narratives. These narratives, Kelting (2009) informs us, detail the lives of women as examples of the way of virtuous womanhood (*satī*), and have been broadly popular amongst lay Jain women since early modern days, if not earlier. Some might then say that the texts I discuss here represent a cluster of *Sītākathās*, and that these are not necessarily comparable to the Jain *Rāmāyaṇas*. But must a *Rāmāyaṇa* only be about Rāma? As we shall see, it is, for most of them, not only the case that Sītā appears in the story, but also that most of what Ramanujan (1991: 45) calls the 'basic elements of the plot' are dutifully covered. However, by employing a variety of the effects Genette recognises as hypertextual operations, they do shift the balance of the story towards Sītā and, in an instance of Genette's transfocalisation, make it more about her quality as a *satī* than about Rāma being a Great Man.

Let us begin with a rather mysterious composition: an anonymous *Sītācaritra*[2] in Sanskrit. I have only managed to access one manuscript of this text, which is held at the British Library. This copy is undated, but the Patan Manuscript Catalogue (Dalal and Gandhi 1937: 175–176) refers to a manuscript of *dharmakathās* dated to 1282 CE that, judging by the matching number of verses for each *sarga*, contains the same *Sītācaritra*. Both manuscripts refer to this *Sītācarit* as a *mahākāvya*, indicating perhaps the strength of Cort's argument. I have not been able to detect a strong sectarian affinity in the work, but the British Library has it catalogued alongside their collections of Śvetāmbara narrative literature (British Library 2006: 124–125). Let us see how this *mahākāvya* begins:

> *astīha mithilānāmapurī devapurīnibhā*
>
> There was a city named Mithilā, a city like that of the gods,
>
> *tasyāṃ janaka ityāsīd asīma-sukṛto nṛpaḥ* || *1.1*
>
> Its king was the limitlessly virtuous Janaka. /1.1/[3]
> (Anonymous, wn.d.)[4]

This is the beginning of the story of how Sītā and her twin brother Bhāmaṇḍala are born to King Janaka and his queen Videhā. The story appears in the 26th canto of the *Pauma Cariya* and tells how the daughter of an earlier king elopes with the son of a *purohit*, only to be taken captive by a princely suitor. Tragedy ensues, and the souls of a goddess and the prince are reborn as Janaka's children, while that of the noble *purohit* is born as a god. This god then takes vengeance on his former enemy, now Sītā's baby brother, by spiriting him away and leaving him to be brought up by a *vidyādhara*, a kind of sprite with the power of flight. This *Sītācaritra*, however, gives us none of this backstory but rather plunges us straight into a *kathā*-like narrative:

2 This text more frequently appears as *Sītācarit* in the catalogues, but I give it the full *–tra* ending here so as to distinguish it from the Brajbhāṣā *Sītācarit*.

3 All translations from Indian languages in this paper are mine.

4 The Sanskrit word divisions here follow the British Library catalogue.

jāta-mātrādato yugmājjahāra kila kaścana

A god then took away the boy from the pair as soon as they were born

devas tatpurvavaireṇa dārakaṃ dāruṇāśayaḥ || 1.6

and pitilessly split them because of their previous enmity. /1.6/

The lack of an introduction to the story of this 'previous enmity' may be taken to indicate that whoever composed the work most likely presupposed that the audiences were familiar with the story already. So why tell it? Let us look at a few more samples from the text and I will make some suggestions.

The next 25 verses detail how things progress for the baby boy, as he grows up and is given the name Bhāmaṇḍala. This is all familiar from the *Pauma Cariya*. Only in verse 30 do we begin to enter the mainstream of the *Rāmāyaṇa* story, as the poet introduces King Janaka's war with the barbarian king Ātaraṃgata/Āyaraṃga:

asti caitādya kailāśanagayoraṃtarālagaḥ
deśo 'rddhabarbaro nāmajanmabhūriva pāpmanaḥ || 1.30
māyūramālanagare tasya deśasya maṃḍane
ātaraṃgatamo nāma mlecha rājo 'sti dāruṇaḥ || 1.31

And there was a land between the Kailāśa mountains;
Called the Ardha-barbara, birthplace of sin. / 1.30
In the ornament of this land, the city of Māyūramāla
The fearful Ātaraṃgatama was king of the mlecchas. /1.31/

Now compare these verses to the corresponding section in Vimalasūri's *Pauma Cariya*:

tattheva atthi deso, ekko cciya addhababbaro nāmaṃ |
nissaṃjama-nissīlo, bahumecchasamāulo ghoro || 27.5
tattha ya maūramāle, nayare parivasai mecchajaṇapaüre |
nāmeṇa āyaraṃgo, rāyā jamasarisadaḍhasatto || 27.6

And there is a land there named Addhababbaro,
Where live many groups of terrible, sinful, undisciplined *mlecchas*. /27.5/
And there, in the town of Maūramāla, where many of the *mleccha* peoples reside.
There king Āyaraṃga lives, firm and capable, resembling Yama. /27.6/
(Vimalasūri 1962)

I do believe there is enough of a similarity between these verses, especially in their third and fourth lines, for us to assume that the poet of the *Sītācaritra kāvya* was familiar with the *Pauma Cariya*, at least enough to think of them as hypertextually related. After these verses, the *Sītācaritra* follows the *Pauma Cariya* quite closely, albeit in a rather abbreviated form. It features four cantos or *sargas* of increasing length. The first three of them focus on the events leading up to Rāma and Sītā's marriage (Canto 1, 93 verses), their exile and the kidnapping of Sītā (Canto 2, 98 verses) and the war of Lankā and the killing of Rāvaṇa (Canto 3, 153 verses). The fourth and final canto, however, spends 210 verses on the story of Sītā's exile, fire ordeal and eventual renunciation.

Again, none of this brings new elements to the story as we know it from *Pauma Cariya*. On the contrary, the *Sītācarit* rather leaves things out: Rāvaṇa, for instance, is given minimal attention, and his earlier births are not even mentioned. What all this does is to subtly rebalance the weight of the story to highlight Sītā and her quality as a *mahāsatī*. Towards the conclusion, this aspect of Sītā's character is underlined:

> *iyaṃ mahāsatī nū naṃ niḥśaṃkāgnau praveṣyati*
> *daivasyeva hi divyasya prāyeṇa viṣamāgatiḥ* || *194*
>
> This mahāsatī fearlessly entered into the fire,
> Which certainly is the thorny road of the divine. /194/

And, significantly, the greater part of the *kāvya* is spent in detailing this part of the story. The Great Men are not mentioned here or earlier in the story. Now what all this accumulates to is a good example of what Genette calls transfocalisation; the narrative does its narrating in a way that brings a particular character of the familiar story to the foreground. Intriguingly, by not bringing in new elements the poet needs to work with what is already there, and Sītā's grand *mahāsatī* moment does not arrive until the very end of the Jain *Rāmāyaṇa* story. This means that the opening of the *kāvya* has to go along with the story of Bhāmaṇḍala instead, and there is a sense throughout of the poet rushing to the final and defining act. Even so, we can see this *mahākāvya Sītācaritra* as an early example, perhaps even an inaugurator, of the tradition of tilting the focus of the Jain *Rāmāyaṇa* story towards Sītā and away from the Great Men-framework. That is not to say that the Great Men-framework is insignificant; like the 'former sin' of Bhāmaṇḍala, the poet probably could assume that the audiences were familiar with it. But, like that 'former sin', it is not a part of what the *Sītācaritra* wants to emphasise.

It should be noted that, despite the *mahākāvya*-moniker in the manuscripts tradition, the poem hardly features any of the *alaṅkaras* one would expect in *kāvya*. Perhaps it would be better to describe it as a *kathā*? Or, should we rather take it as an indication of how, for Jains, the *kāvya* term seems to have included something approximate to 'biography' or similar? I leave this open for now.

At this point, it would have been wonderful to turn to the Prakrit *Sīyacariya* by Bhuvanatuṅgasūri, but, unfortunately, I have not been able to access any manuscripts of this composition. The Patan catalogue (Dalal and Gandhi 1937: 136) tells us of a copy in a late 16th-century manuscript, and another is recorded by Klatt (2016: 895). With 441 verses over 31 pages, this *Sīyacariya* seems to have had a scope comparable to the *mahākāvya Sītācaritra* we just looked at. But while Bhuvanatuṅgasūri's original remains unknown, Samaysundar's *Sītārāmcaupāī* is not. And, luckily, its editors, Nāhṭā and Nāhṭa (1959), state that Samaysundar based his work on the Prakrit *Sīyacariya*. If so, we must here have an example of what Genette calls the transposition of addition, for the *Sītārāmcaupāī* with its nearly 4,000 verses spread over nine *ḍhālas* is a far longer composition than the catalogues record the *Sīyacariya* to be. This seems to be in keeping with Samaysundar's spectacular productivity. A travelling Kharatara Śvetāmbara of the late 16th and early 17th century, Samaysundar composed a great number of works in both Sanskrit and the vernaculars of Rajasthan and Gujarat. He finished the *Sītārāmcaupāī* in Merta in 1631, and it is in the mix of early Rājasthānī, Gujaratī and Hindī that is most conveniently referred to as Maru-Gurjar. Let us see what it contains.

Samaysundar begins with a series of benedictions to the Jinas and the gurus, setting both a more formal scene than the *mahākāvya Sītācaritra*'s *kathā*-like opening, and also perhaps placing us more generally in the wider current of Jain epic narratives. Once these are uttered, we launch into the first *ḍhāla* and the beginning of the narrative proper:

> *jaṃbūdīpa jihāṃ āpe uttama puruṣa nuṃ ṭhāmo re |*
> *bharatakhetra tihā ati bhalau nagara rājagṛha nāmo re || 1.1*
> *gautama sāmi samosaryā giruyā śrīgaṇadhāro re |*
> *sādhu saṃghāti paravaryā śrutakevalī suvicāro re || 1.2*
> *vādivā śreṇika āviyau dyai gaṇadhara upadeśo re |*
> *vāṇī amṛta śrāviṇī niścala suṇai nareśo re || 1.3*

> In the Jambudvīpa, the place of the highest person;
> In the most fine land of Bhārata there is a city named Rājagṛha. /1.1/
> At that auspicious time Lord Gautam, great leader of disciples,
> spent time there with a group of sādhus; he was accomplished and wise. /1.2/
> [King] Sreṇika had come to that wise one, for the advice of the disciple-leader.
> His words to the listeners were nectar; the lord of men listened without doubt. /1.3/
> (Samaysundar 1959: 2)

What we see here is no more than the setting of the Jain *Rāmāyaṇa* that we know already from Vimalasūri; King Śreṇik comes to ask Gautam for advice. But in the

Sītārāmcaupāī, Gautam first lists the 18 sources of sin, which I think are more familiar amongst Śvetāmbara Jains. Having done so, over several verses, Gautam makes the following observation:

> *e aḍhāra pāpa ehavā je karai pāpī jīvo re |*
> *bhavasamudra māhe te bhamai duḥkha dekhai karai rīvo re || 1.7*
> *valī viśeṣa koī sādha nai āpai kūḍau ālo re |*
> *sītā nī pari duḥkha sahai sabala paḍai jajālo re || 1.8*

> These are the 18 sins, which the sinful *jīvas* perform.
> They stray in the ocean of existence; seeing their pain makes one scream out. /1.7/
> Some might speak and lash out at a sādhu with a lie;
> and he will fall into a web of torment as painful as the sorrows of Sītā. /1.8/

This pricks Śreṇik's curiosity, and he begs Gautam to tell him more about this 'blessed' ('*bhagavana*') person. Gautam obliges, and begins telling the story of Sītā's earlier birth as Vegavatī, a *purohit*'s daughter who spread false rumours about a *muni* and was harshly punished for it in a later life. This story gets the narrative under way, and via the story of Bhāmaṇḍala's previous life as a kidnapping prince, we eventually arrive at the familiar entry point of Sītā and Bhāmaṇḍala's birth at the court of Janaka and Vedehī. From this point onwards, we again follow the *Rāmāyaṇa* story as it appears in the *Pauma Cariya* all the way to Sītā's banishment from Ayodhya and the series of events this sets in motion. Unlike the *mahākāvya Sītācaritra*, the *Sītārāmcaupāī* continues the entire story up to and including the episode where Sītā as a deity comes to help Lakṣmaṇa and Rāvaṇa out of hell, which also appears in the final canto of the *Pauma Cariya*. But while the structure and content of the *Sītārāmcaupāī*, apart from its early stages leading up to Sītā's birth, is similar to that of the *Pauma Cariya*, Samaysundar's style tends to place greater emphasis on Sītā's character and the virtues of her actions, at times also interjecting entire cantos of songs full of her praises. What is especially singled out is Sītā's stoicism in the face of misfortune, which she ascribes to errors in a previous life, and her eventual embrace of asceticism. And so the final words of Gautam to Śreṇik, before Samaysundar finishes the composition with an account of his lineages, are an exhortation to venerate Sītā for these *satī* qualities.

At this point we may note how both the *Sītārāmcaupāī* and the *mahakāvya Sītācaritra* employ transfocalising strategies in their respective beginnings. These shift the balance of the narrative over to Sītā, not in terms of focusing on Sītā instead of other characters, but in terms of emphasising her actions and especially her *satī* qualities as the most desirable and instructive in the *Rāmāyaṇa*.

This tendency towards transfocalisation is then borne out further in the mid-17th-century Brajbhāṣā *Sītācarit* by Rāmcand Bālak. Nothing is known about this Bāḷak, and Jain literary histories are sometimes even confused whether he really was a Rāycand (both names appear in the text) and, if so, which of the other Rāycands he might be identified as. Unfortunately, I do not find any of these projections too convincing, especially as they all involve stretching Rāycand/Rāmcand's dates many decades beyond what is probable. What does emerge, however, is that Rāmcand Bālak/Rāycand seems broadly to have been affiliated with the *adhyātmika* movement, which today is perhaps most closely associated with the slightly earlier Digambar merchant Banārsīdās. Bālak's Rājasthānī-inflected Brajbhāṣā, the eastern Uttar Pradesh/western Rājasthān region where manuscripts of the *Sītācarit* are commonly found in Digambar temple libraries, and the lack of interest in lineages and other formal structures in the *Sītācarit* itself, suggest that we may well hypothesise that Bālak was one of the intellectual lay Jains who partook in the study and devotion sessions that marked the *adhyātma* movement of the 17th century.[5]

We may study the opening sequence of the *Sītācarit* in some detail. It opens with the customary series of benedictions and a call to the 'greatest benefactor' to guide Bālak's efforts in setting down the famous qualities of Rāma and Sītā in words. It is when the narrative action gets underway that we see Bālak's ingenuity. After dispensing with the essential events of the war between Rāma and Rāvaṇa in a single *savaiyā*, he turns, in verse 18, to the narrative of Rāma and Sītā's return to Ayodhya. In other words, Bālak begins almost at the ending. And the very first episode he describes in any detail is that of Sītā's dream. Already present in the *Pauma Cariya*, this episode recounts how Sītā dreams of both good and bad omens. Rāma explains the former as the birth of two sons, but is less certain about the latter. Intriguingly, both the *Pauma Cariya* and the *Sītārāmcaupāī* have Rāma describing the dream as 'a bad omen', but in the *Sītācarit* he deems it 'meaningless' (*aṭapaṭau*).

The dream sequence is followed by the spreading of rumours and Sītā's eventual banishment into forest exile. Then, when Sītā is taken to the forest by a reluctant army commander, she gives a lecture on the paramount importance of remaining steadfast on the Jain path, which culminates in her embrace of the role of the *satī*:

tātaiṃ satī subhāva iha dosa na kāhu dehi |
vaṃdhai apa karma bhogavai udai āi phala jehi || *71*

So this is the good nature of the satī; she never blames,
binds herself to the enduring of her actions, from which fruits arise. /71/[6]

When the commander returns to Ayodhya, bringing Sītā's words, Rāma is most dejected, praises Sītā's character and laments his own bad karma, which compelled him to 'destroy her happiness'. From here, we follow the story of Sītā's exile in the forest up to her giving birth to the twin boys. Only in verse 152 does the sage

5 See Cort 2015 for more on this milieu.

6 All references from Bālak's *Sītācarit* are from my forthcoming critical edition, prior to which it has only been available in manuscripts. The edition's four main manuscript witnesses are all dated to the 18th century (Bālak 1711; 1727; 1729; 1761).

Nārada begin telling the twin boys the story of what has happened previously. This takes up most of the remaining narrative, in which Sītā's appearances mostly are kept to a minimum. Only in the last 200 verses (out of about 2,500), as Nārada finishes his telling, do we return to the *Sītācarit*'s frame story of Sītā's exile and so the narrative ends with Sītā's fire ordeal and her asceticism.

In terms of narrative structure, the *Sītācarit* then performs the perhaps most clearly defined transfocalisation of the material we have surveyed so far. It rearranges the ordering of the narrative events themselves so as to frame the entire *Rāmāyaṇa* story within the context of Sītā's banishment and her response to it. Through this device, the *Sītācarit* establishes an interpretative lens through which we first see Sītā's actions as constituting a paradigmatic, exemplary Jain response to a difficult situation. Throughout his telling of the *Rāmāyaṇa* story, Bālak tends to emphasise how the individual character deals with her or his particular situations, taking great care in delineating the agonies of Rāvaṇa. In this, it seems the audiences are encouraged to weigh these characters' responses to those of Sītā, and so it is an added validation when, at the end, Bālak closes his narrative by returning to her and her *satī* qualities. We may then see that the *carit* of the title really does refer to Sītā's 'actions' or 'deeds' as much as to the 'biography' concept; though, of course, the two are closely linked in Jain literature anyway.

Before we turn to take a bird's-eye view of all of these compositions and attempt a return to the introductory questions of this paper, it might also be interesting to take a brief look at yet another example of a Sītā-focused Jain composition. This is the *Sītā Pacīsī*, a *kathā*-like work that appears in a 19th-century *guṭkā* together with a *Rāma Lakṣmaṇa Kathā* (Anonymous 1862). It takes up nine pages of the *guṭkā*, and is mainly a song narrative, featuring *ṭekas*, in a late Brajbhāṣā with some Rājasthānī features. I will not dwell too much on this *Sītā Pacīsī* here, but what we should note is that it contains the elements of the Sītā segment of the *Rāmāyaṇa* story that we already have seen in the other material, and nothing more. Like Bāḷak's *Sītācarit*, it begins at the 'end' – no longer really an ending, but a beginning – with Rāṃa and Sītā's return to Ayodhya. The initial *ṭeka* nicely sums it up when it says that 'Rāma abandoned the faultless Sītā alone in the forest' (*ara niradosa jyānakī raghupati nai choḍī vana mai yekalī*). Some elements of the ensuing narrative appear, mainly the war between the twin boys and Rāma, but the focus remains on Sītā, her response to the forest exile and her final renunciation. As in the *Sītācarit*, much is made out of Sītā's speech to the army commander, and the message she asks him to take back to Rāma is familiar, too:

> *kahau rāma sudharma na choḍaiṃ svarga mukti suṣa dāī* ||
>
> Tell Rāma not to abandon the good dharma, the liberator of heaven, the bestower of bliss. /
> (Anonymous 1862)

Compare Sītā's comments at the same point in the *Sītācarit:*

> *sītā saṃde sau kahyau kahau rāma hū jāni |*
> *loka vadita tuma hūṃ tajī dharma mati tajau jāna || 66*
>
> Doubting, Sītā said, 'Say this to Rāma:'
> 'For the sake of what people say, you have abandoned me; do not abandon dharma too' /66/

If the wording is different, the sentiment is similar, and throughout the *Sītā Pacīsī* we recognise the same stoic, *satī* Sītā of the *Sītācarit*, and her exhortation to remain true to the Jain *dharma*, if not to her. And after gently touching on the various narrative ingredients, the *Pacīsī* ends with Sītā describing her vows of renunciation and their benefits, leaving the audience with an impression of her virtues as an ideal Jain woman, and of how these may be attainable for others through emulation or devotion, or both.

Coming at the end of this brief sprint through a selection of Sītā-oriented Jain compositions, the *Sītā Pacīsī* can be read as an encapsulation of the effects and intentions that seem to be at work in the other, longer stories. By shifting the entry points of the narrative, sometimes even altering the narrative structure itself, these stories transpose and refocus the Jain *Rāmāyaṇa* story, so that it is primarily the story of Sītā and her virtues. As I already have argued, this is not to say that only Sītā remains. On the contrary, the other characters and elements of the story may still remain, and in some of these texts, such as the *Sītārāmcaupāī*, even be described in great detail. What have been shifted are what Said dubbed the relationships of 'continuity or antagonism or a mixture of both', or, in Genette's terms, a transposition between hypo- and hypertext has taken place, which may never be 'innocent'.

Before I turn to an attempt at collating all of these quite scattered examples into digestible questions for further discussion, I would like to add, simply for the sake of comparison and to extend the scope of my later questions, a very brief look at two Jain *Hanumān Caritras*. One of them is by Brahma Rāymalla, a Digambara of the first half of the 16th century. According to biographical traces in his body of work, Rāymalla started his professional life as a manuscript copyist in Delhi, before moving to Jhujhnu in today's Rajasthan. There he took to making his own compositions and left about 15 works in 'Early Hindi' (Mishra 1994: 407–418). This 'Early Hindi' moniker reflects Rāymalla's mix of Brajbhāṣā and Rājasthānī features, but I will not go into the wider question of Jains and Brajbhāṣā here. I accessed several manuscripts of Rāymalla's *Hanumān Carit* in Rajasthan, perhaps indicating the composition's popularity (Rāymalla 1768; n.d.; n.d.). The other is a Sanskrit *Hanumaccaritra* by Brahmājita, who, judging by his own statements, composed this work on the direct orders of his guru Vidyānandin, a Digambara teacher of the early 16th century. A fairly early copy is available at the British Library, and it is at times almost completely covered by annotations in what appears to be Hindī-like vernacular (Brahmājita 1578).

As promised, I will not go into great detail about these texts here, but only note that they both feature the same narrative movement in their respective beginnings. Both begin with a number of benedictions – Brahmājit referencing all of his teachers and intellectual idols, including Kundakunda, and Brahma Rāymalla pleading his own stupidity – before jumping straight into the story of Añjanā. This princess is the daughter of a *vidyādhara* king, and her story appears already in the 15th canto of the *Pauma Cariya.* It tells of how Añjanā is given in marriage to the Prince Pavanañjaya, who suspects her of infidelity and abandons her for 22 years. When that time has passed he comes across a lovesick bird, regrets his actions, and returns to Añjanā. They make love, and he sets off again, leaving her to fall pregnant and be thrown out by a disbelieving mother-in-law. Left to wander alone, Añjanā meets a Jain monk who explains that her present misery is the result of a misdeed in a previous life. Later, Añjanā gives birth to the boy Hanumān, who proceeds to play a major role in the *Rāmāyaṇa* story, and so both *Hanumān Caritras* turn to chronicle these events once Añjana's story is told. This Añjanā story, however, is one of the most popular *satī* stories of popular Jainism. Kelting (2009: 66) notes of the story that the further it 'gets from the *Rāmāyaṇa*, the more it stresses her virtues as a satī'. Exploring just how far it 'gets' in these *Hanumān* narratives will be a task for a different study, but here we may note how the *Rāmāyaṇa* story is prefaced by a *satī* narrative, and that, too, to the extent where this element colours what is to come. Indeed, the *Jinaratnakośa* even records *Añjanācaritra* as a popular, alternate title for the *Hanumaccaritra* (Velankar 1944: 459). And so, for the sake of argument, we may conclude this hurried tour through a variety of materials by paraphrasing Kulkarni and saying that all of these stories of Sītā and Hanumān, these Jain *Rāmāyaṇas*, are essentially *satī* stories. Or are they?

Concluding Questions

At the outset of this rush through *caritras*, *kāvyas*, *caupāīs*, songs and more *caritras*, I promised nothing but questions. Now that we have made it through to the other end, let us see how those questions may look. My argument here has been that the materials under survey, to varying degrees, all lean closer towards the *satī* narrative than the Purāṇa, in terms of intent and, at times, content. Again, that is not to say that the overarching structure of the 63 Great Men is dispelled or forgotten, even though some of the compositions do not refer to it at all. On the contrary, I think it is taken completely as a given here that audiences would be familiar with this superstructure (though the *Pacīsī* in particular seems to be doing fine without it).

What we see in these compositions is, I believe, possibly something akin to the situation described by Bryant (1978) in his study of the poetry of Sūrdās, the early 16th-century Brajbhāṣā *bhakti* poet. Where earlier commentators assumed that Sūrdās' songs fundamentally were translations of the *Bhāgavata Purāṇa*, Bryant argued that close readings of his songs reveal that they actually were relying on the audiences' familiarity with that base text in order to have their full effect. For instance, they knew that at a certain point a demon would enter, and so Sūrdās could end his poem with a description of an ominous cloud.

And here come my questions. May we think of these Jain *Rāmāyaṇa* narratives as continuations of a Jain *Rāmāyaṇa* tradition, continuations that presupposed familiarity and were then free to go in new directions, emphasising other aspects? If so, what does this mean for the way we speak of the Jain *Rāmāyaṇa* tradition? May we, for instance, paraphrase Richman (1991) and speak of 'many Jain *Rāmāyaṇas*'? And what do these new possibilities mean for our evaluation of the importance of early modern Jain literature? I leave these open to discussion.

References

ANONYMOUS. *Mahākāvya Sītācaritra.* British Library, Bühler 301 (India Office Library).

ANONYMOUS (1862) *Sītā Pacīsī.* Apabhraa, BSāhitya Akādamī, 3673/1.

BĀLAK, R. (1711) *Sītācarit.* Śrī Anekānt Gyān Mandir, 10Y23.5-B.

— (1727) *Sītācarit.* M.D. Jain Shodh Samsthan, 225/25.

— (1729) *Sītācarit.* Śrī Digambar Jain Mandir Baḍā Terapanthiya, 2363/2006.

— (1761) *Sītācarit.* Śrī Digambar Jain Mandir Baḍā Terapanthiya, 2368/2083.

BRAHMĀJITA (1578) *Hanumaccaritra.* British Library, Or. 2129.

BRITISH LIBRARY (2006) *Catalogue of the Jain Manuscripts of the British Library: Including the Holdings of the British Museum and the Victoria & Albert Museum,* vol. 3. London: British Library & Institute of Jainology.

BRYANT, K.E. (1978) *Poems to the Child-God: Structures and Strategies in the Poetry of Sūrdās.* Berkeley: University of California Press.

CORT, J.E. (1993) An Overview of the Jaina Purāṇas. In Doniger, W. (ed.), *Purāṇa Perennis: Reciprocity and Transformation in Hindu and Jaina Texts,* 185–206. New York: State University of New York Press.

— (2015) Making It Vernacular in Agra: The Practice of Translation by Seventeenth-Century Jains. In Orsini, F. and Butler Schofield, K. (eds), *Tellings and Texts: Music, Literature and Performance in North India,* 61–105. Cambridge: Open Book Publishers.

DALAL, C.D. AND GANDHI (eds) (1937) *A Descriptive Catalogue of Manuscripts in the Jain Bhandars at Pattan,* vol. 1. Baroda: Oriental Institute.

DE CLERCQ, E. (2005) Paümacariya – Padmacarita – Paümacariu: The Jain Ramāyāna-Purāṇa. *Epics, Khilas, and Puranas: Continuities and Ruptures, Proceedings of the Third Dubrovnik International Conference on the Sanskrit Epics and Puranas, September 2002*, 597–608. Zagreb: Academia Scientiarum et Artium Croatica.

Genette, G. (1980) *Narrative Discourse: An Essay in Method.* Ithaca: Cornell University Press.

— (1997) *Palimpsests: Literature in the Second Degree.* Translated by C. Newman and C. Doubinsky. Lincoln: University of Nebraska Press.

Kelting, M.W. (2009) *Heroic Wives: Rituals, Stories, and the Virtues of Jain Wifehood.* Oxford: Oxford University Press.

Klatt, J. (2016) *Jaina-Onomasticon.* Wiesbaden: Harrassowitz Verlag.

Kulkarni, V.M. (1990) *The Story of Rāma in Jain Literature: As Presented by the Śvetāmbara and Digambara Poets in the Prakrit, Sanskrit and Apabhraṁśa Languages.* Ahmedabad: Saraswati Pustak Bhandar.

Mishra, S. (1994) *Hindī Jain Sāhitya Kā Bṛhad Itihās. Bhāg 2: Satrahvī Śatī (Maru Gurjar).* Varanasi: Pūjya Sohanlal Smārak Pārśvanāth Śodhpīṭh.

Pollock, S. (2006) *The Language of the Gods in the World of Men: Sanskrit, Culture, and Power in Premodern India.* Berkeley: University of California Press.

Ramanujan, A.K. (1991)Three Hundred Ramayanas. Five Examples and Three Thoughts on Translation. In Richman, P. (ed.), *Many Rāmāyaṇas: The Diversity of a Narrative Tradition in South Asia*, 22–47. Berkeley: University of California Press.

Rāymalla, B. (1768) *Hanumān Carit.* Apabhraṃśa Sāhitya Akādamī, 1819.

— (n.d.) *Hanumān Carit.* Apabhraṃśa Sāhitya Akādamī, 4335.

— (n.d.) *Hanumān Caritra.* Nasia Ji Jain Mandir Bharatpur, 306.

Richman, P. (ed.) (1991) *Many Rāmāyaṇas: The Diversity of a Narrative Tradition in South Asia.* Berkeley: University of California Press.

Said, E.W. (1975) *Beginnings: Intention and Method.* New York: Basic Books.

Samaysundar. (1959) *Kavivar Samaysundar Kṛta Sītārām Caupāī.* Edited by A. Nahta and B. Nahta. Bikaner: Sādūl Rājasthānī Risarc Insṭīṭyūṭ.

Velankar, H.D. (1944) *Jinaratnakosa: An Alphabetical Register of Jain Works and Authors.* Pune: Bhandarkar Oriental Series Research Institute.

Vimalasūri (1962) *Paumacariyaṃ: āyariyasirivimalasūriviraiyaṃ. hindīaṇuvāyasahiyaṃ.* Edited by H. Jacobi, 2d ed. Varanasi: Prākṛta Grantha Parishad.

Two Buddhists, Two Jackals and a Flying Stupa

Examination of the Buddhists in the Jain *Dharmaparīkṣā*

Heleen De Jonckheere

Jain narratives, with their instructive tendency, often point out the rights and wrongs by referring critically to other traditions. The satirical narrative *Dharmaparīkṣā*, by the Digambara monk Amitagati, written at the beginning of the 11th century, does this explicitly as it criticises Jainism's opponents through narrative. Although this work emphasises the faults and flaws of the Purāṇic tradition, some space is also reserved for Buddhists. They appear as characters in one of the sub-stories of the *Dharmaparīkṣā* and are explicitly attacked at the end of the text. This paper will discuss in detail what is said about Buddhists in the *Dharmaparīkṣā* and why it is so important to mention them in a text that was composed when Buddhism was already declining in India. I will show that, by opposing Buddhists, Amitagati puts them within the philosophically relevant world for the Digambara Jain community, and that his characterisation of them reveals more about his own community than about Buddhists themselves.

Introduction

In the course of its development, Jainism, a religious tradition that arose around the 6th century BCE in India, was continuously confronted with and influenced by all sorts of ideas and practices that were circulating in the subcontinent. Contacts between the Jain and other traditions, such as Hinduism and Buddhism, resulted both in opposition or influence, and are attested in many texts produced by the Jains or by other traditions.

The *Dharmaparīkṣā*, a textual tradition that is the focus of my research and of this chapter, is an example of how the Jains dealt with their others.[1] As the title reveals – *Dharmaparīkṣā* translates as 'Examination of Religion'[2] – the texts under discussion try to examine and argue why the Jain tradition is 'true' (*samyak*) and why other traditions, especially the dominant Brahmanical tradition, are not. More specifically, the texts make their argument within a narrative structure using stories that refer to and satirically criticise Hindu Puranic and epic episodes. As such, the *Dharmaparīkṣā* can be related to the tradition of *Jaina Purāṇas* and Jain versions of the *Mahābhārata* and *Rāmāyaṇa*. These Jain versions of all-Indian narratives are different from the better-known Hindu versions (with Vālmīki's version as authoritative) on specific aspects, and often explicitly criticise the Hindu version. Besides, the *Dharmaparīkṣā* is often compared to the *Dhūrtākhyāna* of Haribhadra[3] because the works have a similar framework-structure, common narrative motifs, and because both texts are satirical towards religion.[4]

Being a narrative with a satirical undertone criticising other religious traditions, the *Dharmaparīkṣā* was most probably meant to be heard or read by a Jain lay audience, and had the function to convert the laity to Jainism or direct them back to the correct Jain path.

Several versions of the *Dharmaparīkṣā* exist, written from at least the 10th century onwards by Digambara Jain authors. Later (at least from the 15th century onwards), some Śvetāmbara versions were also composed. The oldest *Dharmaparīkṣā* was composed in Apabhraṃśa by Hariṣeṇa in 11 *sandhis* ('chapters' typical for Apabhraṃśa Digambara literature) in 988 CE. However, Hariṣeṇa himself states that he based his composition on an older work in Prakrit by one Jayarāma, but this text has never been found (Upadhye 1942: 595). The most popular version is the *Dharmaparīkṣā* in 21 *paricchedas* ('chapters') by Amitagati, written in 1014 CE, and according to Upadhye (1942) based on the same text as Hariṣeṇa's *Dhammaparikkhā*. Manuscripts of Amitagati's Sanskrit composition can be found in many manuscript collections all over India, and his text is supposedly the inspiration for later versions by others.[5] These later versions were written up to

1 There are several works titled *Dharmaparīkṣā* that all share the same content. I will focus on two of them (see below).

2 Many things can be said about the complexities in translating the word *dharma* that I do not want to discuss here. I chose to translate it as 'religion' because the text is about weighing one religio-philosophical tradition against another.

3 For works referring to the *Dharmaparīkṣā* and the *Dhūrtakhyāna* together, see, for example, Warder (1992: 253), Upadhye (1944) and Osier (2005).

4 Osier writes that the satirical aspect of both texts makes them stand out because this is very uncommon and should especially not be used when refuting other religions (Osier 2005: 33). This view is in my opinion incorrect. Lee Siegel, in his work *Laughing Matters* (1987), shows that there was a strong tradition of humour and satire within Indian literature.

5 This is at least true for the Braj version written by Manohardās in 1649. He explicitly says that he has made a *bhāṣā* ('vernacular') version of the text that Amitagati has written earlier (Schubring 1944: 433; confirmed in reading the manuscripts I collected myself).

the 18th century in Sanskrit, Hindi, Gujarati and even Kannada.[6] They seem to have more or less the same content and differ only in language and style.

This paper will highlight one specific passage of the *Dharmaparīkṣā*, a sub-story within the main frame narrative, that brings the Buddhist tradition to the fore. The aim of the discussion is to give a hypothetical explanation of the meaning the inclusion of the Buddhist tradition might have in the story, by using theories of 'othering' as an analytical perspective. For this purpose, the paper will only include in its discussion the compositions by Amitagati and Hariṣeṇa, because these two texts have been published in a critical edition.[7] Before tackling the passage itself, I want to share some more details about the content of the *Dharmaparīkṣā*.

'There Lies the Mountain Called Vijayardha [...] Inhabited By Vidyādharas'

The *Dharmaparīkṣā* consists of a frame story into which smaller stories are embroidered. The main plot of the text tells the story of two Vidyādharas, *vidyā* or genie possessing humans with the ability to fly, in search of the truth (*samyaktva*; according to Jain conceptions). One Vidyādhara, called Manovega, is a devoted Jain and he is concerned about his friend, the other Vidyādhara, called Pavanavega, who has diverged from the right religious path and is especially drawn towards the Brahmanical religion. In search for help to get his friend back on 'the right track', Manovega goes to Ujjain where he meets a Jain monk, Jinamati. Hearing Manovega's problem, Jinamati advises him to take his friend to Pāṭalīputra, a city dominated by Brahmins, portrayed as experts of the Hindu scriptures. There, Manovega engages in discussions with the Brahmins proceeding from incredible stories he makes up about his life. For every few stories the two Vidyādharas take on a different form, as Vidyādharas are able to, before entering the city, thus playing different characters. Every time they enter Pāṭalīputra they are approached by Brahmins who ask them who they are. Thereupon Manovega replies with incredible stories from his life. When the Brahmins do not believe him, he justifies his stories by referring to parallel episodes from the Hindu epics and *Purāṇas*. In this way he proves the inconsistency of Purāṇic Hinduism. After every such discussion the Vidyādharas go out of the city, where Manovega explains to Pavanavega didactic passages on the Jain doctrine. At the end of the *Dharmaparīkṣā* Pavanavega is converted and accepts the vow of a Jain layman.

From this plot it is clear that the real venom of the *Dharmaparīkṣā* was directed towards the Hindu tradition. The opposition played out by the dialogical structure

6 A list of manuscripts, which is, however, not exhaustive, can be found in Upadhye (1942). Part of my doctoral research is involved with checking and updating this list based on manuscripts and catalogues of manuscripts.

7 However, the edition of Hariṣeṇa's *Dhammaparikhā* seems to contain many mistakes. Therefore, my promoter Prof. Dr Eva De Clercq, and I are planning to prepare a new edition.

of the text is between the Jains and the Brahmins, two groups not only standing each on one side of the conversation, but also on one side of the city (outside vs. inside the city). The fact that the Brahmins remain almost completely silent – except for some awestruck interferences – only strengthens the critical tone towards their tradition.

It is not surprising that the *Dharmaparīkṣā* was mostly written to criticise and laugh with the Brahmanical tradition, as (especially by the 9th/10th century) the Jains lived in a context that was ideologically dominated by Brahmanical Hinduism. Stories and gods traditionally connected to Hinduism became more and more popular within the subcontinent, and thus probably also with the Jain laity. For that reason, the Jain audience had to be reminded that the Brahmanical tradition had unsound ideas of right and wrong, the wrong conduct and invalid stories. This underlying message is made clear in the often morally inspired sub-stories such as the story of Madhukara, the Tomaraking and a cow, the farmer and the aloe, the four fools, the Pulinda (a tribe) and his cat, etc. These stories are then compared with Puranic or epic stories like the story of Yama and Chāyā, the sacrifice of Rāvaṇa, the birth of Vyāsa, etc.

What is now of interest is that at the end of the text, in the second to last sub-story, the *Dharmaparīkṣā* includes the appearance of two Buddhists. This is the case in the compositions by Amitagati and Hariṣeṇa. Because the text is about criticising the Brahmins, the question arises as to why exactly the authors chose to include characters from other religious affiliations (or why the hypothetical author on which they based their compositions chose to do this). Featuring religious others, other than the Brahmins, has no real functionality in refuting the Hindu tradition. In fact, the exemplary stories might be about any kind of person or character. So why exactly are the Buddhists playing a role here?

In order to attempt to understand any reason or function of this Buddhist role in both versions of the *Dharmaparīkṣā*, let us look at the plot of 'the story of the two Buddhists'.[8]

'Dear Friend, I Will Tell You Another Story'[9]

In this story, the two protagonists of the *Dharmaparīkṣā*, the two Vidyādharas Manovega and Pavanavega, once again enter the city of Pāṭalīputra, this time dressed up as two Buddhists (*raktapaṭa/vaṃdaya*).[10] As they enter the city, they are noticed by the Brahmins, who approach them to ask who they are and if they want to discuss with them. Manovega, the more devoted Jain of the two, tells the

8 Amitagati, XV, 68–XVI, 20; Hariṣeṇa, sandhi VIII, 7–11.

9 This is how the Buddhist's story is introduced in Amitagati XV, 68.

10 Amitagati describes them as *raktapaṭa* (XV, 68), Hariṣeṇa as *vaṃdaya* (sandhi VIII, 7: 5).

Brahmins that they are the sons of a Buddhist layman. Once, they were protecting the clothes of Buddhist *bhikṣus* ('mendicant') that were lying in the sun to dry, when two terrifying jackals came near. Immediately, our two heroes climbed upon a stupa to flee from the jackals. However, the beasts lifted up the stupa and flew with it into the sky. The two brothers started crying and upon hearing their cries the *bhikṣus* came back outside. Immediately the jackals went further away (12/32 *yojanas*), and let the stupa fall to the ground. As they were about to devour the two brothers, some hunters with dogs and weapons arrived, scaring away the jackals. Happily saved from these frightening beasts, the two sons decided to start travelling and to become Buddhist monks themselves. Wandering around, they arrived at Pāṭalīputra.

Hearing this absurd story, the Brahmins request our two protagonists disguised as Buddhist monks to tell them what really happened. Manovega takes this occasion to parallel their personal narrative with stories found in the Purāṇas that are just as extraordinary. As the Brahmins are reluctant to admit flaws in the Puranic material, Manovega starts telling them the *Setubandha* story from the Rāmāyaṇa. When Sīta is abducted by Rāvaṇa to Laṅkā, Rāma wants to get her back and therefore orders his monkey-army to go to the south of India to build a bridge there, crossing the ocean, to Śrī Laṅkā. In order to do this, the monkeys lift up multiple mountains and rocks without any difficulty, and even playfully. It is in this element of the *Setubandha* story that we find the parallel with the jackals who elevate the stupa. Hearing Manovega's argument the Brahmins realise that if they do not believe the story of the Buddhists, they should also not believe the story from their own Rāmāyaṇa. After this concession, Manovega takes Pavanavega outside the city and explains to him how the Brahmins and their stories are wrong.

This is how the story is told in both Hariṣeṇa's and Amitagati's *Dharmaparīkṣā*. In itself the telling does not reveal any opinion the Jain authors had towards Buddhism. The narrative does not contain anything explicitly negative about Buddhism. On the contrary, the fact that in the end the two young lay Buddhists turn towards the Buddhist way by pursuing to take *dikṣā* ('initiation') themselves seems at first sight to suggest rather a positive stance.

Osier, who studied the *Dharmaparīkṣā* together with the *Dhūrtākhyāna* as examples of Indian satire, writes that the inclusion of two Buddhists might just be favourable for this kind of marvellous story (2005: 283). However, I find this argument unsatisfactory as it does not explain the relationship between the Buddhist setting and the literary genre of fantastic stories, nor does it give an account of the role a Buddhist reference might play in the whole text. In what follows, I will draw hypotheses based on this role.

First, what can be said about the content of the Buddhist story is that it clearly contains an aspect of mockery. The story in itself is completely absurd: two young Buddhist laymen climbing a stupa, which is then lifted by two animals, does not make any sense at all. The men's decision to become monks after they are saved by hunters accidentally passing by also does not seem to be based on any rational reason. For me these narrative elements clearly suggest that the story was meant to be laughed at, triggering an experience of ludicrousness in the audience. Even then, it is not clear if this laughter is directed towards the Buddhists or if it merely serves the satirical tone in which the whole *Dharmaparīkṣā* is written.

Becoming 'The Other'

Another useful way to attack the question at hand might be to look at the context of the story, namely the structure of the text as a whole and the place of this specific story within the narrative sequence. As mentioned above, the *Dharmaparīkṣā* is a collection of stories set in a frame story, which holds the central narrative. The frame story itself is quite simple and mainly involves the two Vidyādharas taking on different transformations (one of which is into Buddhists) that trigger discussions with the Brahmins. The different forms into which they transform are: (1) two poor sons selling wood; (2) a Pulinda ('a type of tribesman') (Manovega) and a cat (Pavanavega); (3) a fake Digambara *ṛṣi* ('sage') (Manovega; Pavanavega's form is undefined); (4) a Hindu *tāpasa* ('ascetic') (Manovega; Pavanavega's form is undefined); (5) two Buddhists; and (6) two Śvetāmbaras. All of these characters are rather peculiar. Next to the overall eccentricity of the characters it is also noticeable that the last four of these transformations are all 'religious types'. So not only are Buddhists included in the humoristic narrative of the *Dharmaparīkṣā*, but other renunciative traditions are also put on stage.

An effective conceptualisation to make sense of this striking sequence of characters, in my opinion, is that of 'othering'. This concept came to the fore because of the growing belief that a definition of identity should be a dialectal, non-essential one. Within religious studies, the concept of othering has led to questioning 'how religious communities saw themselves through their others, how they have been dealing with the problem of these others, or how religious communities have been articulating a distinct identity in relation to these very others' (Maes 2016: 536). This is exactly what the *Dharmaparīkṣā* is about: it is about guiding the audience towards the Jain path by refuting different ideologies. In other words, it 'others' the religious others.

The term 'othering' implies that there should be someone or something in opposition. But it also implies more, because the other does not exist without the self. The other exists only because the self wants to draw boundaries and wants to limit what is part of the self and what should be excluded from the self. So 'othering' implies a process of placing sameness and difference while negotiating one's own identity (Maes 2016: 535).

It is clear that the *Dharmaparīkṣā* opposes the Brahmanical tradition, as the main character constantly goes into discussion with the Brahmins, but does the text also 'other' other religious traditions, especially Buddhism?

Here the idea of the proximate other developed by Jonathan Z. Smith (2004) leads to interesting insights. The basic idea behind this concept is that it is not the ideological (or geographical) remote other that is of importance, but the proximate other that demands and effects a process of 'othering'. Because the proximate other challenges the intact world-view of the self, it is this other that makes the self reflect on its own identity and then re-establish its identity (Smith 2004: 230–250).

Again, the application of this concept on the Brahmins is easy: they were the dominant religion in the subcontinent and they both took from and influenced other traditions there. In other words, as a proximate other, the Brahmanical tradition was influential on the constitution of the Jain identification and identity. But I believe that the concept of the proximate other can also say something about the sequence of transformations the Vidyādharas take on. First of all, the transformations *an sich* reflect the becoming of 'an other'. When turning into something, you turn into something or someone else. The fact that they transform presupposes that the characters (the Buddhists and others) are 'others'. Moreover, telling the ridiculous life-stories through different characters prevents them from blemishing their own identity as true Digambaras.

Secondly, I believe that the order in which the transformations follow each other reflects a line of others that is progressively proximate. The first two transformations are very far removed from the identity of the Digambara Jain authors or audience. These are more general characters understood as 'socially low' in India. They do not belong to the direct referential world of the authors and audience of the *Dharmaparīkṣā* and therefore do not immediately speak to the feeling of self of the audience. They are radically different. The four religious characters that we come across (only) from the second half of the *Dharmaparīkṣā* reflect different types of 'others'. They are more proximate as they belong to renunciative traditions. They share characteristics and beliefs with the Digambara Jain authors of the text and therefore belong to the realm of relevant others. First in this line is the fake Digambara ascetic. He seems similar to what the author or a reader of the text would identify himself with (*e.g.* Amitagati was a *muni* or 'monk'), but is not the same. The story this character tells about himself shows us that he is not a real ascetic, but only pretending to be one. As such, he is definitely other from a real Digambara Jain and joins the line of somewhat foolish characters to confront the Brahmins. The next transformation as a Hindu ascetic is less disreputable. He is honest in his intentions as an ascetic. Being an honest person, he is thus even closer to the intended audience of the *Dharmaparīkṣā*. As an ascetic he shares the same renunciative ideal as Digambara Jains, but as a Hindu he worships gods (like Śiva) that the *Dharmaparīkṣā* satirises. He also must have been a character that the public of the text was familiar with, which makes him proximate, while still clearly different. Third in line are the two Buddhists who are the characters under discussion in this paper. Buddhists and Jains have been often compared to each other because they originated around the same time, have similarities with regard to practices and especially because both traditions oppose the disclosed character of the Vedas. In this respect they are traditionally presented as proximate others, even though, by the time the *Dharmaparīkṣā* was written, the Buddhist community was already in decline, especially in the region where Haribhadra and Amitagati were active, namely Western India, and it is unclear to what extent the intended public actually came into contact with the living tradition of Buddhism. Finally, the last transformation is into Śvetāmbaras. These others are without doubt the closest to the Digambara Jains. They share many characteristics and beliefs with the intended audience, but are different on a few philosophical and practical aspects. As such they can still be staged telling a ridiculous story about themselves.

This sequence of the four religious types can be seen to reflect a line from less proximate to more and most proximate, even to reflect four types on the spiritual path: from a fake ascetic, to a true ascetic who worships gods, to an ascetic closer to the ideal but refuting the idea of a self, to a person very close to the ideal but mistaken in some aspects. The line eventually ends with the ideal of a Digambara Jain, into which Pavanavega is converted.[11]

To sum up, looking at the Buddhists in the context of the other transformations, we can understand their presence in the text as essential in delineating the proximate others. Although at the time the *Dharmaparīkṣā* was written the Buddhists were possibly not present in the direct environment, they were still considered as relevant others. The position of the Buddhists in combination with the Śvetāmbaras and other ascetics gives the impression that the authors at least wanted to mention the other important traditions before ending the composition with an exposition of *dharma* ('religious ideology'). By mentioning these religious groups, by giving them certain characteristics, they are – maybe – demarcating their religio-philosophical world, existing of only those 'others' who are relevant to themselves, for their own delimitation.

The above analysis has made a first attempt at explaining the presence of the Buddhists in the *Dharmaparīkṣā*, suggesting that the Buddhists are staged as 'other', different from the self (of the text) but also demanding action of the self.

The next step of my analysis will be to draw conclusions on the evaluation of the Buddhists. Trying to find more clues towards an understanding of the Buddhists in the *Dharmaparīkṣā*, I will now examine whether we can draw results from a comparative reading of the texts as they have been written by Hariṣeṇa

11 I realise that this kind of interpretation remains a hypothetical explanation. I do not mean that the authors of the *Dharmaparīkṣā* wrote their compositions with this idea directly in mind. I merely want to suggest that this might have been a way in which the Digambaras understood other traditions, and by that themselves.

and Amitagati. If both authors tell the same story, can we discern some differences between the two versions that might elude the question at hand?

Dharmaparīkṣā vs. Dhammaparikkhā

The specific story about the Buddhists is very similar and unfolds in the same way in both texts. At the beginning of the story, Hariṣeṇa is a bit more elaborate, and he gives some more details when the two Buddhist brothers introduce themselves: for example, he tells us that they come from the city of Vikrama in the east.[12] Further, there is a difference in the distance the jackals cross after the *bhikṣus* have come out: 32 *yojanas* in Hariṣeṇa, whereas they only cross 12 *yojanas* in Amitagati's text,[13] and also in the fact that the brothers pick up the clothes of the *bhikṣus* before climbing the stupa in Hariṣeṇa's text. But these are only small differences.

Stylewise, it can be said that Hariṣeṇa writes in a more dynamic style with shorter sentences and pacier dialogues, while Amitagati uses more metaphors, making the text feel more contemplative. These stylistic differences, however, have more to do with difference in language: Apabhraṃśa, the literary language of Hariṣeṇa's text, tends to be 'lighter' in style than literary Sanskrit, which Amitagati uses.

It seems that a comparative perspective towards this specific story within two versions of the *Dharmaparīkṣā* cannot lead to conclusions about the depiction of the Buddhists, since there are no essential differences between the two versions of the story of the Buddhists.

However, at a later point in the *Dharmaparīkṣā* we do find a relevant difference between Hariṣeṇa and Amitagati related to Buddhism. More precisely, in the 17th chapter of Amitagati's *Dharmaparīkṣā*, we find a passage that directly attacks Buddhist philosophy. This passage is not found in Hariṣeṇa's text and is thus a personal addition to the plot by Amitagati. It comes immediately after the last of the invented stories for which the two Vidyādharas take on the form of Śvetāmbaras.

Whereas at the point in Hariṣeṇa's *Dhammaparikkhā* where Pavanavega asks Manovega for an explanation of *dharma* (Jain *dharma*),[14] in Amitagati's *Dharmaparīkṣā* Pavanavega asks his friend to tell him the characteristics (*viśeṣaṃ*) of the doctrines (*śāstra*) of the Brahmins and others (*ādi*).[15] In response to this

12 Hariṣeṇa VIII, 8, v.6: *etthu ji puvvadesi paṃḍiyaṇāri mahu piu buddhabhattu vikkamapuri* |

13 Hariṣeṇa VIII, 9, v.1–2: *joyaṇa vattīsa kamevi tehiṃ aḍaihiṃ melleviṇu jaṃvuehiṃ* | *bhakkhijja-hu bhukkhavaseṇa jāma sasuṇaha pāraddhiya patta tāma* | Amitagati XV, 79: *śrutvāvayoḥ svanaṃ yāvannirgacchanti tapasvinaḥ| yojanāni gatau tāvad dvādaśatau mahāsyadau* |

14 Hariṣeṇa X.1, v.1: *puṇu uvavaṇu jāeviṇu guṇu maṇṇeviṇu bhaṇiu mittaṃ maruveëṃ* | *purise keṇa vi bhāsiu loya taü dhammu vi kiṃ veëṃ* |

15 Amitagati XVII, 3: *āsīnau pādapasyādho muktvā śvetāmbarākṛtim| mitra dvijādiśāstrāṇāṃ viśeṣaṃ mama sūcaya |3|*

question (in Amitagati) Manovega first explains what aspects are wrong in the Brahmanical doctrine and then turns his criticism towards the Buddhists (the '*ādi*').

According to Manovega, Buddha's 'aggressive' birth 'breaking' the body of his mother shows that the Buddhist tradition approves of violence. The fact that the Buddha eats meat also proves that there is no compassion in this tradition. For Manovega, even episodes such as the Jātaka story, in which Buddha sacrifices himself to a starving tigress who would otherwise eat up her own cubs, do not show compassion, but instead show that Buddha lacks self-control (*samyama*). Then, Manovega attacks core aspects of Buddhist doctrine. If everything is empty, including the Buddha, how can there be attachment and liberation? If the soul does not exist, every act remains meaningless; if everything is just momentary, then nothing really exists. For these reasons Buddha is a fool and he cannot have omniscience.[16] In fact, these criticisms are the main negative Jain philosophers have against Buddhism, as they represent, according to Jain philosophers, the fact that Buddhism undermines ethical responsibility.

From this passage it is clear that Amitagati has a negative attitude towards Buddhism. He not only finds it necessary to explicitly refute the Brahmanical doctrine, which is the main purpose of the text, he also wants to make sure his audience knows that the Buddhist way is not the one to follow either. Amitagati here uses a more negative structure for the plot than Hariṣeṇa, who in the end wants to convince his audience of the merits of Jainism in a positive way. Hariṣeṇa seems to put more trust on the formative power of the stories. For him it is enough to ridicule the Brahmins in order to effectuate the refutability of their tradition. Amitagati, on the other hand, seeks to build a rational base upon which the refutability of the Brahmins and *'ādi'* ('others') can be proved; he wants to give the audience a reason why. Furthermore, by explaining what is wrong in the 'other' traditions, he tells his audience what Jainism is not. He explicates in detail what aspects of behaviour do not belong to the Jain tradition and in this way marks the borders of the Jain identity. For Amitagati, surely, the Buddhists and their ideas and conduct are to be put outside of these borders.

---

16 Amitagati XVII, 70–77: *ūrdhvādhodvāraniryāto bhaviṣyāmi jugupsitaḥ| iti jñātvā vidāryāṅgaṃ jananyā yo vinirgataḥ |70|*
māṃsasya bhakṣaṇe gṛddho doṣābhāvaṃ jagāda yaḥ| buddhasya tasya mūḍhasya kīdṛśī vidyate kṛpā |71|
kāyaṃ kṛmikulākīrṇaṃ vyāghrabhāryānane kudhīḥ| yo nicikṣepa jānānaḥ saṃyamas tasyakīdṛśaḥ |72|
sarvaśūnyatvanairātmyakṣaṇikatvāni bhāṣate| yaḥ pratyakṣaviruddhāni tasya jñānaṃ kutastanam |73|
kalpite sarvaśūnyatve yatra buddho na vidyate| bandhamokṣāditattvānāṃ kutas tatrvyavasthitiḥ |74|
svargāpavargasaukhyādibhāginaḥ sphuṭam ātmanaḥ| abhāve sakalaṃ vṛttaṃ kriyamāṇam anarthakam|75|
kṣaṇike hantṛhantavyadātṛdeyādayo 'khilāḥ| bhāvā yatra virudhyante tad gṛhnantina dhīdhanāḥ |76|
pramāṇabādhitaḥ pakṣaḥ sarvo yasyeti sarvathā| sārvajñyaṃ vidyate tasya na buddhasya durātmanaḥ |77|

Conclusion

If we now, to conclude this paper, think again about the earlier story of the two Buddhist brothers, keeping in mind the explicit refutation that Amitagati includes at the end of his composition, we can state with certainty that the story does not convey anything positive about Buddhism. The idea that the Buddhists are satirised through this absurd story now seems more likely. However, because the explicit refutation of Buddhism only occurs in Amitagati's text and not in the older version by Hariṣeṇa, the two (the story and the refutation) are not necessarily linked to one another. Therefore, we cannot state with certainty that the Buddhists are originally included as characters in order to satirise them.

Moreover, it is important to note here that the appearance of Buddhists as narrative personages is not exclusive to the *Dharmaparīkṣā*. They are also found in earlier narrative strata: the *Āvaśyaka* commentaries, for example, depict the *rattapaḍas* at the centre of several anecdotes (*e.g.* Balbir 1986: 777). This suggests that Jain narrative literary tradition provided the authors of the *Dharmaparīkṣā* with Buddhists as a sort of optional narrative cliché.

The choice to actually use this narrative *topos* in the *Dharmaparīkṣā*, which mainly criticises the Brahmanical tradition, becomes more meaningful when analysed through the concept of 'othering' as it is developed by Jonathan Z. Smith. Seen from that perspective, the use of Buddhists in the story about the jackals and the stupa is a demarcation of the relevant traditional world. By naming them and giving them some characteristics, notably in the context of the sequence of religious transformations, they are marked as a certain religious group with a definite identity. The mere mention of 'the Buddhists' has some implications: one is that the Buddhists are a group with a different religious tradition, another is that they are opposed to an 'us' that also has a definite identity. In a way, the author is saying to his audience, 'we are all Jains and we are not like them'. In fact, the occurrence of the Buddhists shows that they are still thought of in the 10th and 11th century as part of the Indian traditional world relevant for the Digambara Jains. This idea is further strengthened by the refutation of the Buddhists that Amitagati includes in his composition. The Buddhists as 'other' are still important, they still pose enough challenge to the Jain identity. And therefore it is relevant to include them in the Jains' literary texts, to argue with them and to refute them.

References

Balbir, N. (1986) *Études d'Exégèse Jaina: Les Āvaśyaka (Doctorat d'État).* Lille: Université de Lille.

Black, B. and Patton, L. (eds) (2016) *Dialogue in Early South Asian Religions: Hindu, Buddhist and Jain traditions.* New York: Routledge.

Cabezón, J.I. (2006) The Discipline and its Other: The Dialectic of Alterity in the Study of Religion. *Journal of the American Academy of Religion* 74(1), 21–38.

De Clercq, E. and Vekemans, T. (forthcoming) Rejecting and Appropriating Epic Lore. In Flügel, P. (ed.), *Jaina Narratives*, special issue of *Routledge Advances in Jaina Studies*. New York: Routledge.

Dundas, P. (1999/2002) *The Jains*. Second Revised Edition. London: Routledge.

Granoff, P. (ed.) (1993) *The Clever Adulteress and Other Stories: A Treasury of Jaina Literature*. Delhi: Motilal Banarsidass Publishers.

Jain, B. (ed.) (1990) Ācārya Hariṣeṇa Praṇīta Dhammaparikkhā. Nagpur: Sanmati Research Institute of Indology.

Jaini, P.S. (1998) *The Jaina Path of Purification*. Delhi: Motilal Banarsidass Publishers.

Kulkarni, V.M. (1994) *A Treasury of Jain Tales*. Ahmedabad: Shardaben Chimanbhai Educational Research Centre.

Krümpelmann, K. (2000) *Das Dhuttakkhāṇa: Eine jinistische Satire*. Frankfurt am Main: Peter Lang, Europäischer Verlag der Wissenschaften.

Maes, C. (2016) Flirtation with the other: an examination of the processes of othering in the Pali Vinaya. *Bulletin of the School of Oriental and African Studies* 79(3), 535–557.

ManohardĀs: *Dharmaparīkṣā*. Bhandarkar Oriental Research Institute, 616–1875/76.

Mironow, N. (1903) Die Dharmaparīkṣā des Amitagati. Doctoral Dissertation. Leipzig: Kaiser Wilhelm-Universität zu Strassburg.

Monier-Williams, M. (2001) *A Sanskrit-English Dictionary: Etymologically and philologically arranged with special reference to Greek, Latin, Gothic, German, Anglo-Saxon, and other cognate Indo-European Languages*. Offline digital version. Köln: University of Köln.

Neusner, J. and Frerichs, E. (eds) (1985) *To See Ourselves as Others See Us: Christians, Jews, 'Others' in Late Antiquity*. Chicago and California: Scholars Press.

Nichols, R. (2010) Postcolonial Studies and the Discourse of Foucault: Survey of a Field of Problematization. *Foucault Studies* 9, 111–144.

Osier, J.-P. (2005) *Les Jaïna. Critiques de la Mythologie Hindoue*. Paris: Cerf.

Osier, J.-P. and Balbir, N. (2004) Haribhadra, *Ballade des coquins [Dhūrtākhyāna]*. Présentation et traduction du prakrit. Paris: Garnier Flammarion.

Potter, K. (2007) *Encyclopedia of Indian Philosophies*, vol. 10. Delhi: Motilal Banarsidass Publishers.

Schubring, W. (1944) *Die Jaina Handschriften der Preussischen Staatsbibliothek*. Leipzig: Otto Harassowitz.

Shastri, B.P. (ed.) (1998) Ācārya Amitagati viracita Dharmaparīkṣā. Varanasi: Vardhamana Mudranalaya.

Siegel, L. (1987) *Laughing Matters: Comic Tradition in India*. Delhi: Motilal Banarsidass Publishers.

Smith, J.Z. (2004) *Relating Religion: Essays in the Study of Religion*. Chicago: The University of Chicago Press.

Sternbach, L. (1974) Subhaṣita, Gnomic and Didactic Literature. In Gonda, J. and Harrassowitz, O. (eds), *A History of Indian Literature*. Wiesbaden: Otto Harrassowitz Verlag.

Upadhye, A.N. (1942) Hariṣeṇa's Dhammaparikkhā in Apabhraṃśa. In *Annals of the Bhandarkar Oriental Research Institute.* 13(1–4): 592–608.

Upadhye, A.N. (1944) *Dhūrtākhyāna of Haribhadrasūri: Haribhadra's original Prakrit text, Saṅghatilaka's Sanskrit version and an old Gujarati prose rendering etc. With an elaborate critical essay on Dhūrtākhyāna.* Edited by Śrī Jina Vijaya Muni. Ahmedabad: Saraswati Pustak Bhandar.

Winternitz, M. (1933) *A History of Indian Literature*, vol. 2. Calcutta: University of Calcutta.

Blurring the Distinction between *Dhyāna* and *Svādhyāya* in Jayācārya's Writings on Meditation

Samani Pratibha Pragya

This paper explores Jayācārya's (1803–81) short (*choṭā-dhyāna*) and long compositions on meditation (*baḍā-dhyāna*). My research will explore the sources of this meditative practice in the four types of meditation featured in Jaina canonical texts: *ārtta-dhyāna* or meditation on sadness; *raudra-dhyāna* or meditation on distress; *dharmya-dhyāna* or meditation on reality; and *śukla-dhyāna* or absolutely pure or 'white' meditation (Ṭhāṇa, 4.60). I will argue that Jayācārya's meditative practices represent a framework of analytical meditation (*vicaya-dhyāna*) that is a part of *dharma-dhyāna*. Jayācārya's approach is fundamentally soteriological and draws upon scriptural sources rather than other non-canonical predecessors in Jain yogic or meditational treatises.

Introduction

This paper explores Jayācārya's (1803–81) two compositions on meditation, his short treatise on meditation (*choṭā-dhyāna*) and his longer treatise on meditation (*baḍā-dhyāna*). The research will investigate the nature of these practices, and the innovative approach of blurring the line between *dhyāna* ('meditation') and *svādhyāya* ('scriptural study'), which is inspired by the re-use of the canonical texts for meditational formulae. Jayācārya's contribution lies in the reformed usage of the latter, namely the 'scriptural study', as a means of 'meditation'.

My research explores the Jaina canonical and later developed textual sources of these meditative practices and investigates how Jayācārya applies self-study (*svādhyāya*) of texts on meditation practices. I argue that Jayācārya's meditative practices represent a framework of *vicaya-dhyāna* ('analytical meditation'), the term *vicaya* including meanings such as consideration (*paryālocana*), investigation (*anveśaṇa*), thinking (*anucintana*) and inquiry (*mārgaṇā*).[1] Jayācārya's approach is fundamentally soteriological and draws upon scriptural sources rather than other non-canonical predecessors in Jain yogic or meditational treatises. I demonstrate that, in Jayācārya's treatise, the analytical meditation (*vicaya-dhyāna*) details elaborate descriptive instructions rather than mere designations of concepts as found in canonical texts or non-canonical texts by his predecessors such as Haribhadra (8th century CE), Śubhacandra (11th century CE) and Hemacandra (12th century CE).[2]

I further claim that, by blurring the line between scriptural study (*svādhyāya*) and meditation (*dhyāna*), which are categorised under the umbrella of *tapas* as internal penance (ābhyantara-*tapa*),[3] Jayācārya's method of meditation reinforces contemplative meditation in its archaic form.

Svādhyāya, which literally means self-study, has been provided with detailed descriptions in Jaina texts. According to the *Sthānāṅga-Sūtra* (Sthā, 5.220), it exists in five types: 1) imparting training in scripture and its meaning (*vācanā*); 2) inquiry about the word and meaning for clearing doubts (*pracchanā*); 3) recapitulation of text learnt by rote (*parivartanā*); 4) contemplation of the text and its meaning (*anuprekṣā*); and 5) preaching the discipline through various disquisitions (*dharmopadeśa*).

The Jaina canonical texts feature four types of meditation: 1) *ārtta-dhyāna* may be defined as meditation on sadness; 2) *raudra-dhyāna* as meditation on distress; 3) *dharmya-dhyāna* as meditation on reality; and 4) *śukla-dhyāna* as absolutely pure or 'white' meditation.[4] These meditations are mainly related to 'thinking' and 'concentration'. *Dharma* or *dharmya* and *śukla* are the two types of meditation that have been accepted from the canonical period to the present day as being conducive to attaining the liberated state.[5] *Dharmya-dhyāna* (virtuous meditation) has four aspects, namely, 1) investigation of the scriptural commandments (*ājñjā-vicaya*); 2) investigation of suffering (*apāya-vicaya*); 3) investigation of the fruition of karma (*vipāka-vicaya*); and 4) investigation of the shape of the universe (*saṃsthāna-vicaya*).

Before the exploration of Jayācārya's meditative treatises, I will first attempt to illustrate the term '*dharma*' within the frame of his meditation.

---

1 *Tattvārthabhāṣyānusāriṇī ṭīkā*, 9.37.

2 Olle Qvarnström (1998) writes at length about the adoptability of other yogic practices by Hemacandra in his *Yogaśāstra*, but in the case of Jayācārya's meditation the key source is canonical literature.

3 TS, 9.20, *prāyaścitta-vinaya-vaiyāvṛtya-svādhyāya-vyutsarga-dhyānānyuttaram.*

4 Sthā, 4.60, *cattāri jhāṇā paṇṇattā, taṇ jahā- aṭṭe jhāṇe, rodde jhāṇe, dhamme jhāṇe, sukke jhāne.*

5 Ancient and medieval four-fold meditation is discussed at length by Bronkhorst (1993), Ohira (1981) and Qvarnström (1998).

Philosophical Investigation of *Dharma* and *Dharmya*

The Śvetāmbara and Digambara editions of the *Tattvārthasūtra* traditionally use a slightly varied term, namely '*dharma dhyāna*'[6] and '*dharmya dhyāna*'[7] respectively, though theoretically they both are analogous. *Dharma dhyāna* involves 'meditation on ethics', 'contemplation on reality', etc. in Jaina literature. This is explained as 'analytical' in a dogmatic rather than a scientific sense, since it is related to the application of the categories of the *tattvas*.[8] Jainism, a dualistic religion whose ultimate focus is spiritual development, relies on discriminative knowledge (*bheda-vijñāna*) to achieve the experience of the self. The practice of *dharmya-dhyāna* is analytical insofar as it analyses and reflects on the various aspects of the soul, the non-soul, the universe and the scriptures.[9] In other words, these varieties of *dharmya* practice encompass a wide spectrum of knowledge. In this meditative state, knowledge and concentration go hand in hand.

Later, Śubhacandra explains that *dharma-dhyāna* is predicated on the internalisation and application of the ethico-ontology of the series of *tattvas* that, beginning with soul and non-soul, bondage by karma (*bandha*) and so on, have liberation (*mokṣa*) as the last ontological category.[10]

This is how *dhyāna* is conceptualised in the *Tattvārthasūtra*; however, time affects tradition and Jaina meditation is no exception. During the early canonical period, the sole aim of meditation was the termination of karmic bondage by physical mortification and the attainment of liberation. During the late canonical period, meditation was divided into a fourfold system. Of these, the twofold (*dharmya* and *śukla*) meditation is usually accepted as useful for the achievement of liberation. The classical age was a period of systematisation of meditation, whereas the medieval age includes many aspects, such as adaptability, assimilation from other traditions and a new, distinctly Jaina style of meditation developed by the influence of Haribhadra and Hemacandra.

With this background of Jaina meditation in mind, in what follows I will focus on Jayācārya and his works.

---

6 TS, 9.37 uses the term '*dharma*'.

7 SS, 9.36. *Sarvārthasiddhi* is a commentary of TS by Pūjyapāda Devanandi, who uses the term '*dharmya*'. The '*dharmya*' explains reality, the self and non-self.

8 The third category of meditation has two terms '*dharma*' and '*dharmya*', the *dharma* is used in TS and *Sarvārthasiddhi* employs *dharmya*. Here, *dharma* has many meanings, such as nature of reality, and ten types of *dharma* are mentioned in Sthāṇ (10.135) as well.

9 *Tattvārtha-vārtika*, '*dharmādanapetaṃ dharmyaṃ*' (TS_2, 9.37. *Tattavārtha-vārtika*, quoted in Maṅgalaprajñā 2003: 65).

10 JñA, 31.18. *āñchi jīvādayo bhāvāḥ cidacillakṣlamīt | tat svarūpāvirodhena dhyeyā dharma manīṣibhi ||*

Jayācārya and His Works on Meditation

Jayācārya was the fourth head of Jaina Śvetāmbara Terāpanth sect. He was a meditator and a poet.[11] Muni Hemarāja (1773–1848) was Jayācārya's instructor in religious science (*vidyā-guru*). After initiation, Jayācārya spent 12 years with Hemarāja to acquire knowledge of the āgamas and different spiritual arts (Buddhamala 1991: 341). Ācārya Maghavā (1881–92), the fifth ācārya of the Terāpantha sect, wrote quite specifically in *Jaya-sujaśa*, a biography of Jayācārya (1886), that he had learnt meditation from Muni Hemarāja, that he was well versed in *yoga* (*joga-śāstra*) and that he used to practise meditation for long periods of time. Mahāprajña (1920–2010), the 10th ācārya of the Terāpantha sect, states that Jayācārya's life had been highly influenced by Hemarāja. Hence, possibly, meditational sprouting in Jayācārya must be from Hemarāja.

Jayācārya's Choṭā-Dhyāna (Short Meditation)

As the name itself suggests, this is a very short composition, based on the famous Jain 'great *mantra*' (*mahā-mantra*) or 'salutation *mantra*' (*namaskāra-mantra*).[12] The *namaskāra-mantra* in its composite form first appeared in the invocation of the famous *Bhagavatī-sūtra*,[13] but its origin is unknown.[14] It is used for '*mantra* meditation', or veneration of the gurus or teachers, which has become a standard practice amongst all Jains. It is a regular part of the morning and evening veneration to the guru (*guru-vandanā*), which is the third part of the Āveśyaka-sūtra. The practice of equanimity (*sāmāyika*)[15] also starts and ends with reciting the *namaskāra-mantra*. The practice popularly known as ritualised confession (*pratikramaṇa*) begins and is concluded with veneration of the five stages of the spiritual self (*pañcapada-vandanā*).[16] This meditation is based on mental recitation

11 Jayācārya composed 350,000 verses on various subjects of Jain philosophy and religion in Rājasthānī dialect.

12 The *namaskāra-mantra* is well known as *pañca-maṅgala-mantra*. It is famously followed by a stanza which means 'this five-fold obeisance destroys all evil, and is the first auspicious (*maṅgala*) amongst all the maṅgalas'.

13 BhS.1.1, *ṇamo arahantāṇaṃ. ṇamo siddhāṇaṃ. ṇamo āyariyāṇaṃ. ṇamo uvajjhāyāṇaṃ. ṇamo loe savva sāhūṇaṃ.*

14 Gustav Roth (1974) and Mahāprajña (1982) present a detail study about origin and historical development of *namaskāra-mahāmantra*.

15 ĀvN. 1027, *kaya-pañca-namokkāro karei sāmāiyaṃti so'bhihito | sāmāiyaṃgameva ya jaṃ so sesaṃ ato vocchaṃ ||*

16 See Appendix 1 for the full text in Pratibhāprajñā 2017. In Jayācārya (Mahāprajña 1997b: 92–94), the text details this practice in five steps.

on the qualities of five worthy ones (*pañcaparameṣṭhī*). The *namaskāra-mantra* serves as a tool for *svādhyāya* (scriptural readings), various daily rituals and *dhyāna.*

Jayācārya's Baḍā-Dhyāna (Long Meditation)

This composition outlines four main meditational techniques: 1) the method of mindful recitation of *so'ham* with in-breath and out-breath (*sāsā-surat nai soham ro prayoga*); 2) visualisation of the *tīrthaṅkara* (ford-maker) in various colours (*raṅga sahita tīrthaṅkara rai dhāyan rā prayoga*); 3) meditation on the virtues of liberated souls (*siddhāṁ rai dhyāna ro prayoga*); and 4) meditation on the results of different kinds of action (*karma vipāka rai dhyāna ro prayoga*).[17]

This exposé in four categories shows that Jayācārya's knowledge of meditation was really profound, but he also put the theory into practice. The intensity of his meditative practice becomes clear from the following verses of his Ātmā-*sambodha*: 'I (Jayācārya) find myself like the earth, solemn and unshaken as the Mandara Mountain, collecting gem-like qualities of the self, by performing nectar-like meditative practices.'[18] Meditation is compared here to divine nectar, which is beyond worldly things, and yields innumerable virtues of the self, including forbearance (*niṣprakampa*) and equanimity (*samatā*).

The Method of 'So'ham' Breathing Meditation

The process of breathing was used as an object of concentration by Jayācārya, a practice that inspired the 'perception of breathing' (*śvāsa–prekṣā*), introduced later by Mahāprajña.[19] Jayācārya refers to this practice with the term *sāsā-surata* which means 'awareness' or 'mindfulness of breathing'.[20]

Jayācārya employed breathing as a tool to internalise concentration or awareness by shifting conscious attention away from external objects and onto the movement of the breathing process. He says:

17 I also attempt to present my own translation of Jayācārya's meditation and other sources unless they are mentioned.

18 Jayācārya (Mahāprajña 1997c: 105, v.10), *bhū sama jaya! gambhīra, niṣprakampa mandara-girī herai nijaguṇa hīra, dhyāna sudhārasa dhyāya nai.*

19 See '*sāsā-surat nai soham ro prayoga*' in *Baḍā-dhyāna* of Jayācārya (Mahāprajña 1997a: 81).

20 Akin to Mahāprajña's notion of 'perception of breathing' (see Pratibhāprajñā 2017: 216). Jayācārya's meditational practice survives in modern times as traces embedded within Prekṣā meditation, which originates from the same lineage. Jayācārya's meditation was supplementary to Prekṣā-dhyāna, which was recently developed by Ācārya Mahāprajña.

> Firstly, stabilise the lotus-posture (*padmāsana*) etc., eradicate the fickleness of the body and then also eradicate the fickleness of speech. Thereafter, settle the external mind, in, remove all other subjective thoughts, bring about single mindfulness. In order to focus the mind, observe your breathing. Perceive inhalation and exhalation and during inhalation, think of *sa*, during exhalation, *ha*, whilst reciting the word *so'ham* silently. The meaning of *sa* represents the liberated souls' [my state is like the *siddha*]. *Ahaṃ* means 'I am'. Under the effect of the karmic particles, I have become weak and forgotten myself. But I am like the Liberated Soul. Contemplate on the meaning of the words *so'ham* (I am that), *aham so* (that I am). Whilst doing this, the mind stabilises.[21]

These words represent the first written report on the procedures of meditation in the history of the Terāpantha sect. In his composition, Jayācārya describes meditation as a way of stabilising the mind, through awareness of breathing, in order to connect with the soul. He makes an important distinction between the external (*bāhīra*) and the internal (*andara*), which will be discussed later. Jayācārya's practice of *so'haṃ* can be traced back to the Digambara Ācārya Pūjyapāda (6th century CE) in *Samādhitantra/Samādhiśataka* (SŚ, 28). Pūjyapāda states: 'When the self has a disposition into the supreme-self (*siddha*) again and again such disposition of the self gets firm stability into the pure state of the supreme-self.'[22]

Jayācārya claims that from an absolute standpoint (*niścaya–naya*) each individual has a liberated soul that is burdened by karmic bondage. This suggests that liberation is not limited to a few individuals, *i.e.* that anyone and everyone can eventually become liberated. The soul is identified as twofold: a worldly soul (*jīva*) and a liberated soul (*siddha*). The worldly soul must contemplate on the pure soul to annihilate karmic particles, for the way to liberation is through the purification of the soul.[23]

This finds its appearance in the aphorism of later *prekṣā* meditation, 'see yourself through yourself',[24] where the soul is dichotomised as the observer and the

---

21 Jayācārya (Mahāprajña 1997a: 81, *Prayoga*-1), *prathama to padmāsanādika āsana thira karī, kāyā noṃ cañcalapaṇo meṭī, vacana noṃ piṇa cañcalapaṇo meṭaṇo | pachai mana bāhira thakī andara jamāvaṇo- viṣayādika thaki mana nai miṭāya nai ekanta* āṇaṇo | *te mana ṭhikāṇai āṇavā nimata svāsā surata lagāvaṇī | svara-praveśa-nirgamana ūpara cintavaṇā karaṇī—praveśa meṃ sakāra, nirgamana meṃ hakāra 'so'haṃ' śabda aṇabolyāṃ ucarai | so kahatāṃ te sidha no svarūpa—jiva, te sarīkho | ahaṃ kahatāṃ—hūṃ chūṃ | karmāṃ basa nirabala hoya rahyo,* āpo *bhūlyo chūṃ | piṇa hūṃ te sidha sarīkho chūṃ | 'so'haṃ' 'ahaṃ so' iṇa śabda rai artha ūpara cintavaṇā karaṇī | ima karatāṃ mana nī sthiratā huvai |*

22 Pūjyapāda, (SŚ, 28), *so'hamityātta saṃskārastasmin bhāvanayā punaḥ, tatraiva dṛḍhasaṃskārāl-labhate hyātmani sthitim.*

23 Cf. Kundakunda's potential unacknowledged influence on Terāpanth (discussed by Peter Flügel), http://eprints.soas.ac.uk/7443/1/Terapanth_Enc-rel_02.pdf.

24 DVS, Culikā, *saṃpikkhae appagamappaeṇaṃ.*

observed. Here there seems to be a different approach to Jayācārya's meditation. Jayācārya's emphasis was on experience of the self as pure, his meditation being associated with the liberated ones (*siddha*), while *prekṣā* meditation suggests the meditator should perceive the impure self, leading to a pure state of being where the pure soul is the perceiver.

Another form of *so'ham* meditation was later created in the Sthānakavāsī tradition by Ācārya Ātmārāma (1882–1962) and also became a core practice in the recently developed *ātmā-dhyāna* by Śivamuni.[25]

Colour-Visualisation of the Tīrthaṅkara

Meditation on the ford-maker (*tīrthaṅkaras*) is a traditional practice in Jainism, being a part of the *Āvaśyaka-sūtra*, obligatory for ascetics and laity to some degree. This meditation on the *Caturviṃśatistava* (*Logassa*)[26] is a concentration on words and not visual form. Jayācārya's visualisation of the 24 *tīrthaṅkaras* in various colours appears to be an interiorisation of the popular tradition of seeing the image (*darśana*). This type of practice falls under the category of meditation on form (*rupastha-dhyāna*). Each *tīrthaṅkara* has its own colour, used in various worship (*pūjā*) rituals. Jayācārya described the five colours of the *tīrthaṅkaras* in his work *Caubisī.* [27] *Caubisī* is a set of 24 hymns in the praise of *tīrthaṅkaras* which is extremely popular in Jaina tradition.[28] The purpose and method of such visualisation is to focus on visible colours to enable 'seeing' and 'purifying' the non-visible subtle body and the self.

The discussion of the colours of the *tīrthaṅkara* goes back to Hemacandra's work, the *Abhidhāna-cintāmaṇi*[29] (AC, 1.49). The colour of Mahāvīra as per Hemacandra is golden, which does not match the colour ascribed in the Digambara tradition. Jaini, pointing to *Ravisena's Padmapurāṇa*, mentions that Mahāvīra shone like a crystal in the assembly hall (*samavasaraṇa*). Bronkhorst (1993: 11), comparing the Jaina and Buddhist traditions, describes the Buddha

---

25 This practice is discussed further in Pratibhāprajñā (2017: chapter 5 section 5.8).

26 A eulogy of 24 Tirthaṅkara being a part of Pratikramaṇa ritual or *Āvaśyaka-sūtra*.

27 Jayācārya (Mahāprajña, 1997d: 4, v. 10–11).

śvetavaraṇa canda suvidhi jina, padma vāsupūjya lāla,
muni suvrata riṭhanema prabhu, kṛṣṇa varaṇa suviśāla.
mallinātha phuna pārśva prabhu, nīla varaṇa vara anga
ṣodasa śeṣa jineśa tanu, sovana varaṇa sucanga.

28 Nirvāṇa-śrī and Yogakṣema-prabhā (1994/2009: 81–92) note 109 such Caubisīs were composed by various *ācāryas*.

29 AC, 1.49,

raktau ca padmaprabhavāsupūjau, ṣuklau ca candraprabhapuṣpadaṅtau
kṛṣṇau punarnemimunī vinīlau, śrīmallipārśvau kanakatviṣo'nye.

as golden. This also reveals that *tīrthaṅkaras* and Buddha have been identified with colours, though specification of colours does not seem to exist unless the explanation is symbolic. Ellen Gough (2012),[30] in her research, has brought to light this issue of colour dispute between Digambara and Śvetāmbara traditions. The reasoning behind the different colours of all the *tīrthaṅkaras* also remains unresolved.

Another way of visualising the environment in which the *tīrthaṅkara* is present is the image of the assembly hall where the *tīrthaṅkara* delivers his sermon (*samavasaraṇa*). It can be visualised or imagined in a pictorial way, as though one can feel the presence of a *tīrthaṅkara* (Mahāprajña 1997a: 81). Jayācārya describes this practice in the following way:

> Thereafter meditate on the ford-makers (*tīrthaṅkaras*). Whichever body colours the twenty-four *tīrthaṅkara* were, visualise them with those colours. Where you sit leave a distance of two, three or four arms' length and establish the *tīrthaṅkara*. Imagine that the Lord is sitting here. He is in a stable posture. From the five colours (black, blue, yellow, red or white), visualise whichever colour your mind chooses. Knowing (as if) the *tīrthaṅkara deva* is sitting in this colour, and I am meditating upon Him. Śrī *tīrthaṅkara deva* was this colour. He lived for many years at home. After initiation he bore many hardships ...[31]

Meditation upon the *tīrthaṅkaras* is an important exercise for the theory of transference of qualities (*guṇa-sankramaṇa*). The meditator can begin to mimic the qualities of *tīrthaṅkaras* through the technique of visualisation. The idea is that, with repeated practice over a long period, it is possible to achieve what one wishes or focuses upon. Jayācārya elucidates the concept of the preaching assembly hall of the ford-makers (*samavasaraṇa*). Similar descriptions could be found in commentarial literature such as the discussion of *aṣṭa-prātihārya* in the Āvaśyaka-niryukti (ĀvN, 362.1).[32]

---

30 In her article 'Shades of Enlightenment: A Jain Tantric Diagram and the Colours of the *tīrthaṅkaras*', Ellen Gough (2012) discusses the debate between the Śvetāmbaras and Digambaras concerning the colours of the *tīrthaṅkaras*. However, her study is restricted to sectarian debates, and there is no reference to the practice of visualisation upon the *tīrthaṅkaras* during meditation.

31 Jayācārya (Mahāprajña 1997a: 81, *Prayoga-2*), *raṅga sahita tīthaṅkara rai dhāyan rā prayoga: tivārai pachai tīrthaṅkara noṃ dhayān karaṇo | caubīsa tīrthaṅkara je raṅge thayā te tīrthaṅkara raṅga sahita ciṅtavaṇā | āpa baitho tiṇa āgai do hātha tīna hātha yā cāra hātha rai āṅtarai tīrthṅkara nai thāpaṇā | jāṇai iṇa ṭhikāṇai śrī bhagavaṇta virājyā chai | thira āsaṇe chai. Kālo nīlo pīlo rāto tathā dhavalo ai pāṇcūī raṅga māṃhai āparo mana hovai soī raṅga rī cintavaṇā karaṇī | jāṇai iṇa raṅge tīrthṅkaradeva virājyā chai, so hūṃ piṇa uṅāro ija dhyāna dhyāvūṃ chūṃ | śrī tīrthaṅkara deva ise raṅge huṅtā | so ghaṇā varsāṃ tāi to ghara meṃ rahyā. Pachai dikhyā lai nai, ghaṇā parisaha sahī nai ...*

32 ĀvN, 362.1, *ceiduma*
pīḍhachandaya, āsaṇa chattaṃ ca cāmarāo ya jaṃ ca'ṇṇaṃ karaṇijjaṃ, karenti taṃ vāṇamantariyā.

> The Lord seems as if he is sitting on a throne of snow rock crystal. Above his head are three parasols (*tri-chatra*) and an *aśoka* tree. Flanked by him are flywhisks, divine kettledrums, a halo and religious wheel to adorn him. Ahead of him is the finery of the four-fold congregation. There, the heads of the demigods and goddesses, men and women are gathered and seated. They look upon him, transfixed, and they become ecstatic.[33]

Jains theorise their Jina or the *tīrthaṅkaras* as engrossed in extremely pure meditation for long durations in stable postures with stillness in mind, body and speech. Through performing the highest level of penance and in their meditation posture these *jinas* achieved perfection and attained omniscient knowledge. *A tīrthaṅkara* is considered to be endowed with infinite knowledge, perception and conduct. His modes and qualities of conduct are held to be extremely pure. He is assumed to know and perceive all of the substances of the cosmic space (*loka*) and super-cosmic space (*aloka*) with his infinite knowledge (Mahāprajña 1997a: 81–82). These reflections refer to the description found in texts like *Samavāyāṅga*, which describes 35 verbal signs of superhuman magnificence (*vacanātiśaya*) (SamS, 34; AC, 1.65–71), 34 special qualities (*atiśaya*) (SamS, 34–35; AC, 1.65–71) and other qualities of the *tīrthaṅkaras* Jayācārya summarises this description in the following way:

> His dripping nectar like voice is enlightening. It is the exceedingly loving voice of the Lord. The ocean of ambrosia water is sweet but the voice of the Lord is sweeter, it contains the thirty-four supreme qualities (*atiśaya*). The *tīrthaṅkara* is as pure as the moon, is like an earthen lamp light illuminating. He is like the ocean deep and carries its stillness. He crosses the worldly ocean and enables others to cross. He is the great shepherd man (*gopāla*). Apart from that, there are numerous other qualities that he has. As the meditation becomes purer, more qualities appear and as more qualities are praised the meditation becomes purer. Thereafter whichever colour was contemplated that colour begins to appear; it is as if the *tīrthaṅkara* has taken seat at this location. This type of omniscient God (*arahant-deva*) having destroyed all his *karmas* becomes a liberated soul (*siddha*).[34]

---

33 Jayācārya (Mahāprajña 1997s: 81, *Prayoga-2*), *te bhagavān jāṇai phaṭika siṅghāsaṇa ūpara virājamāna chai | mastaka ūpara tīna chatra asoga vṛkṣa chai | pāsai cāmara, devadundabhī, bhāmaṇḍala, dharmacakre karī sobha rahyā chai | mukha āgala cyāra tīrtha rā thāṭa chai | jihāṃ indra-indrāṇī, deva, nara-nāryāṃ rī paraṣadā baiṭhī chai | te bhagavaṅta nai dekhai chai, dekha dekha nai harṣe chai |*

34 Jayācārya (Mahāprajña 1997a: 82, *Prayoga-2*), *imaratadārā vāṇī prakāsa karai chai | atyaṅta vallabha bhagavān rī vāṇī chai | mīṭho khīra samudra no pāṇī te thī piṇa bhagavān rī vāṇī ghaṇī mīṭhī chai | paintīsa guṇe karī sahita chai | te bhagavāna caṅdra jisā niramala, dīpaka jyūṃ udyota rā karaṇahāra chai | samudra samāna gambhīra chai | āpa tarai chai, aurāṃ nai tārai chai | mhā guvāla purasa chai | iṇa rīte aura aneka guṇa chai | dhyāna niramala caḍhai jarai guṇa ghaṇāṃ pragaṭa thāya anai ghaṇā guṇagāna karai tivārai dhyāna niramala caḍhai | tivārai jehavo raṅga ciṅtavai tehavoī dīsaṇa lāga jāvai,*

Visualisation extends to the physical environment of the *tīrthaṅkara*, his physical body, physical suffering, etc. This is done as a means of developing one's imagination in a way that enables clear, discriminating perception of the nature of things, in particular, differences between the inner and outer worlds, and the importance of turning inwards only once the outer world has been mastered.

Jayācārya's meditation presents a deep devotion, which is based on the description of the *tīrthaṅkara*'s hagiography from the later developed canons. He incorporates the techniques of visualisation and colour, which are well-known tantric elements. He does not present this meditation as a worship (*pūjā*) ritual, but creates an environment for the *tīrthaṅkara*'s presence.

Visualisation of the *tīrthaṅkara*'s physical appearance, physical struggles, his environment, etc. relies on textual tradition, especially canonical literature, and is recommended as a means of turning and focusing the mind (*manas*) inwards. Although key tantric elements are incorporated in the visualisation of the images of *tīrthaṅkaras* such as the use of colour meditation and the employment of mantras like *so'haṃ*, these techniques serve as a means of imagining and aligning one's own nature with regard to thought, speech and bodily appearance to be the same as that of the enlightened ones (*arhat*), something that is the goal of every Jaina seeker who follows the path of liberation. This shows that some of the elements of Jayācārya's meditation, such as visualising the colours of the *tīrthaṅkara* and meditation on the middle point of the eyebrow, remain rooted in traditional Jaina literature.[35]

The colour meditation undertaken by Jayācārya seems to be merely an expanded form of the canonical and post-canonical literature description of analytic meditative practice (*dharma-dhyāna*). One of the four analytical meditations (*dharma-dhyāna*) is based upon the cosmos and its content (*saṃsthāna-vicaya*) (TS_1, 9.37). A detailed visualisation process is presented by Śubhacandra in Jñānārṇava (Jñā, 34.1), where meditation on the form of *arhat* is *rūpastha-dhyāna*. Visualisation is embedded within the colours and forms. Jayācārya's effort to explicate the traditional philosophical ideas of *vicaya dhyāna* renders a detailed illustration of colour meditation. Jayācārya asks one to visualise the colour of one's own choice and to accordingly choose the *tīrthaṅkara* relating to that colour. He emphasises the importance of selecting colours that are comfortable to oneself, rather than merely having a devotion to any specific *tīrthaṅkara*.

The two types of practices mentioned above are forms of meditation that involve concentration (*ekāgratā*) and visualisation of an image of a *tīrthaṅkara* with colour (*tīrthaṅkara raṅga sahita ciṅtavaṇā*), breathing (*śvāsa*) and mantra recitation. However, in some practices, concentration, mantra recitation and sutra repetition are common in both *dhyāna* and *svādhyāya*. In the next part,

nai ima jāṇai śrī bhagavaṅta ija iṇa ṭhikāṇai virājyā chai| īsā arihaṅta deva sarva karma khapāya nai siddha thayā |

35 As we found in Hemacandra and Śubhacandra's works.

I demonstrate how the canonical textual sources are used by Jayācārya as a contemplative and reflective practice within meditation. Normally, these textual sources are a part of *svādhyāya*.

The Practice of Meditation on Liberated Souls (Siddhas)

Meditation on liberated souls is a traditional feature of Jaina practice due to its soteriology. Jayācārya's meditation on *siddha* has its presence in earlier texts like *Ṣaṭkhaṇḍāgam* (Ṣaṭ, 13.5.4.29–31)[36] and *Dravyasaṃgraha* (DS, 51) of Nemicandra. *Ṣaṭkhaṇḍāgam* noting the *siddha* as the focus of meditation describes its qualities. *Dravyasaṃgraha* states: 'He [*siddha*] has destroyed the eight karmas and the body, he is knower (and) perceiver of the world and the non-world. He has a human form, his soul is perfect. He abides at the top of the world. Meditate (upon him)' (DS, 51, tr. Balbir). Jayācārya discusses it at length referring to the eight qualities of the *siddha*. He writes:

> This liberated soul (*siddha*) is free of birth, illness, death, grief, disease, sorrow, poverty, karma, doubt etc., with eight attributes present. He is always merged in the infinite happiness of the soul. He is free from the sticky black muddied world and the ocean of great affliction. On the liberated soul (*siddha*), meditate consciously with a focused and steady mind.[37]

The purpose of this meditation is to realise that one's own true nature is similar to that of the *siddhas*: it is a kind of meditation on the sameness (*tādātmya*) of the ordinary soul and the enlightened one. The theory underlying this practice is that, due to the impurity caused by attachment of karmic particles to the pure soul, its real nature has become obscured under the worldly conditions generated by *karma*. The pure soul, in this case, can be recognised by meditation on its true nature, represented by the liberated souls of the *siddhas*. The practice that leads to this realisation is meditation on the fact that attachment, aversion, passions and the influx of *karmas* are 'not mine', that I am separate from them and consist of infinite knowledge, perception, conduct, spiritual energy, that I am the pure, enlightened and everlasting soul. The qualities of the soul to be meditated on as truly mine are:

---

36 Ṣaṭ, 13.5.4.29–31 *paccāharittu visaehi indiyāiṃ maṇaṃ ca tehiṃto, appāṇammi maṇaṃ taṃ jogaṃ paṇidhāya dhāredi 29. akasāyamavedattaṃ akārayattaṃ videhadā ceva, acalattamalepattaṃ ca hoṅti accaṃtiyāiṃ se 31.*

37 Jayācārya (Mahāprajña 1997a: 82, *Prayoga*-3), *te sidha bagavāna janama, jarā, maraṇa, soga, roga, duḥkha, dālidra, karma, bharma rahita chai, āṭha guṇā sahita chai | te anaṅta ātmika sukhāṃ meṃ sadā lahalīna chai | kalakalībhūta saṃsāra mahākalesa no sāgara, te thakī chūṭā chai | te siddha bhagavāna no dhyāna ekāgra cita mana thira rākhanai karaṇo |*

> My soul is; 1. immutable (*a-jara*), 2. beginning-less (*an-ādi*), 3. infinite (*an-anta*), 4. imperishable (*a-khaya*), 5. immovable (*a-cala*), 6. entire (*a-kala*), 7. sinless (*a-mala*), 8. inaccessible (*a-gama*), 9. nameless (*a-nabhī*), 10. formless (*a-rūpī*), 11. karma-less (*a-karma*), 12. bondage-free (*a-baṅdhaka*), 13. in an unrising state of karma (*an-udaya*), 14. karmas that cannot be brought forward (*an-udīraka*), 15. free from threefold activities of mind, body and speech (*a-yogī*), 16. free from sensual enjoyment (*a-bhogī*), 17. disease-less (*a-rogī*), 18. un-pierceable (*a-bhedī*), 19. devoid of sexual feelings (*a-vedī*), 20. unbreakable (*a-chedī*), 21. devoid of sorrow (*a-khedī*), 22. passionless (*a-kaṣāyī*) 23. beyond colouring (*a-lesī*), 24. bodiless (*a-śarīrī*), 25. devoid of speech (*a-bhāṣī*), 26. the state of not consuming (*an-āhārī*), 27. free from obstruction (*a-vyābādha*), 28. always stable (*a-gurulaghu*), 29. beyond the senses (*an-iṅdrī*), 30. devoid of vital force (*a-prāṇī*),[38] 31. free from birth (*a-yonī*), 32. liberated soul (*a-saṃsārī*), 33. immortal (*a-mara*), 34. alone (*a-para*), 35. succession-less (*a-paraṃpara*), 36. non-pervasive (*a-vyāpī*), 37. independent (*a-nāśrita*), 38. un-shakeable (*a-kaṃpa*) 39. free (*a-viruddha*), 40. devoid of karmic influx (*an-āśrava*), 41. invisible (*a-lakha*), 42. sorrow-free (*a-śoka*), 43. being in detachment (*a-saṅgī*), 44. shapeless (*an-ākara*), 45. knower of cosmic and super cosmic space (*lokālokajñāyaka*) and 46. pure (*sudha*).[39]

The source of this negation form of description can be found in the texts like Ācārāṅga (ĀS, 5.6.123–40),[40] *Ṣaṭkhaṇḍāgama* (Ṣaṭ, 13.5.4.31)[41] and *Samayasāra* (SSā, 1.49).[42] The meditation on these 45 extended qualities of the pure soul presents the absolute view of reality (*niśacaya naya*), which is aligned with Kundakunda's approach. Kundakunda says, 'He who perceives the soul as unbound, untouched, not other than itself, steady without any difference and not-combined, know him as the absolute view of reality (*niścaya-naya*)' (SSā, 1.14).[43]

---

38 The term *prāṇī* is used for those living beings who possess two or three senses.

39 Jayācārya (Mahāprajña 1997a: 82, *Prayoga*-3), 1. *ajara* 2. *anādi* 3. *anaṅta* 4. *akhaya* 5. *acala* 6. *akala* 7. *amala* 8. *agama* 9. *anabhī* 10. *arūpī* 11. *akarma* 12. *abaṅdhaka* 13. *anudaya* 14. *anudīraka* 15. *ayogī* 16. *abhogī* 17. *arogī* 18. *abhedī* 19. *avedī* 20. *achedī* 21. *akhedī* 22. *akaṣāyī* 23. *alesī* 24. *asarīrī* 25. *abhāsī* 26. *anāhārī* 27. *avyābādha* 28. *agurulaghu* 29. *aneṅdrī* 30. *aprāṇī* 31. *ayonī* 32. *asaṁsārī* 33. *amara* 34. *apara* 35. *aparampara* 36. *avyāpī* 37. *anāśrita* 38. *akampa* 39. *avirudha* 40. *anāśrava* 41. *alakha* 42. *asoka* 43. *asaṅgī* 44. *anākara* 45. *lokālokajñāyaka* 46. *sudha.*

40 ĀS, 5.132–40, *ṇa kāū; ṇa ruhe; a saṃge;...arūvi sattā; se ṇa sadde, ṇa rūve, ṇa gandhe, ṇa rase, ṇa phāse.*

41 Ṣaṭ, 13.5.4.31, *akasāyamavedattaṃ akārayattaṃ videhadā ceva, acalattamalepattaṃ ca hoṅti accaṃtiyāiṃ se.*

42 SSā, 2.49, *arasamarūvamagaṅdhaṃ avvattaṃ cedaṇāguṇamasaddaṃ, jāṇa aliṃgaggahaṇaṃ jīvamaṇiddiṭṭhasaṃṭhāṇaṃ.*

43 SSā, 1.14, *jo passadi appāṇaṃ abaddhapuṭṭaṃ aṇaṇṇayaṃ ṇiyadaṃ| avisesamasaṃjuttaṃ taṃ suddhaṇayaṃ viyāṇīhi.*

The practitioner should therefore not attach himself to sensory objects that are of the nature of karmic particles (matter), because the pure, intelligent and blissful nature is completely different from them. In this way, one must think of the difference between the nature of the soul and matter in meditation by considering that one's soul is like that of a *siddha*, but is suffering because of karmas. The eight qualities of the soul are obscured by the eight karmas, the source of pain and pleasure for all worldly beings. Therefore, one should neither become attached to such pleasures nor be tormented by such pains. Jayācārya's process of meditation is analytical (*vicaya*), and a meditator discriminates himself from the physical, karmic existence. It is a process to connect the pure self with non-metaphysical reality.

The assimilation of the true qualities of the soul, what one really is, is meant here to displace the obscured understanding of the soul of the practitioner. Repetition of the true qualities of the soul is meant to achieve both insight and understanding of one's real nature by ostensibly cutting through and displacing erroneous notions of the soul, *i.e.*, of oneself, that have been cultivated in this life on the basis of one's basic karmic predilections. Practice, mental, verbal and bodily, is a means of practical understanding of oneself, which when performed incessantly and intensely, can mentally and finally 'cut through' and achieve the knowledge of separation of soul and body (*bheda-vijñāna*).

As the terminology designating the liberated soul used by Jayācārya is found in Jaina texts such as the *Ācārāṅga* and the *Ṣaṭkhaṇḍāgama*, this indicates that he did not 'invent' the content or the methods of meditation but, at best, elaborated the received paradigms. His innovativeness in re-contextualising the 'textual content' for a meditational purpose, thus rendering a 'new structured content' for traditional analytical meditations (*vicaya-dhyāna*) that had only survived through their names, is his contribution. As per the close study of Jayācārya's meditation, it is evident that his meditation is grounded on the Śvetāmbara canonical sources as his description of hell (*naraka*)[44] and the assembly hall of a *tīrthaṅkara* (*samavasaraṇa*)[45] can be traced to the Āvaśyaka-niryukti. Jayācārya's life and work seem to be influenced by canonical sources even more prominently if we explore, for example, his contribution 'Bhagavati kī Joḍa', which is a commentary on the *Bhagavati-sūtra*. He also composed a partial commentary on Prajñāpanā, which has not been published.[46]

It is only the methodological approach of *vicaya* meditation that Jayācārya has taken from the fourfold meditational model found in the *Tattvārtha* tradition. However, no evidence is currently available that can enlist specific sources he has explored.

44 For more detail, see *Niryāvalikā-sūtra*.

45 *Āvaśyaka-niryukti* (ĀvN, 362.1).

46 The commentary on Prajñāpanā by Jayācārya is kept in the *Lāḍanū Bhaṇḍāra*.

Meditation on the Results of Karma (Vipāka)

The aim of *karma vipāka* meditation by Jayācārya is to gain understanding through meditative concentration on the role of *karma* in our lives, since, according to Jaina doctrine, it is due to the karmic influx (*āśrava*) that the soul has an embodied existence. For this reason, the characteristic features of karmic bondage (*bandha*), namely the type of bondage of karmic matter to the soul (*prakṛti-bandha*), the duration of bondage of *karma* (*sthiti-bandha*), the intensity of bondage of *karma* (*anubhāga-bandha*) and mass of material particles accumulated on the soul (*pradeśa-bandha*),[47] are focused on in meditation, to gain an understanding of the inexorable suffering of the soul in the cycle of rebirth, in particular, the suffering of one-sensed beings, the *nigodas*.[48]

The nature and structure of *karma* and its consequences are detailed by Jayācārya in *karma-vipāka* meditation to gain insight into the elimination of accumulated *karma* in the following way. He begins the text by classifying the different characteristics of *karma* that are to be annihilated by the practice of meditation. He then goes on to discuss the suffering of *nigoda*, which Jaina doctrine posits as the least developed type of living being, having the shortest life span, in contrast to other life forms. This being has no opportunity to take part in religiosity and to improve its capacity to be liberated. These descriptions drawn from the commentary of Prajñāpanā by Malayagiri (*vṛtti patra* 39–40) are to bring awareness of the Jaina belief of the infinitely long journey one has gone through in such a minuscule form.

Jayācārya then moves to a critique firstly of human beings devoid of mental faculty (*asaṃjñi*) who accumulate heavy *karma* and, secondly, of the physiology of the human body, especially during a woman's pregnancy. This critique can be linked to the description from *Uttarādhyayana-sūtra*, which says 'birth is misery' (Utt, 19.15).[49]

The horrific image he portrays of these states may not be acceptable to all modern meditators, who may seek a more positive visualisation of these conditions during their practice. Finally, he details the requirements for reaching the internal joy of liberation and ridding oneself of karmic bondage, which is to be achieved by living an ascetic life. Some of the key practices he details are summarised below.

---

47 TS, 8.4, *prakṛti-sthiti-anubhāva-pradeśās tadvidhayaḥ*.

48 Jayācārya (Mahāprajña 1997a: 83, *Prayoga*-4). The concept of *nigoda* (a single one-sensed body) is described as follows by Jayācārya: 'There are innumerable numbers of nigoda present even within a minute needle point. Each category has uncountable, ultimate indivisible and detachable parts of the substance (*pradeśa*). Further, each category consists of uncountable layers (*pratara*). Each layer has uncountable rounds (*golā*). Each round has uncountable bodies. Each body has infinite living beings. These beings have the shortest life span. Oh being! You have taken 65536 times birth in a muhūrta (48 minutes) and having undergone the extreme pain of space and existence, borne the extreme suffering of birth and death for infinite times and even then you have not become vigilant until now.'

49 Utt, 19.15, *jamma dukkhaṃ jarā dukkhaṃ*.

He explicates the Jaina philosophy of rebirth in different subtle forms of life. He conveys the embodiment of the soul in countless types of living being and hence the suffering it encounters as follows:

> You remained in the earth, water, fire and wind for innumerable eras of time. For infinite time cycles, you have been dying, dying over and over, and being reborn. You have experienced immense lacerations, piercing and great pain. As two-sensed, three-sensed, four-sensed and five-sensed creatures, those with a thinking mind, those without the power to think, you have had many lifespan experiences. That is why you have borne/suffered lacerations, piercing, fire-bearing weapons causing pain, greatly terrifying, extreme pain/ sorrow.[50]

This description drawn from *Uttarādhyayana-sūtra* (Utt$_1$, 10.5–13)[51] attempts to unveil the philosophical concept of life cycles according to which Jains believe one has gone through innumerable births in the primitive form before reaching to this developed form. This is buttressed with a description of past embodiments in regions of hell:

> Oh Soul, in hell you spent a lifespan of thirty-three ocean measured periods (*sāgaropama*)[52] and till then you experienced the pain of the place, created by the demonic demi-gods, fighting amongst each other with weapons, ill health, eternal hunger, inexhaustible thirst, infinite cold, interminable heat, everlasting itching, and under the dependence of other you bare extreme intense pain. Innumerable times you have experienced great sharp pain, the sorrow caused by *vaitaraṇī*,[53] the river of hell, and the suffering and pain,[54] sharper than a sword, like leaves of the Semul (*śālmali*)[55] tree.[56]

50 Jayācārya (Mahāprajña 1997a: 83, *Prayoga-4*), *valī pṛthavī, pāṇī, teu, vāū meṃ asaṅkhyāto kāla rahyo | asaṅkhyta kālacakra tāṅi tihāṅja marī-marī ūpano | ghaṇī chedana-bhedana mahā vedanā bhogavī | valī beṅdrī, teṅdrī, caureṅdrī, pañceṅdrī, sannī asannī māṅhai aneka bhavāṃ bhamyo | tyāṃ chedana-bhedana agnādika sastra nī vedanā mhāvikarāla atyaṅta duḥkha sahyā |*

51 Utt, 10.5–13. *havikkāya-maigao, ukkosaṃ jīvo u saṃvase, kālaṃ saṃkhāīyaṃ, samayaṃ goyama mā pamāyae* 5/...

52 Tulasī 2009: 363. 'Amacro-time-unit, which is measured through a similie (*upamā*); that period of time which is equivalent to 10xcrorexcrore palyopama (innumerable years) (AnuCū, 57)'.

53 A very dreadful river, full of very hot water, filled with pus, blood, hair and bones.

54 The text continues: 'Cakravartī Brahmadatta (universal sovereign) took 28,523,880,000 breaths in seventh hell, a lifespan of thirty-three ocean measured periods (*sāgaropama*). He had bound himself with heavy karmas because of his obsession with worldly enjoyment. Therefore, for each and every breath's enjoyment he received beatings for over 1,156,925 (*palyopama*) a time-unit of innumerable years to get rid of the karmas that had stuck with him because of one breath's enjoyment of cakravarti-life.'

55 A tall tree with thorns and red flowers; known as a tree of torture in hell.

56 Jayācārya (Mahāprajña 1997a: 83, *Prayoga-4*), *re jīva! valī naraka māhai sāgarā nā āukhā paryanta khetra-vedanā, parmādhāmī nī kīdhī vedanā, āpasa meṃ sastrādika nī asātā, anaṅta bhūkha, anaṅta*

The textual details found in *Sūtrakṛtāṅga-sūtra* (SKS_1, 5.8) about, for example, the river of hell, elucidate the karmic consequences such as rebirth in different hells, which further leads to more bondage. Jayācārya describes these at length, with sharp emphasis on the inexorable operation of karmic consequence even for a being destined to become a *tīrthaṅkara*, and such consequences can only be avoided by a strict vigilance that avoids karmic influx.

In his exposition of human life Jayācārya details, on the one hand, the horrors of embryonic existence, but on the other hand highlights the significance of a human birth, which the disciple is instructed not to waste but to use for the renunciation of the body and illusionary pleasures, described as being inherently base, by turning to asceticism. Meditation on the relentless suffering that karmic accumulation inflicts on the soul, and the types of behaviour that are associated with each form of embodied suffering, is thus detailed.

Jayācārya uses anecdotes to serve as easy, simple sources for contemplation. He draws on exemplary figures (Jayācārya 1997: 88) from textual sources such as Brahmadatta Cakravartī from *Uttarādhyayana* (Utt, 13) who falls into the seventh hell, Kālikumāra from the *Nirayāvalikā* (Nir, 1.25)[57] who ends up in hell because of his lavish sinful life, and Dhana Kumāra from the *Anuttaropapātikadaśā* (AnupD, 3.1–62)[58] who is reborn in the *Sarvārthasiddhi devaloka* after ascetic practice.

Jayācārya's horrifying illustrations are fearful, and this seems to contradict the modern approach of meditation, but he eventually reinforces positive examples (for example, Dhana, who is reborn in heaven on account of his good deeds). He thus seems to be trying to convey the philosophy of taking responsibility for one's own life. These anecdotes drawn from scriptures describe details of action and its consequence, hence rendering philosophical concepts for contemplation, again from the scriptures. These verses from the *Uttarādhyayana-sūtra* (Utt, 20.36–37)[59] state that the source of hellish pain and heavenly pleasure is within oneself. Although Jayācārya begins with tough lessons, he ends gently, as if telling a story with a moral.

Jayācārya's approach may trigger a shock and awareness that can serve to instigate an intense aspiration in the practitioner to rid himself of *karma* by gaining an understanding of the behaviour and practices that lead to, and manifest in, each type of embodiment, and by contrast, the types of conduct and practices that avoid such suffering. Overall, it is an attempt to imprint the Jaina philosophy at a

---

tiraṣā, anaṅta sīta, anaṅta tāpa, anaṅta khāja, paravasapaṇai mahā trīvra pīḍā, vaitaraṇī nā duḥkha taravāra thī piṇa atyaṅta tīkhā patra chai jehanā, te sāmalī vṛkṣa nā kaṣta-vedanā anaṅtī bāra bhogavī |

57 Nir, 1.26, *Goyamāi! cautthīe paṅkappabhāe puḍavīe hemābhe narage dasasāgarovamaṭṭhiiesu neraiesu neraiyattāe uvavaṇṇe.*

58 AnupD 3.59–62, *savvaṭṭhasiddhe vimāṇe uvavaṇṇe.*

59 Utt, 20.36, *appā naī veyaraṇī, appā me kuḍasāmalī, appā kāmaduhā dheṇū, appā me nandaṇaṃ vaṇaṃ.*

subtle level through meditation, which eventually could serve to be transformative, inspiring the meditator to change his or her way of life.

Concept of the Soul

The depiction of the body and rebirth as a source of untold suffering and horror paves the way for Jayācārya's discussion of the necessity of turning inwards towards one's own soul:

> In this respect the provider of happiness, your own soul, is your friend. Besides your soul, no one is your friend. Oh soul! You are your own friend. Why do you desire for an external friend? Attachment towards other friends is a cause for the *karma*. This form of pure quality of your soul is a giver of unwavering happiness like a friend. This soul is the doer of action, this soul is the disperser of *karma*, your soul is your friend, your soul is the enemy, your soul is the giver of grief, like '*vaitaraṇī* river'. The grief (equivalent to that) of the '*kūḍa-sāmalī* tree' is caused by the soul. The soul is like the divine cow (*kāma-dhenu*) in comparison, like the divine garden (*nandanavana*) joy giving, is the soul. So by controlling the soul, a being can receive the invaluable joy of salvation.[60]

Further Remarks on Jayācārya's Baḍā-Dhyāna

Jayācārya's text *Baḍā-dhyāna* is a part of *dharma-dhyāna*, which is divided into four categories:

(1) The first *dharma-dhyāna* investigates the essence of the scriptural commandment, ājñā-vicaya. This type of meditation focuses on the traditional concepts of meditating on the *tīrthaṅkaras*, *siddhas* and their teaching.
(2) The second *dharma-dhyāna* investigates the nature of physical and mental suffering, known as *apāya-vicaya*. Jayācārya presents painful situations of underdeveloped living beings, such as one-sense to five-sense organisms (*e.g.* bacteria, insects, birds, etc.).

---

60 Jayācārya (Mahāprajña 1997a: 85, *Prayoga-4*), *te bhaṇī sukha nī dātā e potā nī ātmāija mitra chai | ātmā ṭāla anero koī mitra na thī | re jīva! tāharo mitra tūṅhīja chai | bāhiralā mitra syūṃ vāchai? Bījā mitra moha vaśya karma nā kāraṇa chai | e sudha nija guṇa rūpa ātmā acala sukha nī dātā mitra chai| e ātmāija karma nī kartā, e ātmāija karma nī vikheratā, potā nī ātmāija mitra, ātmāija dusamaṇa, vetaraṇī nā dukha nī dātā potā nī ātmā chai | kūḍa sāmalī nā dukha nī dāyaka ātmā chai | ātmā kāmad-henu tulya, naṅdana vana nā sukha nī deṇa hāra potā nī ātmā chai | te māṭai ātmā nai basa kiyaṃ jīva amolaka mukti nā sukha pāmai |*

(3) The third *dharma-dhyāna* investigates the effect of karma, *vipaka-vicaya*, which Jayācārya explained under the fourth meditation, which is *Karma vipāka rai dhyāna ro prayoga.*
(4) The fourth *dharma-dhyāna* investigates the shape of the universe and its contents, *sansthāna-vicaya*, which is used in Jayācārya's '*Raṅga sahita tīrthaṅkara rai dhyāna rā prayoga*' by meditating on the *samsthāna* of the *tīrthaṅkara's* body (TS_1, 9.37). Tatia presents a parallel concept in Buddhist tradition, which is known as analysis of *dharma* '*dharma-pravicaya*' for the eradication of impurities (*kleśa*) (Ṭātiā 1986: xxvii).

The *Baḍā-dhyāna* also includes specifically Jaina exercises of renunciation of sensory objects and cultivation of the soul's virtues, including turning attention inwards on the soul.[61] Jayācārya's elucidation of these detailed practices suggests that Jayācārya had himself practised these in the ascetic community. From personal experience, I have noticed many elderly men and women practising Jayācārya's meditation method within scriptural study, while others use Jayacarya's words of meditation, spoken aloud, as a form of spiritual composition, rather than adopting silent meditation.[62] This also reveals that the survival of these contemplative meditation practices within the congregation is neither uniform nor profound. This might have been because of changing language trends,[63] the lack of a trend to meditate without it being specified in a certain ritual,[64] or for some other unknown reasons.

Jayācārya's meditation practice was traditionally based on scriptural content categorised as *dharma-dhyāna*. He seems to have taken a number of different types of practices, which can be broadly classified into three categories: (1) enstasy practice, such as meditation on the pure self as found in *so'ham* and *siddha* meditation; (2) visualisation with devotion as found in *tīrthaṅkara* meditation, which is again geared to experiencing the self in that state; and (3) contemplation on the cause of misery, etc., as in karma meditation. All these approaches of visualisation, contemplation and enstasy are found in the *prekṣā* technique as well. In most cases, *prekṣā* is about perception rather than visualisation. Visualisation is a dominant component in one of the eight limbs, this being *anuprekṣā* and *leśyā-dhyāna*. The *anuprekṣā* is primarily visualisation, and eventually might lead to the enstasy state, where the goal and meditator duality dissolves.[65]

61 Translation of the *Dhyāna-vidhi* in Jayācārya (Mahāprajña 1997b: 96–97).
62 Many monks and nuns had listed Jayācārya's meditation as they learned it by heart (*kaṇṭhastha*). This meditation was a part of daily *svādhyāya*. For further detail see Navaratnamala (1984/2005).
63 The language of Jayācārya is comprehensible, but certain terms are not fully apprehendable, even for the common Hindi readers for the usage of typical Rājasthāni words.
64 Certain rituals include a practice of meditation. Normally, Jaina ascetics meditate twice a day as part of the *pratikramaṇa* ritual, requisite for their ethical code.
65 For further details of the eight limbs of *prekṣā* meditation, see (Pratibhāprajñā 2017, chapter 4).

Conclusion

The approach by Jayācārya was fundamentally scriptural, yet not drawn from sources related to meditation. His intention was to reframe scriptural descriptions into a meditational context. This aim to create and document a methodological content, with set wordings for *vipaka* and *sansthāna vicaya dhyāna*, was innovative and one of the first attempts found in Jaina literature. Ohira remarks that during the canonical period one can see a 'dependent position of *dhyāna* to *tapas*' (Ohira 1982: 89). *Svādhyāya* also falls under the category of internal *tapas*. *Svādhāya* and *dharma-dhyāna* have similar performative aspects, such as *vāyaṇā* – teaching of canons, *paḍipucchaṇā* – questioning to resolve doubts, *pariyaṭṭaṇā* – revising the canons and *aṇupehā* – contemplating the meaning of *sūtra*. These four aspects are the part of *svādhyāya* as well as *dharma-dhyāna*.[66] Furthermore, it is worth mentioning that, in the Jaina yogic field, knowledge (*jñāna*) and meditation (*dhyāna*) are two states of the same consciousness (*cetanā*). Knowledge is the flowing state of *cetanā* and meditation is fixed *cetanā*.[67]

Jaina meditation goes back to the history of traditional *Āvaśyaka* meditation, where *dhyāna* and *svādhyāya* go hand in hand. The act of reciting *sūtras* mentally whilst maintaining a motionless meditative pose combined these two practices of *dhyāna* and *svādhyāya*.[68] The main content of *dharma-dhyāna* focuses more on knowledge and less on meditation. Traditionally, the concept of contemplation (*anuprekṣā*) is a well-documented part of righteous meditation (*dharma-dhyāna*). Therefore, I conclude Jayācārya's meditative system blurred the distinction between *svādhyāya* and *dhyāna*.

Abbreviations

AC	*Abhidhāna-cintāmaṇi* (see Hemacandra 1946)
AnupD	*Anuttaropapātikadaśā* (see Nathamala 1974)
ĀS	*Ācārāṅga-sūtra* (see Mahāprajña 1974/1992)

---

66 Sthā, 4.67. *Sthāṅāṅga-sūtra* mentions a list of four, which supports the virtues meditation. The list is the same as *svādhyāya*, but with the exclusion of preaching, the discipline through various discussions (*dharmopadeśa*).

67 Manonuśāsanam Vyākhyā (Mahāprajña 1979: 43), *calam cittam jñānam, sthiram cittam dhyānam.*

68 Notably, during my visit to Ācārya Vidyānanda (b.1925) a prominent Digambara monk, at Kundakunda Bhāratī (2006) New Delhi, I observed a quote painted on the wall: 'the self-study [of scripture] is meditation' (*sajjhāya meva jhāṇaṃ*). I noticed that after having food (*āhāra*) on a regular basis, Digambara ascetics perform the practice of equanimity (*sāmāyika*); during the 48-minute period of *sāmāyika* they do *svādhāya*. *Sāmāyika* can be performed through the *svādhyāya* (self-study) of some scriptures (*śāstra*), repeating whatever *sūtras* were learned by heart (*parivartanā*) and contemplation of the text and the meaning (*anuprekṣā*), in a meditative style, on the same *sūtras* (Pratibhāprajñā 2017: 197–199).

ĀvN	Ācārya Bhadrabāhu. *Āvaśyaka-niryukti* (see Kusumaprajñā 2001)
BhS	*Bhagavatī-sūtra* (see Mahāprajña 1994/2007)
DS	Nemicandra. *Dravyasaṃgraha* (see Balbir 2010)
DVS	Ārya Sayyaṃbhava. *Daśavaikālika-sūtra* (see Nathamal (1964/1974)
JñA	Śubhacandra. *Jñānārṇava* (see Bākalivālā 1975)
Nir	*Nirayāvalikā* (see Mahāprajña 1989)
SamS	*Samavāyāṅga-sūtra* (see Nathamal 1974)
Ṣaṭ	*Ṣaṭkhaṇḍāgama*
SŚ	Ācārya Pūjyapāda. *Samādhi-śataka* (see *Śāstrī* 1995/2010)
SS	Ācārya Pujyapāda. *Sarvārthasiddhi* (see *Śāstrī* 2005)
SSā	*Ācārya* Kundakunda. *Samayasāra*
Sthā	*Ṭhāṇam* (see Mahāprajña 1976)
TS	Umāsvāti. *Tattvārtha-sūtra* (see Ṭāṭiā 1994)
Utt	*Uttarādhyayana-sūtra* (see Mahāprajña 1967/2000)

References

ANONYMOUS (1971) *Samayasāra With English Translation and Commentary Based upon Amṛtacandra's Ātmakhyāti. English Introduction and translation by Prof. Chakravarti.* Fourth edition. Jñnanpith Moortidevi Jain Granthamala. English Series. New Delhi: Bhāratīya Jñānapīṭha Prakāśana.

BĀKALIVĀLĀ, P. (ed. and trans.) (1975) Śubhacandra. *Jñānārṇava.* Agāsa: Śrīmada Rājacandra Āśrama.

BALBIR, N. (ed. and trans.) (2010) Nemicandra. *Dravyasaṃgraha.* Mumbai: Hindī Grantha Kāryālaya.

BRONKHORST, J. (1993) Remarks on the History of Jaina Meditation. In Smet, R. and Watanabe, K. (eds), *Jain Studies in Honour of Jozef Deleu,* 151–162. Tokyo: Hon-no-Tomosha.

BUDDHAMALA, M. (1991) *Terāpanth kā Itihās: Terāpanth ke Pratham Cāra Ācārya.* (Khaṇḍa-1). Edited by S. Sudarśana and M. Śārdūla. Third Revised Edition. Calcutta: Jain Śvetāmbar Terāpanth Mahāsabhā Prakāśana.

FLÜGEL, P. (2002) Jaina Terāpantha Śvetāmbara Tradition. In Melton, J.G. and Bauman, G. (eds), *Religions of the World: A Comprehensive Encyclopaedia of Belief and Practices,* 1266–1267. Santa Barbara: ABC Clio.

GOUGH, E. (2012) Shades of Enlightenment: A Jaina Tantric Diagram and the Colours of the Tīrthaṅkaras. In Flügel, P. (ed.), *International Journal of Jaina Studies (online).* 8.1, 1–47.

HEMACANDRA (1946) *Abhidhānacintāmaṇi. Abhidhānacintāmaṇināmamālā: Svopajñaṭīkā Sārthaśabdānukramaṇikā-bhyāṃ Samalaṅkṛt.* Ahmedabad: Sāhitya Vardhaka Sabhā, Prāptisthānāni, Śrī Amṛtasūrīśvarajī Jñānamandira.

HĪRALĀLA, J. (ed.) (1994) *Ṣaṭkhaṇḍāgamaḥ by Puṣpadanta and Bhūtabali with the commentary Dhavalā by Vīrasena, edited with Hindi translation, notes and indexes.* vol. 13. Solāpūr: Jain Saṁskriti Samrakṣaka Saṅgha.

Kusumaprajñā, S. (ed.) (2001) *Āvaśyaka-niryukti*, vol. 1. Lādnun: Jaina Viśva Bhāratī Institute.

Mahāprajña, Ā. (ed.) (1967/2000) Commentary by Ācārya Tulasī. (vācanā). *Uttarādhyayana-sūtra: Mūlapāṭha, Saṃkṣipta Chāyā, Hindī Anuvāda, Tulanātmaka Ṭippaṇa*. Third Edition. Lādnun: Jaina Viśva Bhāratī.

— (ed.) (1979) Manonuśāsanam Hindī Vyākhyā. *Manonuśāsanam by Ācārya Tulasī.* Third Edition. Curu: Ādarśa Sāhitya Saṅgha Prakāśana.

— (ed.) (1976) Commentary by Ācārya Tulasī (vācanā) *Ṭhāṇam. Mūlapāṭha, Saṃskṛta Chāyā, Hindī Anuvāda Tathā Tṭippaṇa.* Lādnun: Jain Viśva Bhāratī Institute, Lādnun.

— (1982) *Ekalā Calo Re.* Lāḍnūṁ: Jaina Viśva Bhāratī.

— (1982/2002) *Manana Aura Mūlyāṅkana.* Edited by M. Dulaharāja. Lādnun: Jaina Viśva Bhāratī.

— (1982/2010) *Main Kucha Honā Cāhatā Hūṁ.* Edited by Muni Dulaharāja. Lādnun: Jaina Viśva Bhāratī.

— (1989) Commentary by *Ācārya* Tulasī (vācanā). *Nirayāvalikā in Uvaṅgasuttāṇi.* Rājasthāna: Jaina Viśva Bhāratī, Lādnun.

— (ed.) (1994/2007) *Bhagavatī-Sūtra: Khaṇḍa 1, 4 (Śataka 1, 2, 12-16). Mūla-Pāṭha, Sanskrit Chāyā, Hindī Anuvāda, Bhāṣya Tathā Abhayadevasūri-Kṛta Vṛtti Evaṃ Pariśiṣṭa Śabdānukrama Ādi Sahita.* Commentary by Ācārya Tulasī. Lāḍanūṁ: Jaina Viśva Bhāratī.

— (ed.) (1997a) *Baḍā-dhyāna.* In Jayācārya [Jītamala], Ārādhanā, 1–36. Third Edition. Hindi translation by Sādhavī Pramukhā Kanakaprabhā. Lādnun: Jaina Viśva Bhāratī.

— (ed.) (1997b) *Dhyāna-vidhi.* In Jayācārya [Jītamala], Ārādhanā, 85–97. Third Edition. Hindi Translation by Sādhavī Pramukhā Kanakaprabhā. Lādnun: Jaina Viśva Bhāratī.

— (ed.) (1997c) Ātma-Sambodha. In *Jayācārya, Ārādhanā.* 105–106. Third Edition. Lādnun: Jaina Viśva Bhāratī.

— (ed.) (1997d) Caubīsi. In *Jayācārya, Ārādhanā.* 1–36. Third Edition. Lādnun: Jaina Viśva Bhāratī.

Mahāprajña, Y. (ed.) (1974/1992) Commentary by Ācārya Tulasī. (vācanā.) *Ācārāṅga-sūtra in Aṅgasuttāṇi 1.* Second Edition. Lādnun: Jaina Viśva Bhāratī.

— (ed.) (1987) Commentary by Ācārya Tulasī (vācanā). *Āvaśyaka-sūtra In Nvasuttāṇi.* Lādnun: Jaina Viśva Bhāratī.

Malayagiryācārya (1918) *Prajñāpanā Vṛtti.* Mehasāṇā: Āgamodaya samiti.

Maṅgalaprajñā, S. (2003) *Ārhatī Dṛṣti.* Delhi: Ādarśa Sāhitya Saṅgha.

Nathamal, M. (ed.) (1964/1974) Commentary by *Ācārya Tulasī.* (vācanā) *Daśavaikālika-sūtra: Mūla-Pāṭha, Sanskrit Chāyā, Hindī Anuvāda tathā Ṭippaṇa.* Lādnun: Jaina Viśva Bhāratī.

Nathamala, M. (ed.) (1974) Commentary by Ācārya Tulasī. (vācanā.) *Anuttaropapātikadaśā in Aṅgasuttāṇi: Nigganthaṃ Pāvayanaṃ.* Āgama-Sutta Granthamālā. Lādnun: Jaina Viśva Bhāratī, Lādnun.

Nathamala, M. (ed.) (1974/1992) Samavāyāṅga-sūtra. In *Aṅgasuttāṇi* 1. Commentary by Ācārya Tulasī. Lādnun: Jaina Viśva Bhāratī.

Navaratnamala, M. (1984/2005) Śāsana Samudra Bhāga-16 part 1–2. Second Edition. Lādnun: Jaina Viśva Bhāratī.

NĀRVANA, S. and YOGAKṢEMAPRABHĀ, S. (2009) Caubīsī: Eka Aitihāsika Adhyayana. In Jain, Ś. (ed.), *Vītarāga Vandanā*: 81–92. New Delhi: Ādarśa Sāhitya Saṅgha.

OHIRA, S. (1981) Śukla Dhyāna. In Malvania, D., Nagin, J.S. and Ahmedabad, L.D. (eds), *Studies in Indian Philosophy: A Memorial Volume in Honour of Pandit Sukhalalji Sanghavi*, 267–277. Ahmedabad: Institute of Indology.

OHIRA, S. (1982) *A Study of Tattvārtha Sūtra with Bhāṣya*. Ahmedabad: L.D. Institute of Indology.

PRATIBHĀPRAJÑĀ, S. (2017) Prekṣā Meditation: History and Methods. SOAS University of London, PhD dissertation.

QVARNSTRÖM, O. (1998) Stability and Adaptability: A Jain Strategy for Survival and Growth. *Indo-Iranian Journal* 41, 33–35.

ROTH, G. (1974) Notes on the Paṃga-Namokkāra-Parama-Maṅgala in Jaina Literature. *The Adyar Library Bulletin (Mahāvira Jayanti)* 38(17) 1–18.

ŚĀSTRĪ, N. (ed.) (1995/2010) Ācārya Pūjyapāda. *Samādhi-śataka*. Jivarāja Jaina Granthamālā Hindī Vibhāga Puṣpa-41. Solāpur: Jaina Sanskṛti Saṅgha.

ŚĀSTRI, P.H. (ed.) (2005) Ācārya Pujyapāda. *Sarvārthasiddhi*. 13th edition. New Delhi, Bhāratīya Jñānapīṭha Prakāśana.

ṬĀṬIĀ, N. (1986) *Jaina Meditation- Citta Samadhi: Jain-Yoga*. Lādnun: Jaina Viśva Bhāratī.

ṬĀṬIĀ, N. (ed. and trans.) (1994) *That Which Is. Tattvārtha-sūtra of Umāsvāti/Umāsvāmī with the Commentaries of Umāsvāti/Umāsvāmī, Pūjyapāda and Siddhasenagaṇi*. San Francisco: Harper Collins.

TULASĪ, Ā. AND MAHĀPRAJÑA, Y. (1997) Prastuti. Jayācārya [Jītamala], *Ārādhanā*, 17–38. Edited and translated into Hindi by Sādhvī Pramukhā Kanakaprabhā. Lādnun: Jain Viśhva Bhāratī.

TULASĪ, G. (Synod Chief), MAHĀPRAJÑA, Ā. (Lexicographer), YUVĀCĀRYA, M. AND MUKHYANIYOJIKĀ, S. (eds) (2009) *Jaina Pāribhāṣika Śabdakośa: A Dictionary of Technical Terms in Jainism*. English translation by Muni Mahendra Kumāra. Lādnun: Jaina Viśva Bhāratī & Jaina Viśva Bhāratī University.

WILEY, K. (2000) Colours of the Soul: Byproducts of Activity or Passions. *Philosophy East and West* 50(3), 348–366.

Devotee, King and Creator

Kailāsa as ποιητής in Śrīkaṇṭhacarita IV*

Chiara Livio

The *Śrīkaṇṭhacarita*, a great poem (*mahākāvya*) composed by the Maṅkha in 12th-century Kashmir, discusses the deeds of Śrīkaṇṭha (Śiva), specifically the mythological episode of the destruction of Tripura. The text consists of 25 cantos (*sargas*), many of which contain the lengthy descriptions (*varṇanas*) so typical of the classical Indian poetry (*kāvya*). Among them, the 64 stanzas of the fourth *sarga* are entirely dedicated to the *varṇana* of Kailāsa, the bright and snowy Himalayan mountain. In this section, the poet (*kavi*), while enumerating the natural features of the surrounding environment, presents the mountain as an active entity with anthropomorphic traits. Kailāsa not only plays the role of a worshipper of the god (*devapūjaka*), but also acts as a king (*rājan*) and a creator (*prajāpati*). The first two characteristics of worshipper and king had already been employed elsewhere in other *mahākāvyas*, and the author follows this tradition. Nevertheless, the role of creator seems to be quite unexpected.

In the fourth *sarga*, in fact, the *prajāpatis* are two: the first and utmost is the god Śiva, whereas the second is Kailāsa, which at times takes the place of the actual divinity. The creative power of the mountain, however, requires better definition. Maṅkha seems to depict Kailāsa as the alter ego of a poet, busy with the creative process of composing a *kāvya*. After all, 'who else would be able to make the past visible, if not *creators*, as are the *poets*? They are distinguished for their *charming creations*'.[1]

---

* I am grateful to my supervisor Raffaele Torella and to Daniele Cuneo, for his precious help and thoughtful suggestions. I sincerely thank Lidia Szczepanik-Wojtczak and Alessandro Battistini for their constructive critique and for reviewing my English translations of the *Śrīkaṇṭhacarita*.

1 Kalhaṇa's *Rājataraṅgiṇī* (RT) I 4, as translated by Slaje (2008: 217).

The *Śrīkaṇṭhacarita*, its Author and the Fourth Canto

The *Śrīkaṇṭhacarita*,[2] a *mahākāvya* in 25 *sarga*s, on the story of the destruction of Tripura by Śiva,[3] was composed by Maṅkha in the 12th century during the reign of the king of Kashmir, Jayasiṃha (1128–55),[4] and commented by Jonarāja almost 300 years later.[5] According to Walter Slaje, we can narrow down the timeframe of the composition to the years 1140–44 (2008: 217),[6] when the poem was finished and read before a circle of intellectuals at the house of Maṅkha's brother, Alaṅkāra. The information about the poet and his life in the Valley can be derived not only from Kalhaṇa, the well-known author of the chronicle of the kings of Kashmir, and Maṅkha's contemporary, but also from the first three cantos, and the last, of the *Śrīkaṇṭhacarita*, which the poet devotes to a detailed autobiographical account. He worked at Jayasiṃha's court as an intellectual figure[7] as well as the minister of 'Justice and Foreign Affairs'[8] and, according to Kalhaṇa, Maṅkha was also a distinguished member of the community, who financed the construction of a monastic institute (*maṭha*) along with a statue for Śiva.[9] Although coming from a wealthy inter-religious

2 Maṅkha's work had been discovered by Bühler (1877). The available edition of the text of the *Śrīkaṇṭhacarita* with the commentary by Jonarāja is Durgaprasada and Paraba's (1887), along with the second revised edition (1900) and its reprint (1983). Studies on the text had been conducted by Bhatt (1973) and Mandal (1991). The only published translations of the *Śrīkaṇṭhacarita* are the ones of the 25th canto by Kreyenborg (1929) and of 1.56, 2nd, 3rd, 14th, 15th and 25th cantos by Slaje (2015). I will employ hereafter the sigla ŚKC for the *Śrīkaṇṭhacarita* text, and J. for Jonarāja's commentary.

3 The *Tripuradahana* story is narrated in *Brāhmaṇas*, *Mahābhārata*'s *Karṇaparvan* and *Purāṇas*. See Bhatt (1973: 10–20) and Mandal (1991: 21–22). For a summary of the contents of the 25 *sargas*, see Bhatt (1973: 1–9) and Mandal (1991: 26–41).

4 The last book of the RT closes in the 22nd year of Jayasiṃha's reign. See Stein (1900: vol. 2, 271).

5 Jonarāja was a pandit at the court of sultan Zayn al-'Ābidīn during the 15th-century Kashmir. He wrote the commentary to the *Śrīkaṇṭhacarita* by Maṅkha, to the *Kirātarjunīya* by Bhāravi, and he composed the so-called *Dvitīyā Rājataraṅgiṇī*, a continuation of Kalhaṇa's masterpiece. See Slaje (2014), Obrock (2015: 72–90) and Bhatt (2013).

6 See Slaje (2015: 14).

7 Maṅkha was a disciple of Ruyyaka, the well-known Kashmiri author of the *Alaṅkārasarvasva* (ŚKC XXV 26–30). The poet composed also a dictionary of synonyms, the so-called *Maṅkhakośa* (MK). For a detailed analysis of the attribution of other works to Maṅkha, see Mandal (1991: 55–98).

8 Maṅkha was a minister (*prajāpālanakāryapūruṣa*) at the court of Jayasiṃha. See ŚKC III 66, Bhatt (1973: 80) and Slaje (2015: 124–125). As we learn both from the author himself and from Kalhaṇa's chronicle, not only was the *kavi* included in King Jayasiṃha's politics, but also other members of his family. Both Maṅkha and Alaṅkāra, his brother, were chosen as ministers, and they became part of the king's entourage, while already involved in the social life of the Kashmiri community (See RT VIII 2422–2423, 3354). Nonetheless, scholars have different opinions regarding the bonds between the *mahākavi* and his patron. Some passages of the text have been discussed as a criticism of the improper conduct of the king; in addition, Kalhaṇa was not complimentary when dealing with the reign of Jayasiṃha. See Pollock (2001: 399).

9 See RT VIII 3354 and Slaje (2015: 32).

family,[10] there is no doubt about Maṅkha's faith; he was a Śaiva devotee and this is reflected not only in his attested act of devotion, but also in the choice of the subject for his great poem. Maṅkha's magnus opus is visibly Śaiva-centred, which can be seen throughout his *mahākāvya.* For example, in the first canto the poet declares the intention to celebrate 'that king whose court is the mountain Kailāsa';[11] the whole fifth *sarga* appears to be a eulogy of Bhagavat, the Lord Śiva; moreover, the more philosophical sections of the text[12] are permeated by the Śaivite influence.

The fourth canto of the *Śrīkaṇṭhacarita,* the 64-line-long *kailāsavarṇana,*[13] follows a similar pattern. This section contains a meticulously elaborate description of one of the most sacred mountains for Hindu devotion, the Kailāsa, commonly referred to as the seat and house of Śiva, his wife Pārvatī and his mount and devotee Nandin. As generally prescribed for all the *mahākāvyas,*[14] the presence of a *sarga* partly or completely dedicated to the description of a mountain (*śailavarṇana*) is not surprising.[15] In the fourth *sarga,* Maṅkha tries to distinguish himself by selecting the Kailāsa out of all the other mountains. Certainly, the *kavi* did not choose this Tibetan mountain for its real physical appearance, and there is no indication that he travelled throughout the Himalayan range to gain first-hand knowledge of the Kailāsa. More likely, the reason for Maṅkha's relocation of the mountain in Kashmir must have been the evocative power its name possesses.[16] Kailāsa, the very abode of the god, formed the most suitable background for the narration of the deeds of Śiva. While picturing the beauties on the slopes of such a holy site, Maṅkha is implicitly celebrating the god whose actions are narrated in the *Śrīkaṇṭhacarita.*

Despite being topical for its theme, namely the description of a mountain in a *mahākāvya,* the fourth canto remains unique. Firstly, regarding the structure, the

10 His father had converted to the Harihara cult on his deathbed, and two of his brothers were Vaiṣṇava and Bauddha respectively. See Slaje (2015: 16).

11 [...] *kailāsādrisabhāpater iti mayā maṅkhena maṅkhāyate* (ŚKC I 56). See also Slaje (2015: 38–39) and Pollock (2001: 399).

12 See Mandal (1991: 165–166).

13 The 'description of the Kailāsa' has never been translated before. My translation of the *sarga* is based on the second revised edition of the ŚKC (see fn. 2). The titles of each section can be found in the *index* of the edition itself, which sources them from Jonarāja's colophons in the manuscripts. It is possible to divide the *sarga* into two metrical sections: ŚKC IV 1–45 (*anuṣṭubh*) and ŚKC IV 46–64 (various: 46, *vaṃśastha*; 47, *viyoginī*; 48, *mālinī*; 49, *puṣpitāgrā*; 50, 51, 56, 57, 59–62 *śārdūlavikrīḍita*; 52–64, *sraghdharā*; 53, *upajāti*; 54, 55, 58, 61, *vasantatilakā*; 60, *mañjubhāṣiṇī*; 63, *śikhariṇī*). See Mandal (1991: 131–137).

14 KĀ I 16: *nagarārṇavaśailārtucandrārkodayavarṇanaiḥ* [...].

15 The Kashmiri poetic literature abounds in examples. The most famous and longest are Kālidāsa with the snowy Himālaya in the incipit of his *Kumārasaṃbhava* (see Smith 2005 and Boccali 2011), Bhāravi with the fifth canto of the *Kirātārjunīya* (see Peterson 2016), and Ratnākara's description of mount Mandara in the *Haravijaya* (see Smith 1985 and Peterson 2016).

16 Maṅkha's choice falls under that process called by Pollock 'Sanskrit cosmopolitanism', which involves 'duplicated locations everywhere' (Pollock 2006: 121–122, 572; Gomez 2016: 4).

word *kailāsa* appears only in the first line (ŚKC IV 1) and it is recalled afterwards only by relative and demonstrative pronouns. This way of maintaining the text cohesiveness is not new to classical Indian poetry, but what impresses the most here is its extent. From the second line until the final verse, the proper name of the mountain is not mentioned again.[17]

Secondly, it becomes immediately apparent that the lexicon and images are related to the semantic sphere of *light*. From the first line, Kailāsa is described as surrounded by a peculiar white or yellow brilliance, produced either by the moon, or by the reflections of its rays on the icy slopes, or by the mountain's snow itself.[18] This brightness is the *fil rouge* of the whole *sarga*, and each line, without any exception, contains at least one reference to it.

Lastly, the roles played by the mountain in the text are far from being conventional. As stated earlier, the realistic description of Kailāsa is not a priority for Maṅkha, who focuses more on the ingenious elaboration of its characteristics instead. The mountain is turned into an active and anthropomorphic character, with human-like traits and behaviours.

On the basis of the identification of the mountain with a living individual, three main motifs coexisting in the *sarga* have been traced: first, Kailāsa as Śaiva devotee performing rites for the deity; second, Kailāsa as king of the other mountain ranges; third, Kailāsa as active creator of mesmerising beauties on its own slopes. In order to define and qualify in a more efficient way these three different aspects of the character-Kailāsa, I employ the following terms: *devapūjaka* (worshipper of the god), *rājan* (king) and *prajāpati* (in the broader sense of creator). These words should be used carefully, considering their meaning. They are meant to categorise and differentiate the various roles of the mountain, but we must keep in mind their crucial interactions, since they may overlap.

The Mountain-Devotee

The representation of the Kailāsa as *devapūjaka* is immediately evident in the fourth *sarga*, and Maṅkha elaborates this theme both explicitly and implicitly; on the one hand by employing a technical lexicon that displays the steps of a rite

17 The same procedure is adopted by Maṅkha in the V *sarga*, where the subject *devaḥ* is mentioned only in the first line. See ŚKC V 1.

18 A similar description of a mountain surrounded by shining brightness can be found in the fifth canto of Bhāravi's *Kirātarjunīya* (see translation in Peterson 2016), where Himālaya possesses the same features of Kailāsa. Bhāravi's *mahākāvya* must have been one of Maṅkha's models, and it is clear from the ŚKC itself that the author was well acquainted with the work of his predecessor. In fact, Bhāravi's name is mentioned by Maṅkha in ŚKC II 53, along with Meṇṭha, Subandhu and Bāṇa (see Slaje 2015: 78–79).

performed by Kailāsa;[19] and on the other hand by evoking the role of the mountain with other artifices, which recall the character or the action of a devotee. The latter can already be observed in the introductory *śloka,* which places the Kailāsa within the dominion of Śiva:

> *śaśiśubhrāḥ kiran bhāso hāso dhanapater diśaḥ* |
> *girir astīha kailāso nivāso vṛṣalakṣmaṇaḥ* || ŚKC IV 1 ||[20]

> Spreading lights, bright for the Moon,
> smile of the North, Dhanapati's direction,
> abode of the God whose mark is the bull,
> here stands the mount Kailāsa.[21]

As we can see, Kailāsa is described by means of two appositions:

a) *hāsa* ('smile') *of* the North, *dhanapater diśaḥ*. The circumlocution 'direction of the Lord of Wealth' links the cardinal point to the God Kubera-*dhanapati,* and, by implication, to Śiva: Kubera is said to reign above Alakā, which, according to Maṅkha,[22] lies on the slopes of the mount Kailāsa, Śiva's abode.
b) *nivāsa* ('abode') *of* Śiva, 'the god whose mark is the bull'.

What matters in the first *śloka* is not a specific quality of the mountain – for instance, its shape, height, population and the like – but the fact that it is defined as the possession of someone else (the North, Śiva). The genitive case is here fundamental to understand Maṅkha's view. Kailāsa exists by virtue of its belonging to Śiva's dominion, and such possession is a first statement of the kind of relationship between the God and the mountain. The latter, imagined in a secondary and lower position, seems to be already reflecting the state of a bowing devotee. The celebration of the divinity is the primary aim of the mountain, and it can be clearly seen through the actions described throughout the *sarga*:

> *viśvātmane svanāthāya digambaradaśājuṣe* |
> *vayatīvāmbaraṃ dikṣu yas tatair aṃśutantubhiḥ* || ŚKC IV 34 ||[23]

> With the threads of his rays
> spread across the celestial directions,

19 See *infra* ŚKC IV 37–42.
20 Metre: *anuṣṭubh.* See fn. 15 and Mandal (1991: 131–137).
21 All the translations of the ŚKC are mine, unless otherwise indicated.
22 See *infra* ŚKC IV 60.
23 Metre: *anuṣṭubh.* See fn. 15 and Mandal (1991: 131–137).

Kailāsa seems to weave a garment
for his Lord Viśvātman,
delighted in [his] nude condition.

Śiva is Kailāsa's 'Lord' (*nātha*), and for his naked lord (*digambara*[24]) the rays emanated by the white and snowy Kailāsa become the threads for weaving a 'garment' (*ambara*) made of sky. The action of the light, a dress for the naked god, along with his attribute *viśvātman*, make the image pulse at a cosmic level, where the devotee assumes divine traits. As stated before, the brightness is a constant throughout the fourth *sarga*, and in the case of Kailāsa as *devapūjaka* it stresses even more its pious undertakings. It is through its rays of light that the mountain shows its extreme and unparalleled devotion (*bhakti*).

This *bhakti*, however, has its roots in a non-superhuman context. Despite the presence of two unearthly participants – Śiva and Kailāsa – the actions of the mountain evoke at times a completely human ritual.[25] One of the most effective examples is the description of a *pūjā* ceremony in the following cluster of stanzas (*kulaka*), which mirrors the everyday Hindu rite performed in the temples all over India:

ḍhaukitānantakusumaprakaraḥ pārśvapādapaiḥ |
kīrṇārgho girijāsiṃhakarajonmuktamauktikaiḥ ||
dhūpadhūmam abhivyañjan bharair navapayonmucām |
dattadīpālikaḥ śṛṅgaprajvalattapanopalaiḥ ||
snānāni yacchann acchinnam ucchaladbhir itas tataḥ |
nityaniḥṣyandamānendudṛṣatsūtibhir ambubhiḥ ||
sadhātunirjharārabdhasamālabhanavibhramaḥ |
stuvan darīmukhair vātalaharīmukharīkṛtaiḥ ||
śubhopakalpitabalir nānāvidhaphalarddhibhiḥ |
taṭaprastutasaṃgītabhaṅgīko divyacāraṇaiḥ ||
yo bhasmasmerasarvāṅgo nibhṛtāṃ sthitim aśnute |
nityasaṃnihitaṃ devadevam abhyarcayann iva || ŚKC IV 37–42 ||[26]

The offer of a heap of blossoms,
endless due to the trees on its sides;
with the reception tribute increased by the pearls,
fallen from the claws of the mountain-daughter's lion;[27] (37)

24 It is not clear, and all in all doubtful, whether Maṅkha is using the term *digambara* as related to the homonymous Jaina sect. For Maṅkha's references to Jaina tradition, see Mandal (1991: 164).

25 For Maṅkha's usage of a terminology related to the *pūja* ritual within a *kāvya* context, see ŚKC V.

26 Metre: *anuṣṭubh*. See fn. 15 and Mandal (1991: 131–137).

27 *girijāsiṃha*° the lion as vehicle of Pārvatī, daughter of Himālaya.

Displaying the incense smoke
through the abundance of the young clouds;
with the line of lights,
the inflamed solar stones of its peaks; (38)
Offering ablutions through the waters
which spring out tirelessly, here and there,
generated by the perpetually flowing lunar stones; (39)
With the grace of the [*tilaka*] unguent,
the [flowing] waterfall reddened by minerals;
raising hymns from the mouth of the caves,
through the sound of the wind howling; (40)
With the auspiciously prepared oblation
made of many kinds of diverse fruits;
tuning its own frequencies sung in chorus on its slopes
with the divine celestial singers; (41)
The mount Kailāsa, with the body fully covered in ashes,
silently reaches immobility,
worshipping the God of Gods
perpetually close to him. (42)

As mentioned earlier, the services performed here by Kailāsa find their equivalent in human practice. Maṅkha makes the mountain, an insentient entity, the human agent of the ritual through the rhetorical figure of the *utprekṣā*.[28] However, the *bhakti* of Kailāsa is eventually more powerful than the one of a common devotee. The mountain is eager to offer its own body parts, the natural elements on his slopes, as material for the rite: the flowers of its trees, the waters of its springs, the brightness of its inflamed peaks and the like. More specifically, lines 37–41 can be also read in the light of a metaphorical identification (*rūpaka*) (Table 5.1) which conflates on the one side the naturalistic aspect of the mountain, on the other side the *pūjā* ritualistic procedures.

The two sides reunite in the last stanza, in which Kailāsa, white both as a mountain covered in snow and as worshipper covered in ashes (*bhasma*), is explicitly occupied by a single action, the celebration (*abhyarcan*) of Śiva, the god of the gods (*devadeva*).

These cited verses, presenting Kailāsa as a Śaiva devotee, are suggestively indicative of the poet's faith, which he clearly intends to reflect in his work. Moreover, it is significant that Maṅkha dedicates such a long passage to the mountain-worshipper, placing it in an important position, almost half-way through the canto.

28 See Gerow (1971: 131–138).

Table 5.1: Correlations between nature and ritual in ŚKC IV 37–41

Nature	*Ritual*
trees (*pādapa*)	flower offerings (*kusuma*)
pearls (*mauktika*)[1]	pearls as welcoming gifts (*mauktika*)
young clouds (*navapaya*)	smoke of incense (*dhūpadhūma*)
sunstones (*tapanopala)*	lanterns (*dīpā*)
rivers/springs (*ambu*)	ablutions (*snāna*)
waterfalls (*nirjhara*) with red minerals (*dhātu*)	unguent for the *tilaka* (*samālabhana*)
caves (*darī*) sounding for the wind (*vāta*)	hymns (*stuvat / stuti)*
fruits (*phala*)	fruits for the oblation (*bali*)
divine inhabitants singing (*divyacāraṇa*)	act of singing together (*prastutasaṃgīta*)

[1] On the natural side, the *mauktikas* are the pearl-shaped bones contained in the elephants' temples and taken by the lions after their killing. See KS I 6 and Kale (1981: 5) (notes): 'These pearls are often described by poets as sticking to the nails of lions splitting open the temples of elephants'.

The Mountain-King

Being Śiva's devotee is just part of the complex figure of the mountain. Maṅkha not only depicts Kailāsa from a religious perspective, but he makes the character evolve towards utter humanisation. This mountain becomes in all respects a fully legitimate *rājan.*

It is not the first time that such identification occurs in a *mahākāvya*, and Kālidāsa's description of Himālaya must have been one of Maṅkha's models. In Kālidāsa, the mountain range is qualified as king of the mountains (*girirājan*),[29] having supremacy among the other ranges (*śailādhipatyam*).[30] In these lines of the *Kumārasaṃbhava*, such qualification is often accompanied by the luminous splendour of the surrounding environment, and 'it must be remembered that, for ancient *kāvya* conception, the colour associated with fame and glory (*yaśas*) is the brilliant white'.[31] Reviving and expanding Kālidāsa's topic, Maṅkha aims to place the mountain within bright scenery to stress the importance of Kailāsa as the rich and splendid chief of its kingdom:

29 KS I 13.

30 KS I 16.

31 Boccali (2011: 81), translation from Italian by the present author. According to Rājaśekhara's *Kāvyamīmāṃsā* (1946: 219–220), a bright whiteness (*śauklya*) characterises both glory (*yaśas*) and smile (*hāsa*).

ābaddhapariveṣasya raśmibhiḥ sphaṭikāśmanām |
pradakṣiṇapravṛtteva rājate yasya jāhnavī || ŚKC IV 10 ||[32]

Gaṅgā, Jahnu's daughter,
circling around [the mountain]
as if performing a *pradakṣiṇa*,
shines for Kailāsa,
with his vest fastened
by the crystal lustre.

For the first time, in this line Maṅkha shifts from the glorification of Śiva, the king of the gods, to the glorification of Kailāsa. The mountain is transformed into the object of devotion and the devotee is no longer the Kailāsa but the goddess Gaṅgā. This celestial river, having recognised the superior nature of the mountain, performs a circumambulation (*pradakṣina*) by flowing around it. Like the previous *pūjā*, this *pradakṣina* is a completely human rite, which consists of walking around a deity's statue or temple as an act of reverence. In this case, the venerated entity is the *rājan* Kailāsa. The commentator Jonarāja aptly explains the reasons for such rite in two ways. On the one hand, the mountain is considered superior to Gaṅgā because of its overwhelming whiteness (*śvetatva*), which requires a form of obeisance by the river. On the other hand, this procedure can be seen simply as a sign of friendly respect (*bandhutvam*).[33]

However, evidence for the dignity of the mountain can be found not only in the *pradakṣina* image, but also in the 'vest' (*pariveṣa*) that encloses Kailāsa. This garment, which may consist of snow, light or both,[34] is kept together (*ābaddha*) by the crystal rays spreading from the mountain slopes,[35] and seems to resemble the one offered to eminent figures to recognise/legitimate their power. A similar image occurs again in ŚKC IV 24, where another vest is clearly of this type:

yo madhya madhya saṃkrāntanavābhrakaṇaśāritaiḥ |
lauhitīkataṭair bhāti svapraśastipaṭair iva || ŚKC IV 24 ||[36]

With his crystal slopes,
variegated by the rain drops

32 Metre: *anuṣṭubh.* See fn. 15 and Mandal (1991: 131–137).

33 *śvetatvāvajayo bandhutvaṃ vā pradakṣiṇe hetuḥ* J.

34 *pariveṣa* = *pariveṣṭana* J. = vest that goes around, *i.e.* halo.

35 The image of the 'rays-hands' expanding upwards from a mountain recalls again the *Kumārasambhava* (see KS I 16). Here the correlation between the verticality of the image (expressed by the rays that proceed towards the sky) and the highness of the mountain (*i.e.* its royalty) has already been emphasised. The influence of the mountain dominion is extended not only to the earth, but in every direction. See Boccali (2011: 100).

36 Metre: *anuṣṭubh.* See fn. 15 and Mandal (1991: 131–137).

falling from the clouds
[and] thickening in the very centre
of the valleys,
Kailāsa shines,
As if wearing garments for his own *praśasti*.

Undoubtedly this garment (*paṭa*) is presented to stress the importance of Kailāsa. The play of light and shadows created by the drops (*kaṇas*) on the hillsides of the mountain makes it worth wearing such variegated vest. As a mark of royal glorification (*praśasti*), this garment is the ultimate recognition of the mountain's superiority. Moreover, by employing a meaningful term like *praśasti*, Maṅkha is certainly willing to evoke the actual panegyrics composed for the kings.[37]

The higher status of Kailāsa and its legitimation as king, however, is not only caused by his richness and power. Maṅkha includes in this description also a positive moral judgement of the mountain, which appears to be a magnanimous king of true integrity, as it can be noticed in the following stanza:

dikṣu dyutibhir eṇāṅkagabhastiprativastubhiḥ |
yaśāṃsi varṣatā yena rājanvanto mahībhṛtaḥ || ŚKC IV 13 ||

Thanks to Kailāsa,
showering in all directions
a golden rain of glory
through the brilliant rays of his light,
equal to moonbeams,
the mountains are ruled by a just monarch.

The keyword, *rājanvanto*, is perspicaciously explained by Jonaraja. According to the commentator, Kailāsa personifies a good king (*surājan*),[38] whose dharma expects him to bestow glory (*yaśas*) as a gift for his people.[39] This raining *yaśas* is produced by Kailāsa's rays, which are spread equally across his kingdom. In the second hemistich, it is evident that Maṅkha imagines the other mountains (*mahībhṛtaḥ*) as the population residing in Kailāsa's dominion.

37 See Lienhard (1984: 18). According to Schmidt (1928: 270), the compound must be read as *sva-praśastipaṭa*, with *praśastipaṭa* = *praśastipaṭṭa*, meaning, in ŚKC IV 24, 'Rhumes-urkunde' (see *praśastipaṭṭa*, m. 'ein schriftliches Edict' in Böhtlingk 1883: 172). In this case, the line changes its meaning, but still along similar lines: with the falling of the drops of rain, the Kailāsa is like a slab for the inscription of its own panegyric. Jonarāja, however, is more prone to interpret the passage in the first sense (*ābhrakaṇas* as *varṇasthānīyāḥ*, 'representing a mantle').

38 *kailāsaḥ śailānāṃ surājetyarthaḥ* J.

39 *rājño yaśovarṣaṇam ucitam* J.

As stated earlier for *pūjā* and *pradakṣina*, Maṅkha tends to project in his *mahākāvya* contemporary practices and customs. This tendency can be seen in this case as well, and it is interesting to observe that the author's notion of kingdom seems to derive from his historical context. The compound *mahībhṛt* (literally 'earth-supporter'), in fact, not only refers to the mountains, but it can also be translated as 'vassal', who administers the lands for the king. It is known from Kalhaṇa[40] that groups of nobles (the *dāmaras*) owned some territories as vassals during the 12th century in Kashmir. Although the kings of the Lohara dynasty were ruling as the primary political force in the Valley, they were not the only power. It is likely that Maṅkha, minister at the court of Jayasiṃha and thus familiar with his politics, intentionally evoked here the situation of the reign.

Nevertheless, it should be mentioned that the righteousness of Kailāsa might not be applicable to the behaviour of the present ruler. Kalhaṇa is once again the source for our historical references, and he describes this period as one of the worst for Kashmir history.[41] The king was morally corrupt and violent upheavals were extremely common. Considering the completely positive description of king Kailāsa in the fourth *sarga* and the incompatibility with Jayasiṃha's controversial leadership, two solutions can be concluded. On the one hand, Maṅkha might have depicted Kailāsa as Jayasiṃha's counterpart, to stress the contrast between good and bad kings and to alienate his work from the current Kashmiri situation. On the other hand, the figure of a righteous *rājan* might have been placed in the canto *for* Jayasiṃha as a sort of *speculum principis*, which aims to present to the king the vision of an ideal and correct model of sovereignty.

The Mountain-Creator

As we can see from the overture of the *sarga* – which we might consider as the infant stage of Kailāsa's evolution – the mountain is a mere product of a creator (*dhātṛ*). The mountain is presented as only one of the newborn objects in Śiva's possession:

> *bimbitair yo mṛgair bhāti sphuṭasphāṭikasānuṣu* |
> *kautukena kṛto dhātrā rāśibhiḥ śaśinām iva* || ŚKC IV 2 ||[42]

> With the silhouettes of the deer
> mirrored on the limpid crystalline slopes,

40 Stein (1900: vol. 1, 14–20).

41 According to Stein (1900: vol. 1, 17): '[...] it will be seen that the greatest portion of Kalhaṇa's life passed in what was for Kaśmīr one long period of civil war and political dissolution'.

42 Metre: *anuṣṭubh*. See fn. 15 and Mandal (1991: 131–137).

the mountain shines,
as if it was playfully made by the Creator
through the gathering of groups of moons.

Kailāsa is placed in the omnipresent luminous context, and the bodies of the actual deer wandering on the mountain are reflected as shadows on its bright slopes. Such play of light and shadow doubles the presence of the animals on the mount, which is therefore covered not only with the physical deer, but also with the dark silhouettes of such animals.

Being bright and still possessing such marks – the deer's shadows – the Kailāsa is comparable to the gathering together of a heap of moons (*śaśinām*), whose spots are said to resemble the shape of a deer.[43] However, if in other ŚKC passages such brilliance seems to be a wonder radiated by the Kailāsa itself, the astonishing brightness of the mountain is now the result of the action undertaken by a god. Jonarāja names this agent (*dhātrā*) 'world-creator' (*jagatkartrā*), Śiva.

Such dichotomy between agent and patient (Śiva and Kailāsa) is crucial, and Maṅkha seems willing to describe two different entities that, in the end, reveal themselves to be *one*. On the one hand, the god is the only power, on the other hand, the mountain slowly gains ground, somehow overlapping with Śiva during the creative process. In some lines Kailāsa is brought to a more conscious action, in the first place by becoming Śiva's double.

saguhāṃ prakaṭāhīnakaṭakāṃ dadhad ākṛtim |
sadāpinākam ākramya sthitaḥ pādavaladgaṇaḥ ||
dadhāno'dhigataśvetasānugrahaśarīratām |
svasāmyam iva yo nītaḥ sevāprītena śaṃbhunā || ŚKC IV 8–9 ||[44]

With his figure made of whole ridges
opened with caves,
approaching the sky,
standing still
with groups of mountains around his feet,
assuming the state of a body
with white peaks pointing upwards,
Kailāsa obtained a status equal to
Śaṃbhu's, pleased with [this] service,
displaying bracelets of strong snakes,

43 The usage of the term *śaśin* 'containing a hare/rabbit' (*i.e.* its shape) for 'moon' is coherent in this line: Maṅkha is not using the compound *mṛgāṅka*, 'the deer marked' – which would have made the image clearer – to avoid the *doṣa* of *paunaruktya* with *mṛgair* in the first hemistich. I am grateful to Dr Alessandro Battistini for his insightful suggestion.

44 Metre: *anuṣṭubh*. See fn. 15 and Mandal (1991: 131–137).

Table 5.2: Kailāsa resembles Śiva according to Jonarāja in ŚKC IV 8–9

The mountain	*The god*
with whole ridges opened (*prakaṭa-ahīna-kaṭaka°*)	with bracelets of strong snakes displayed (*prakaṭa-ahīna-kaṭaka*)
together with caves (*sa-guhā*);	in the same appearance of Kumāra (*sa-guha*);
well reaching the sky (*sad-āpi-nāka*);	always with the bow (*sadā-pināka*);
with the groups of mountains (*gaṇaḥ*);	with the troops of Gaṇas (*gaṇaḥ*);
with corporeality assumed (*graha-śarīratām*)	with corporeality (*śarīratām*)
[the corporeality] of the peaks (*sānu*)	which is a grace (*anugraha*)
which are white (*śveta*)	for the seer Śveta (*śveta(sa)*)

having the same appearance of Guha,
always holding the bow,
standing still with the Gaṇas around his feet,
who granted the seer Śveta[45]
the grace of a corporeal form.

As we can see from the *yugma*, the Kailāsa (*yaḥ*) becomes identical to the Benevolent,[46] Śiva. Through a pun (*śleṣa*) that covers the first three hemistichs (*padas*), Maṅkha allows us to perceive the two faces of the same coin; the mountain is really acquiring the same attributes as the god, as we can see from the following table (Table 5.2).

The praise of the mountain as Śiva's alter ego continues in the following couplet (*yugma*), where, again by means of a *śleṣa* (see *infra* Table 5.3), the physical *varṇana* of the Kailāsa is presented alongside its human and royal aspects, resulting in the unique image of a celebrated *rājan*:

mānasāskandanapaṭuḥ spṛśannutkaṭakāntatām |
dadhānaḥ sukhadaṃ rūpaṃ siddhasādhyagaṇāśritaḥ ||
sālakāntasthitir nīlakaṇṭhādhyāsanapāvanaḥ |
ya ivābhāti yaccitram[47] *aharyakṣais tu sevyate* || ŚKC IV 26–27 ||[48]
Vigorously ascending the lake Mānasa,
or over the Mind,
with the summit of the ridges expanding upwards
or with the immense beauty shaken,

45 For references to the sage Śveta and the sources of the myth, see Bhatt (1973: 51).

46 ŚKC IV 9: *svasāmyam* [...] *nītaḥ* [...] *śaṃbhunā*.

47 I intended the *yac* in *yac-citram* as referred again to Kailāsa. Jonarāja does not gloss the compound.

48 Metre: *anuṣṭubh*. See fn. 15 and Mandal (1991: 131–137).

Table 5.3: The two sides of the mountain in ŚKC IV 26–27: the natural and the human

Natural aspect	*Human aspect*
with the lake Mānasa (*mānasa°*)	with the mind (*mānasa°*)
with the summit of the mountain ridges (*°kaṭaka-anta*)	with the immense loveliness (*°utkaṭa-kāntatām*)
with the beautiful valleys (*su-khadam* [=] *droṇī°* J.)	with the pleasant aspect (*sukhadam rūpam*)
with the inhabitants of Siddhas, Sādhyas and Gaṇas	with groups of Siddhasādhyas (*siddhasādhya-gaṇa°*)
with the beauty of the Sal trees (*sāla-kānta*)	with the city of Ālaka in its territory (*sa-alakā-anta°*)
the abode of the peacocks (*nīlakaṇṭha-adhyāsana*)	the blue-necked/Śiva's seat (*nīla-kaṇṭha-adhyāsana*)
venerated not only by the lions (*a-haryakṣais tu sevyate*)	venerated every day by the Yakṣas (*ahar yakṣais tu sevyate*)

with pleasant valleys
or with a gorgeous aspect,
frequented by Siddhas, Sādhyas and Gaṇas
or by groups of Siddhasādhya,
standing beautifully for the Sāla trees
or with the city Alakā within its borders,
being the pure abode of the peacocks
or Śiva's pure seat,
venerated not only by the lions,[49]
or continuously by the Yakṣas,
Kailāsa appears as the painting of himself.

While unifying the two readings of the lines, namely the natural and the mythical, the last verse helps to stress once again the uniqueness and the insuperable nature of Kailāsa. Jonarāja stresses the fact that the comparison itself is non-consistent if we consider this: between the subject of comparison (*upamāna* – Kailāsa in his natural aspect) and the object of comparison (*upameya* – Kailāsa in his human

49 *haryakṣāḥ siṃhās tatsadṛśaiḥ prāṇibhiḥ sevyate* J. The commentator interprets the *a* of *a-haryakṣais* with *sadṛśa*. 'by beings *who are like* lions, having yellow eyes' in the light of *paryudāse nañ*, *i.e.* '*nañ* in the sense of *paryudāsa*'. When the privative particle *na/a* is compounded with a noun, it sometimes has the meaning of the 'exclusion; negation with a view to exclude' (see Abhyankar and Shukla 1986: 244). Along with the particle *tu*, 'but', it is possible to interpret the verse as follows: 'venerated *not only, exclusively*, by the lions, *i.e.* by all the beings which are equally worth/fit for celebrating it'.

aspect) there are no substantial differences,[50] since they are considered both the same entity.[51] The word 'painting' (*citram*)[52] is significant in this context: King Kailāsa paints/writes/shapes his own natural kingdom – which is nothing but himself – ultimately contemplating his own nature as the source of incomparable wonders. As an active individual, Kailāsa acquires a new creative power and, as evidenced by some passages, it is even winning in the comparison with Prabhu-Śiva, the mighty one:

> *atyunnatasya pādeṣu kṣapāsu luṭhatendunā* |
> *yasya prabhur api spardhāṃ naiti candraśikhāmaṇiḥ* || ŚKC IV 22 ||[53]

> Not even Prabhu,
> with the moon-jewel on his head,
> dares to compete with the real Moon,
> dangling during the nights
> at the feet of Kailāsa,
> extremely elevated.

According to the above passage, Śiva and the mountain share the same attribute, the moon. However, the moon (*candra*) of the god is placed on his matted hair as ornament (*maṇi*), whereas Kailāsa's moon (here: *indu*) is the real one, dangling at his feet. Maṅkha intertwines the naturalistic perspective with a human-like aspect. On the one hand, the mountain is so elevated (*atyunnata*) that, by looking at it from land-level upwards, the moon seems to be just halfway towards its summit. On the other hand, *atyunnata* means 'extremely elevated', no longer in the sense of physically high, but referring to the moral noble conduct of Kailāsa, which is even more valuable than the god. The mountain's moon (*indu*), in fact, is not staying on his top at the peak of the mountain like Śiva's *candra*, but lies at his feet in a reverential act.

All the previous lines suggest the mountain's growing self-awareness in the poet's imagination, which leads to its progressive detachment from the god's control. After having seen the Kailāsa described firstly as *devapūjaka* and afterwards as *rājan* – but each time under Śiva's watchful eye – the mountain starts to play the role of a completely autonomous character, *prajāpati* (creator). Kailāsa is actively involved in the creation of an incredible world. The word *prajāpati* occurs as part

50 *atrābhede 'pi bhedāropeṇa dvitvakalpanayā sāmyoktir upamānāntarābhāvasūcanārthā* J.

51 I argue that Jonarāja intends here a simile of the type *ananvaya*, in the sense given by Gerow (1971: 148): 'self-comparison; an *upamā* in which the subject doubles as object'.

52 The word *citra* might allude also to the pictorial poetry known as *citra-kāvya*. This second meaning would directly hint at the action of Kailāsa as (*citra*)*kavi* (see *infra*, 'From creator to poet').

53 Metre: *anuṣṭubh*. See fn. 15 and Mandal (1991: 131–137).

of the compound *śailaprajāpati*, intended as 'creator of the mountains',[54] in the following stanza:

> *śivavāhakhuropajñajātarūpasamṛddhibhiḥ* |
> *kṣaṇān merusahasraṃ yaḥ sūte śailaprajāpatiḥ* || ŚKC IV 15 ||[55]

> By means of the shining gold
> invented[56] by Nandi's hooves,
> He, the *prajāpati* of the mountains, creates,
> in the twinkling of an eye, a thousand Merus.

The above meaning of '*prajāpati* of the mountains' is ambiguous. First, it stresses anew that Kailāsa is the lord of the kingdom whose subjects are the other mountains. Second, the usage of such a compound justifies the image of the line. The creator of the mountains cannot form anything but another mountain (*meru*). Jonarāja likewise points to the importance of the action of the Kailāsa, since 'the creation is under the control of the *prajāpati*'.[57]

From Creator to Poet

The long and baroque description of the mountain's tour de force is drawing to an end, and it is time for Maṅkha to reveal the true meaning of the canto. At first sight, the choice of presenting the mountain as king (a man of high social status), as devotee and as creator seems to be quite unexpected, since Kailāsa is playing all these roles at once. Moreover, it remains unclear why the mountain is referred to as creator, in a canto where the presence of Śiva, the utmost *prajāpati*, should have been sufficient. To solve these inconsistencies, it is necessary to discuss what has been left out until now: *what* is Kailāsa creating? In the previous sections, I argued how the author intended to present the mountain as immersed in its own creative process. However, the outcomes of Kailāsa's brilliant activity are yet to be determined. The first evidence of what Kailāsa-creator aims to construct appears in ŚKC IV 60:

54 *yaḥ śailā eva prajās tāsāṃ patiḥ* J. 'He, who really is the lord of these ones, *i.e.* those beings which are the mountains'.

55 Metre: *anuṣṭubh*. See fn. 15 and Mandal (1991: 131–137).

56 *śivavāhasya vṛṣabhasya kharāṇām upajñādyajñānaṃ khuropajñaṃ* J. The rocky slopes of the Kailāsa are said to become golden/made of gold by contact with the hooves of Nandin, Śiva's wandering vehicle. *upajña* seems to be used in the sense of 'invented', 'created': the gold was not present – thus it was unknown – before the passage of the bull.

57 *prajāpateś ca sṛṣṭir āyattā* J.

yam adūratas trijagadekakautukavyavahārasargavidhinavyavedhasam |
alakā vimudrabahusaudhasauhṛdād animeṣalocanacayeva vīkṣate ||
ŚKC IV 60 ||[58]

The city Alakā, as if covered in watchful eyes
because of [her] friendship
with the numerous unlocked palaces,
observes – not from afar – him, the new *Vedhas*,
performing the *creation* of wonderful activities,
unique in the world-triad.

In this stanza, the word *vedhas* has replaced the word *prajāpati* without any semantic shifting. Jonarāja clearly states that the two terms are considered synonyms by commenting *nava-vedhas* with *abhinava-prajāpati*, thus indicating that Kailāsa is the 'new creator'.

Maṅkha makes clever use of the word 'wonder' (*kautuka*),[59] which serves to indicate both the results of the mountain's creation and its purpose, namely triggering a reaction to something marvellous and astonishing.

The response of the mythical city of Alakā to the mountain's newly born world is noteworthy. Her majestic unsealed palaces (*vimudrabahusaudha*), with doors and windows unlocked,[60] transform the city in the main spectator of Kailāsa's swarming activities, with eyes wide open in amazement. One might well surmise that the audience is clearly the assembly (*sabhā*) gathered at Alaṅkāra's house, whereas the actor is the poet, reciting his *mahākāvya*. Furthermore, some phonetic references to the *kāvya* technical terms can be perceived in this line: *kavya* reminds of *kavi* and *kāvya* (first hemistich); *sarga* is a 'canto' in *mahakāvyas* (second hemistich); *sauhṛda* evokes *sahṛdaya*, the poetic connoisseur, a man of taste (third hemistich).[61] On this basis, my contention is that Maṅkha intentionally compares Kailāsa's creation to the composition of a *kavi*.

58 Metre: *mañjubhāṣiṇī*. See fn. 15 and Mandal (1991: 131–137).

59 The word *kautuka* had appeared before in the *sarga* (ŚKC IV 2) in connection with the creative performance of the other creator, Śiva.

60 I choose for *vimudra* the meaning 'open, unsealed' after Slaje (2018: 10): 'Maintenance of internal security was another yardstick of good rule. When, time and again, Kashmir had "no protection from the attacks of robbers, and when the weak were slain by the strong", it was, says Kalhaṇa, "as if the country had been without a king". Since ambushes en route and brutal assaults by bands of outlaws on villages were common, a king was expected to guarantee his subjects their safety. There were indeed some rulers who successfully hunted bandits down and killed them, making the valley in its entirety "so free from robbery, that at night the doors were left open in the bazaars, and the roads were secure for travellers"'.

61 See DĀ I 1 (43).

My hypothesis is reinforced by the last stanza of the canto, undeniably the most important one. Not only does it summarise all the images previously expressed by the poet, but it also gives the audience the key for interpreting them:

> *dvirbhāvaś candrabhāsāṃ taruṇakumudinīnāthacūḍāṭṭahāsa*
> *anuprāsaḥ śailaputrīnavahasitasudhāvipruṣāṃ paunaruktyam* |
> *svargaṅgāvīcivīpsā rucir upacinute cāturīṃ yasya tasya*
> *kṣoṇībhartur guṇeṣu pratipadapaṭhanaṃ ko vinirmātum īṣṭe* || ŚKC IV 64 ||[62]

> The *repetition* of the heavenly Gaṅgā's waves,
> the *reduplication* of Candra's moonbeams,
> the *alliteration* of Śiva's loud laughter,
> who is carrying on his forehead the female lotuses' husband,
> the *repeated sound* of the drops of the nectar,
> the ones of Gaurī's fresh smile –
> Who could fully compose the recitation, word by word,
> of every single element of the mountain,
> whose light already enhances his dexterity.

The first peculiarity that appears is the employment of four technical terms: 'repetition' (*vīpsā*), 'reduplication' (*dvirbhāva* or *dvitva*), 'alliteration' (*anuprāsa*) and 'repeated sound' (*paunaruktya*). All of these words belong to the grammatical and poetical vocabulary[63] and they are meant to place the action of the mountain within the context of a written composition. Kailāsa, the best of the poets, reduplicates by means of the light (*ruci*) – his splendid poetic genius (*pratibhā*)[64] – the elements on his slopes: Gaṅgā's waves, Candra's moonbeams, Śiva's laughter and Gaurī's smile.

Apparently, the identity of the *kavi*'s action with a *prajāpati*'s one is Maṅkha's aim, but it must be noted that this is not his invention. By referring to 12th-century Kashmir, Slaje (2008: 216–218) has rightly pointed out that Kalhaṇa had already addressed the *poets* as *creators* in two lines of his *Rājataraṅgiṇī*. In the first one,[65] the *kavi-prajāpati*s are 'distinguished for their charming creations'; in the second,[66]

62 Metre: *sragdharā*. See fn. 4 and Mandal (1991: 131–137).

63 See Abhyankar and Shukla (1986).

64 Maṅkha is not extraneous to the notion of *pratibhā* as 'poetic genius' (see ŚKC II 29, 43; Warder 1992: 83; Slaje 2015: 60–61, 70–71).

65 RT I 4: *ko'nyaḥ kālam atikrāntaṃ netuṃ pratyakṣatāṃ kṣamaḥ* | *kaviprajāpatīṃs tyaktvā ramyanirmāṇaśālinaḥ*. 'Who else would be able to make the past visible, if not *creators*, as are the *poets*? They are distinguished for their charming creations [of literature]' (translated by Slaje 2008: 216–218).

66 RT I 45: *tasmin kāle dhruvaṃ teṣāṃ kukṛtaiḥ kāśyapībhujām* | *kartāraḥ kīrtikāyasya nābhuvan kavivedhasaḥ*. 'Certainly, it was due to the evil deeds of those kings of Kaśmīr, that at their time there

the *kavi-vedhasas* are the creators of 'body of fame' for their patrons, the kings of Kashmir.

If we compare these passages with ŚKC IV 15 and 60, in which the words *prajāpati* and *vedhas* appear, we might observe a similarity in the terminology and in the images involved. Both authors employ phrases which have to do with a creative power: Kalhaṇa uses 'charming creations' (*ramya-nirmāṇa*), whereas Maṅkha confers on the Kailāsa the 'creation of wonderful activities' (*kautuka-vyavahāra-sarga*). Jonarāja comments the word *sarga* with the term *nirmāṇa*,[67] further equating Maṅkha with Kalhaṇa. Moreover, it should not be forgotten how Maṅkha describes the mountain Kailāsa in ŚKC IV 64, exactly as a poet intent on the composition of charming creations. After all, is not the mountain, like a *kavi* – as Abhinavagupta would say – characterised by a *pratibhā*, 'an intellect able in the creation [*nirmāṇa*] of ever new things'?[68]

Kalhaṇa is not the first author who mentions the figure of the poet as creator, and both Kalhaṇa and Maṅkha are indebted to the scholarly tradition of Kashmir. Certainly, as Walter Slaje suggests (2008: 218, fn. 47), we cannot avoid mentioning the well-known passage from Ānandavardhana's *Dhvanyāloka*, which seems parallel to Maṅkha's description of Kailāsa's activity: 'in the shoreless world of *kāvya*, the poet is the unique creator (*kavir ekaḥ prajāpatiḥ*) he revolves all this world exactly as it pleases him; [...] A good poet, as he wishes, makes even the inanimate beings act as they were animate and the animate ones as if they were inanimate'.[69] The ability of the poet to create mesmerising, uplifting and yet seductive wonders finds its equivalent in Kailāsa's action, and at times the similarity is just striking:

> *yatra sphaṭikatejobhir bhargasya ca galatviṣā* |
> *rajany api dinam manyā rātrim manyam bhavaty ahaḥ* || ŚKC IV 12 ||[70]

> On Kailāsa,
> for the lustre of the crystals
> and for the poison of Śiva's throat,
> the night, thinking herself to be day,
> really becomes day –
> who believes to be night.

were no *poets* present, [who] *as creators*, [would have] created a body of fame [for them]' (translated by Slaje 2008: 216–218).

67 *kautukavyavahārāṇāṃ adbhutakarmaṇāṃ nirmāṇe.*

68 Abhinavagupta's *Locana* at DĀ I 6: *pratibhā apūrvavastunirmāṇakṣmā prajñā.* See also Slaje 2008: 219 (fn. 51).

69 DĀ III 42: *apāre kāvyasaṃsare kavir ekaḥ prajāpatiḥ | yathāsmai rocate viśvaṃ tathedaṃ parivartate || [...] bhāvān acetanān api cetanavac cetanān acetanavat | vyavahārayati yatheṣṭa sukaviḥ kāvye svatantratayā.* See Ingalls ed. (1990: 639).

70 Metre: *anuṣṭubh.* See fn. 15 and Mandal (1991: 131–137).

Moreover, for the concept of *kavi-prajāpati*, as Slaje states, 'reference should be made to Ratnākara's *Haravijaya* [...], on the *śleṣas* of which Alaka remarks: ... *kaviḥ prajāpatir api*'.[71] Ratnākara, a Kashmiri *mahakāvi* like Maṅkha, not only suggests a parallelism between poets and creators, but also, places this discussion in the same context, the 'description of a mountain'. In the *Haravijaya*, two whole *sargas* (IV and V) are dedicated to the *varṇana* of mount Mandara and, according to Smith (1992: 53–54), this mountain plays the role of a poet-creator whose actions are parallel to the process of *kāvya* composition. Therefore, what David Smith had already stated both for Kalidāsa and Ratnākara seems to be valid for Maṅkha: 'the labour the poet attributes to the Creator mirrors his own [...] The description, like creation itself, is a job of work' (1992: 51), where 'Creator' was certainly Mandara-Ratnākara,[72] and, in this case, Kailāsa-Maṅkha.

Concluding Remarks

Despite what seems to be evident at a first reading, the *kailāsavarṇana* is no mere description of a mountainous scenery. It reveals and intertwines various aspects of Kailāsa, which make almost impossible a single and complete interpretation regarding the aim of the canto. The roles played by the mountain (*devapūjaka*, *rājan* and *kavi-prajāpati*) often overlap, and it is not always possible to determine when Maṅkha is focusing on only one of the three, is combining two of them or coalescing the three in a more complex unity. Unfortunately, Jonarāja does not offer indications on how to interpret the canto in the light of these characteristics.

For the first role (Kailāsa as worshipper of the gods) one can safely state that the mountain's devotion to Śiva is a projection of Maṅkha's sentiment. This can be gleaned from both the references to the rituals (*pūjā*, *pradakṣina*), which also reveal the poet's knowledge of these specific forms of worship, and possibly from Maṅkha's own religious life.[73]

For the second role (Kailāsa as king), the matter appears more complex. In the fourth canto, the idea of *rājan* assumes a completely positive connotation. This seems inconsistent if we consider the questionable actions of the king of Kashmir and the political instability of the Valley.[74] Moreover, an open praise of the king

71 See also Slaje 2008: 217, fn. 45: 'Reference should also be made to Ratnākara's *Haravijaya* (*druhiṇasya kāvyam iva sargagocaraṃ sphutacitravrttikam avadbhir adbhutam | viśadaṃ bhavadbhir abhitanyatetarām abhitaḥ purāṇakavinā kṛtam yaśaḥ* || HV VI 8 ||), on the *śleṣas* of which Alaka remarks: ... *kaviḥ prajāpatir api*'.

72 Smith (1992: 52) analyses also the *incipit* of the KS, where 'implicit within the description of the Himālaya is its resemblance to the processes of *kāvya*'.

73 See above, 'The *Śrīkaṇṭhacarita,* its author and the fourth canto'.

74 The presence of a king in the *mahākāvya* should refer to Maṅkha's current patron Jayasiṃha, but what Stein writes about Kalhaṇa's work is also valid: the acknowledgement of the royal power seems

of Kashmir is absent in the whole *Śrīkaṇṭhacarita*. As opposed to the non-existent celebration of Jayasiṃha, Maṅkha makes no attempt to hide his own relevance as poet, which can be verified in various passages of the work. Two out of many: the tirade against the bad poets (ŚKC II) and the description of the poetic *sabhā*, the audience of intellectuals gathered precisely because of the reading of his text (ŚKC XXV). These sections, atypical for *mahākāvya*s, reveal Maṅkha's persistent desire for self-praise. It would not be surprising if the poet implicitly considered himself a *rājan* and intended the fourth *sarga* as an auto-celebrative section as well.

With regards of the third role (Kailāsa as poet-creator), the predominance of Kailāsa at the expense of Śiva has already been observed. In the fourth canto, the god is not the main protagonist, and the mountain progressively takes over his role as 'new creator' (*navyavedhas*, ŚKC IV 60). In my interpretation, this shift in perspective should not be interpreted as Maṅkha's disregard for the god, but in the light of the religious traditions of Kashmir Śivaism. According to the non-dualists, reality is Śiva's emanation, everything can be recognised as part of the god and, ultimately, as the god himself. Therefore, Kailāsa's power cannot but be the result of such identification; absorbing all the attributes of Śiva, the mountain becomes ultimately an autonomous creator.

More specifically, Maṅkha seems to refer to the Kashmiri Pratyabhijñā school when he employs a certain lexicon and imaginary related to light, luminosity and reflection. As already observed by Raffaele Torella (2007: 194) 'a large group of synonyms or quasi-synonyms, a close-knit constellation of "luminous" terms' appears in Utpaladeva's and Abhinavagupta's texts, the main representatives of the Pratyabhijñā. The notion of light is vital, the world (reality) is constructed by a light that is 'not differentiated [from the subject]: being light constitutes the very essence of the object' (Torella 2007: 928). From this standpoint, Śiva, the ultimate light, radiating the objects of the world, kindles their 'inner luminous nature' (*ibidem*) and makes them recognise themselves as part of the cosmic brilliance. With the risk of overinterpretation, it can be argued that Maṅkha applies this idea to the *kailāsavarṇana* as well. On a poetical level, in fact, the luminous mountain (the object) gradually acquires a higher level of subjectivity only because of (and after) the impulse of the luminous god, the 'universal spirit' (*viśvātman*, ŚKC IV 34).

As previously evidenced by some lines in the fourth canto, the nature of Kailāsa's creative power can be equated to that of a poet. Three main points are worth repeating. First, *the action* of Kailāsa is defined by the word *sarga* (ŚKC IV 60), with its intended ambivalence of 'cosmic creation' and 'chapter of a poem/ canto'.[75] Second, *the means* for his action is the light, which plays a major role, as

'to have been inserted merely on the ground of the conventional respect due to the actual ruler' (Stein 1900: 17). See above, 'The mountain-king'.

75 It must be noted that Maṅkha compares the role of creator to the role of poet in the sixth canto as well. There Caitra-Vasanta (the king 'Spring') is described as the supreme poet and demiurge of the worlds, as can be seen in ŚKC VI 48: *śanaiḥ śanair āttavatā navīnajagattrayollekhamahākavitvam* |

the most important passages are completely dedicated to the brightness of Kailāsa. Third, it is the light itself that creates and shapes *the products* of the mountain's creation, which are the spectacular reflections on his slopes. Kailāsa's *action*, *means* and *products* correspond to the elaboration of a *kavi* (action), through the light of the poetic genius (means) of a marvellous *mahākāvya* (product). It must be noticed that the overwhelming reference to a blinding light is Maṅkha's strategy to infuse his poetry with emotion, that is, to present the *bhāva* ('permanent emotion') and thus trigger the *rasa* ('sentiment') in the spectator.[76] Specifically, the fourth canto looks like a textbook illustration of the couple *vismaya* (*bhāva*) – *adbhuta* (*rasa*): the 'emotion of amazement' (*vismaya*) stimulates the 'savouring of marvellous' (*adbhuta*)[77] through the bright yellow light.[78] The best example of the representation of this emotional state can be found in ŚKC IV 60,[79] where the city of Alakā is described with her eyes wide open and unwinking, in thrilling excitement, joyful and restless.

The two aspects of 'Kailāsa as cosmic creator' and 'Kailāsa as cosmic poet' converge if we consider that other texts offer examples of Śiva, the creator par excellence, represented in the guise of a cosmic poet.[80] The image is coherent with what stated so far, since Kailāsa assumes anew a trait that belongs to the god as well. In this perspective, the whole *kailāsavarṇana* must be read as the ultimate

---

caitreṇa cakre bata campakaughair abhyastasaurabhyasuvarṇasargaḥ || 'The golden creation of a sarga beautifully composed, with the fragrance of its pleasantness accumulated by the multitude of campaka trees, was created by Caitra, who acquired, little by little, the status of a *mahākavi*, intent on the descriptive creation of a new incredible world'.

76 The *rasa-bhāva* theory was firstly conceived by Bharata in his *Nāṭyaśāstra* and later extended to *kāvyas*. For *rasas* and *bhāvas* in *mahākāvyas* in particular, see KĀ I 18 (*rasabhāvanirantaram*). Obviously Maṅkha is well aware of this poetic process (see ŚKC II). In my wording, I have implicitly hinted at Abhinavagupta's interpretation of the *rasa* theory, but any discussion of the various interpretations of *bhāvas* and *rasas* lies well beyond the scope of the present paper. For the most recent overall treatment of related issue, see Pollock (2016).

77 A quick reference to the 'sentiment of wonder' had been made by Mandal (1991: 126). The scholar, however, attributes the *bhāva-rasa* couple '*vismaya-adbhuta*' only to few lines of the fourth canto and not to the whole section.

78 In the theatrical practice, golden-yellow (*pīta*) was the colour attributed to the couple *vismaya-adbhuta* (see NŚ VI 43). Although the fourth canto does not contain explicit reference to the colour yellow, it must be noticed that it is indicated by the context itself. Similarly, the golden-white colour (*gaura*), linked to the sentiment of heroism (*vīra*) and thus to kingship, is well displayed. However, there is no question that the first (*pīta*) is predominant, as there are many more stanzas dedicated to the description of the 'marvellous' than to the 'heroic'.

79 See above, 'From creator to poet'.

80 Two of the best examples of the action of Śiva as the cosmic *kavi* have been quoted by Cuneo (2016: 43–45 and fns 31–32) from Bhaṭṭa Nārāyaṇa's *Stavacintāmaṇi*: 'You have initiated the drama of the three worlds, containing in its womb the seed of the numerous entities emitted [by you]. Is there any other poet but you, O Destroyer [*i.e.* Śiva], who might be capable of bringing it to its conclusion?' (*Stavacintāmaṇi* 59); 'O Lord, is there any sensible man who is not amazed by your power, capable to conceive, at every moment, the ever-new conditions of the world picture?' (*Stavacintāmaṇi* 80).

representation the *kavi*'s creative process. Along these lines, it is not hard to notice that Kailāsa's activity is nothing but the reflection of Maṅkha's effort in writing the *Śrīkaṇṭhacarita*. And, as the ancient Greeks suggest – in which other way can one successfully be a poet, if not through the ποίησις – the *sarga* – of a great poem?[81]

Abbreviations

KĀ	Daṇḍin's *Kāvyādarśa*
KS	Kālidāsa's *Kumārasaṃbhava* (see Kale 1981)
MK	Maṅkha's *Maṅkhakośa*
NŚ	Bharata's *Nāṭyaśāstra*
RT	Kalhaṇa's *Rājataraṅgiṇī*
ŚKC	Maṅkha's *Śrīkaṇṭhacarita* (see Durgaprasada and Paraba 1887)

References

Abhyankar, M.K.V. and Shukla, Shukla, J.M. (1986) *A Dictionary of Sanskrit Grammar*. Gaekwad's Oriental Series, no. 134. Baroda: Oriental Institute.

Bansat-Boudon, L. (1992) *Poétique du théâtre indien. Lectures du Nāṭyaśāstra*. EFEO 169. Paris: Publications de l'École Française d'Extrême Orient.

Bhatt, B.N. (1973) *Śrīkaṇṭhacaritam – A Study*. M.S. University of Baroda Research Series, vol. 14. Baroda: M. S. University of Baroda.

Bhaṭṭa, V. M. (2013) *Śrījonarājakṛtā Kirātārjunīyaṭīkā*. Delhi: Nāga Pabliśarsa.

Boccali, G. (2011) La descrizione del Himālaya nel *Kumārasaṃbhava* (I, 1–17) di Kālidāsa. *Indologica Taurinensia* 37, 75–106.

Böhtlingk, O. (1883) *Sanskrit-Wörterbuch in kürzerer Fassung bearbeitet von Otto Böhtlingk*, vol. 4, St. Petersburg: Buchdruckerei der Kaiserlichen Akademie der Wisseschaften.

81 See also Bansat-Boudon (1992: 319 fn.) on Bhaṭṭa Tauta: '[...] the poet, he [Bhaṭṭa Tauta] says, must be in this world the artisan of the Word [...]' (translation from French by the present author). Moreover (Bansat-Boudon 1992: 319 (fn.): *tathā cāha bhaṭṭatotaḥ – nānṛṣiḥ kavir ity uktam ṛṣiś ca kila darśanāt | vicitrabhāvadharmāṃśatattvaprakhyā ca darśanam || sa tattvadarśanād eva śāstreṣu pāṭhitāḥ kaviḥ | darśanād varṇanāc cātha rūḍhā loke kaviśrutiḥ || tathā hi darśane svacche nitye 'py ādikaver muneḥ | noditā kavitā loke yāvaj jātā na varṇanā ||* 'It is said that a *kavi* is necessarily a seer (*ṛṣi*); and a seer is one who has vision (*darśana*). Vision is the intuition (*prakhyā*) of the qualities. To be termed "kavi" in the *śāstras*, it is enough if one possesses this vision of Reality. But in common parlance the term "kavi" becomes current if one possesses expression (*varṇanā*) as well as vision. Thus, though the *ādi kavi* (*i.e.* Vālmiki), being a sage, ever possessed vision, the world did not accord him the appellation of "kavi" until his Expression was born' (Bhaṭṭa Tauta as quoted by Hemacandra in *Kāvyānuśāsana* p. 379, English translation by Sreekantaiya (1937: 74).

Bühler, G. (1877) *Detailed Report of a Tour in Search of Sanskrit Mss made in Kaśmir, Rajputana, and Central India.* Bombay: Royal Asiatic Society (Bombay Branch).

Cuneo, D. (2016) Detonating or Defusing Desire. From Utpaladeva's Ecstatic Aestetics to Abhinavagupta's Ecumenical Art Theory. In Bäumer, B. and Torella, R. (eds), *Utpaladeva, Philosopher of Recognition*, 31–76. New Delhi: DK Printworld.

Durgaprasada, P. and Paraba, K.P. (eds) (1887) The Śrīkaṇṭhacarita of Maṅkhaka, With the Commentary of Jonarāja. *Kāvyamālā* 3. Bombay: Nirṇaya Sāgara Press.

Gerow, E. (1971) *A Glossary of Indian Figures of Speech.* The Hague: Mouton.

Gomez, K. (2016) *Beyond Sacred Landscapes: Poetic Illuminations of Local Experience in Maṅkha's Śrīkaṇṭhacarita.* South & Southeast Asian Studies. Berkeley: University of California Berkeley.

Ingalls, D.H.H. and Masson, J.M. (ed. and trans.) (1900) *The Dhvanyāloka of Ānandavardhana with the Locana of Abhinavagupta.* Cambridge: Harvard University Press.

Kreyenborg, E. (1929) *Der XXV Gesang des Śrīkaṇṭhacaritam. Ein Beitrag zur altindischen Literaturgeschichte.* Münster: Philos–Diss.

Kale, M.R. (ed.) (1981) *Kalidāsa's Kumārasaṃbhava, Cantos I–VIII.* Delhi: Motilal Banarsidass.

Lienhard, S. (1984) *A History of Classical Poetry. Sanskrit-Pali-Prakrit.* Wiesbaden: Otto Harrassowitz Harrassowitz Verlag.

Mandal, B.C. (1991) *Śrīkaṇṭhacarita, A Mahākāvya of Maṅkhaka. Literary Study with an Analysis of Social, Political and Historical Data of Kashmir of the 12th Century AD.* Calcutta: Sanskrit Pustak Bhandar.

Obrock, L.J. (2015) *Translation and History: The Development of a Kashmiri Textual Tradition from ca. 1000–1500.* South & Southeast Asian Studies. Berkeley: University of California Berkeley.

Pasedach, P. (2011) *The Haravijaya of Ratnākara and the Commentaries thereon by Utpala and Ratnakaṇṭha: Sargas 1 and 2.* Hamburg: Wissenschaftliche Hausarbeit zur Erlangung des akademischen Grades eines Magister Artium der Universität Hamburg.

Peterson, I.V. (2016) *Arjuna and the Hunter.* Murty Classical Library of India 9. Cambridge: Harvard University Press.

Pollock, S.I. (2001) The Death of Sanskrit. *Comparative Studies in Society and History* 43(2), 392–426.

Pollock, S.I. (2006) *The Language of the Gods in the World of Men. Sanskrit, culture, and power in premodern India.* Berkeley: University of California Press.

Pollock, S.I. (2016) *A Rasa Reader: Classical Indian Aesthetics.* New York: Columbia University Press.

Rājaśekhara (1946) *Kāvyamīmāṃsā.* Edited by N. Stchoupak and L. Renou. *La Kāvyamīmāṃsā de Rājaśekhara.* Paris: Imprimerie Nationale.

Schmidt, R. (1928) *Nachträge zum Sanskrit-Wörterbuch in kürzerer Fassung von Otto Böhtlingk bearbeitet von Richard Schmidt*, Leipzig: Otto Harrassowitz.

Slaje, W. (2008) In the Guise of Poetry – Kalhaṇa Reconsidered. In Slaje, W. (ed.), *Śāstrārambha. Inquiries into the Preamble in Sanskrit*, 207–244. Weisbaden: Harrassowitz.

Slaje, W. (2014) *Kingship in Kaśmīr (AD 1148–1459): from the pen of Jonarāja, Court Paṇḍit to Sulṭān Zayn al-'Ābidīn*. Studia Indologica Universitatis Halensis 7. Halle (Saale): Universitätsverlag Halle-Wittenberg.

Slaje, W. (2015) *Bacchanal in Himmel und andere Proben aus Maṅkha*. Weisbaden: Harrassowitz.

Smith, D. (1985) *Ratnākara's Haravijaya. An Introduction to the Sanskrit Court Epic*. Oxford: Oxford University Press.

Smith, D. (1992) Construction and Deconstruction, Narrative and Anti-Narrative: The Representation of Reality in the Hindu Court Epic. In Shackle, C. and Snell, R. (eds), *The Indian Narrative: Perspective and Patterns*, 33–59. Wiesbaden: Otto Harrassowitz.

Smith, D. (2005) *The Birth of Kumāra by Kālidāsa*. New York : New York University Press, JJC Foundation.

Sreekantaiya, T.N. (1937) Imagination in Indian Poetics. In Law, N.N. (ed.), *The Indian Historical Quarterly* 13, 59–84. Calcutta: Calcutta Oriental Press.

Stein, M.A. (1900) *Kalhaṇa's Rājataraṅgiṇīā or Chronicle of the Kings of Kashmir*, vol. 1 and 2. Westminster: Archibald Constable and Co.

Torella, R. (2007) Studies on Utpaladeva's *Īśvarapratyabhijñā-vivṛti*. Part IV: Light of the subject, light of the object. In Kellner, B., Krasser, H., Lasic, H., Torsten Much, M. and Tauscher, H. (eds), *Pramāṇakīrtiḥ. Papers dedicated to Ernst Steinkellner on the occasion of his 70th birthday*, 925–939. Arbeitskreis für Tibetische und Buddhistische Studien. Wien: Universität Wien.

Torella, R. (2008) *Il pensiero dell'India. Un'introduzione*. Roma: Carocci Editore.

Torella, R. (2017) Śaiva Nondualism. In Tuske, J. (ed.), *Indian Epistemology and Metaphysics*, 183–205. London: Bloomsbury.

Warder, A.K. (1992) The Wheel of Time. *Indian Kāvya Literature* 7. Delhi: Motilal Banarsidass.

The Tree Adoption Ritual as Presented in the *Dharmanibandhas*

Amandine Wattelier-Bricout

According to V. Narayanan,[1] the proverb 'One tree is equal to ten sons' found in Indian tradition can inspire today's ecologist behaviours in India. Actually, the first occurrence of this phrase is not found in the Matsyapurāṇa (154.512), but in the unpublished chapter 158 of the original Skandapurāṇa (SP), probably composed near the end of the sixth century in the centre of North India. In their section about trees, Dharmanibandha authors quote, *inter alia*, this proverb, some verses in chapters SP158 and other sources, including lost works, which all suggest the existence of a particular ritual dedicated to trees, which is neither the gift nor the planting of a tree, but its adoption as a son.

What is the aim and the particularity of this ritual? How can one adopt a tree? What are the differences between the procedures described? Is it possible to sketch a historical survey of this ritual?

By studying how Dharmanibandha authors handle their tree chapters, the article offers a new assessment on the value of each Nibandhas work and enables reliable identification of sources dealing with tree adoption. Once these sources are determined, their comparative study first reveals that one can save one's ancestors through tree adoption, which could be understood as another soteriology. Then, working through the complexity of the ritual procedures, it establishes a relative chronology of the different occurrences of the tree adoption. Finally, it tries to trace the continuation of this ritual in later sources, showing its impact on Indian culture.

1 Narayanan (1997: 291–332).

Introduction[2]

The aim of this article is to evaluate the scope of a particular ritual dedicated to trees, which is neither the gift nor the planting of a tree, but its adoption as a son. *Dharmanibandha* works, which are compendia of quotations from various *smṛti* works, such as *dharmaśāstras* or *purāṇas*, organised in thematic order, offer evidence of this ritual described in several *Purāṇas*, including lost works. Given that the different Nibandha authors did not quote the same works and did not arrange their quotations in the same manner, their comparison will enable us to access a wide variety of sources in the textual tradition available to them, to fully appreciate the value of their references to this ritual and to understand why some of them merely mention tree adoption while others do not touch upon it.

In this study, my objective is threefold: first, to understand the aim and particularity of a tree adoption; second, to compare the adoption procedures described, in order to establish a relative chronology of the different occurrences of this ritual; and, third, to trace the impact and the continuation of this ritual in later sources.

To do this, I will compare the passages concerning the gift, the planting and the adoption of trees as found in the *Dharmanibandha* literature, as well as in the non-quoted parts of Purāṇic literature, in order to establish the theoretical basis of tree adoption, the procedure and the material used during this ritual. In this way, I will be able to observe which features are specific to the tree adoption, how these evolved in time and how they influenced other ritual practices and myths.

Presentation of the Text Material

The *Dānanibandha* literature, which is a part of *Dharmanibandha* literature dedicated to gifts is very extensive and not completely accessible.[3] Among these prolific works,[4] I consulted Lakṣmīdhara's *Dānakāṇḍa* in his *Kṛtyakalpataru*, Ballālasena's *Dānasāgara*, Hemādri's *Dānakhaṇḍa* in his *Caturvargacintāmaṇi*,

2 I would like to thank J. Törzsök and I. Ratié and the reviewers of the Puṣpikā team for their comments and for their help in revising the content and the English text of the draft of this paper.

3 One can find a very useful list of works on *Dāna* in Rangaswami Aiyangar's edition of Lakṣmīdhara's *Kṛtyakalpataru* (1941: 127–129).

4 In comparison with the talk presented in September 2017 which included a study based on three authors (Lakṣmīdhara, Ballālasena and Hemādri), this article offers new conclusions, a wider range of sources having been consulted. So this paper deals with some *Skandapurāṇa* quotations which are not in the list of *Dharmanibandha* testimonies established by Adriaensen, Bakker and Isaacson (1998: 5–16). The references of *Skandapurāṇa*'s quotations discovered through this research and not belonging to the tree-ritual thematic were forwarded to the *Skandapurāṇa* project team.

Madanasiṃha's *Dānavivekoddyota*, part of his *Madanaratnapradīpa*, Govindānanda's *Dānakriyākaumudī* and Nilakhaṇṭha Bhaṭṭa's *Dānamayūkha* for the purpose of the present study.

Of these six authors,[5] four are particularly notable because they devote a whole chapter to rituals about trees: Lakṣmīdhara, Ballālasena, Hemādri and Madanasiṃha. Lakṣmīdhara's *Kṛtyakalpataru* (henceforth KKT) is not the first compilation,[6] but 'of the numerous extant works that deal exclusively with *Dāna* (the Sanskrit term for "gift/giving"), the *Dānakāṇḍa* is almost certainly the oldest'.[7] His KKT was perhaps[8] written in Kannauj under the reign of Govindacandra, between 1109 CE and 1168 CE. According to Aiyangar (1941: 127), Ballālasena wrote his *Dānasāgara* (DS) in 1168 CE, whereas Hemādri composed his *Dānakhaṇḍa*, part of his *Caturvargacintāmaṇi* (CVC), in Devagiri between 1260 CE and 1270 CE. As for Madanasiṃha, the editor of his *Dānavivekoddyota*, part of his *Madanaratnapradīpa* (MRP), informs us that the author must belong to the 14th or 15th centuries, whereas Kāṇe (1930: 363–365) argues that the work was composed 'probably about 1425–50'[9] near Delhi. Therefore, this study presents tree adoption in texts whose date of composition[10] ranges from that of the *Purāṇas* to the 15th century, the latest date of the relevant *Dharmanibandha* literature. As said before, *Dharmanibandha* literature has the advantage of showing textual traditions in a thematic manner, but I did not settle for this literature when searching tree-ritual evidences. I will examine some evidence of tree rituals from *Purāṇas* not quoted by the *Nibandha* authors. As far as these sources are concerned, three scenarios are possible: either these texts had not been written when the *Dharmanibandhas* were composed, they were ignored by the compilers or they were simply unknown to them.

5 Surveying the *Dānanibandha* literature has helped me to discover about 50 quotations of the *Skandapurāṇa* and a chapter titled *taruputrakavidhiḥ* in the *Dānavivekoddyota* of Madanasiṃha (part of the *Madanaratnapradīpa*, edited by Deśapāṇḍe (1964–67)).

6 Aiyangar 1941: 120–123.

7 Brick 2009: 62.

8 For more information about the date of the *Kṛtyakalpataru* and the biography of Lakṣmīdhara, see Brick (2009: 63–70): he lays out the different points of view and arguments of several scholars, including those of Aiyangar (1941: 8–15) and Kāṇe (1930: 315–318).

9 Kāṇe (1930: 390) bases his conclusions on a single manuscript (the critical edition dates from 1964). He also says that the MRP is 'quoted as a great authority by the writers of the 16th and 17th centuries, such as Nārāyaṇabhaṭṭa, Kamalākarabhaṭṭa, Nīlakaṇṭha and Mitramiśra'. Mitramiśra knew the MRP and referred to it, which raises new questions about the quotations of the SP in his *Virāmitrodaya*. In the part titled 'The *Dharmanibandha* citations' of the introduction of volume 4 of the critical edition of the SP (2018: 13–18), this potential borrowing from the MRP by Mitramiśra was not considered since the quotations of the SP in the MRP were not known.

10 The dates of composition of the *Purāṇas* are very difficult to establish. In this respect the work of Rocher (1986) is very useful because for each *Purāṇa* he gives a complete panorama of the points of view of different scholars.

How do the Four Authors Deal with Tree Rituals?

In this type of literature it is very common to use the works of predecessors and the act of copying is so important that many scholars have more often emphasised the similarities of two works than their independent nature and agenda. For example, it is often agreed that Hemādri used the work of his predecessor Lakṣmīdhara and that he largely drew on the *Kṛtyakalpataru* to write his *Caturvargacintāmaṇi*.[11] This raises the following questions: is it interesting to compare several compilers just to obtain more sources on tree rituals or can we learn more about these rituals by comparing the layout of their quotations?

To answer these questions, I will observe in a chronological order how each compiler handles tree rituals in relation to his predecessor(s). Lakṣmīdhara is the oldest of the four compilers studied in this paper. As Kāṇe points out, Lakṣmīdhara probably quoted from his predecessors, 'but as those works are not yet available, no positive conclusion can be drawn about its borrowing for the present'.[12] So I will consider here the KKT as the oldest compilation dealing with tree rituals.

The index of Ballālasena's *Dānasāgara* informs us that he used works of his predecessors, but not the KKT. After studying them, I have not retained the quotations of Ballālasena's *Dānasāgara* in my analysis. Indeed, his two chapters on trees are extremely short and give no evidence of an adoption ritual.[13] Nevertheless, this very absence is interesting in itself because it shows that this author selected his sources. Brick (2009: 78) confirms this selective approach of Ballālasena and describes it as a kind of religious puritanism, while De Simini (2015: 613–614) highlights the fact that Ballālesana 'tries to find connections between the instructions given by his authorities and the actual religious performance, an attempt that has to be read in the context of the restauration of orthodox beliefs that this monarch was promoting', and he 'wishes to expunge the "impure" elements derived from the influence of Tantric Śaivism on the Smārta Tradition'. For example, Ballālasena considers the *Devīpurāṇa* as an 'heretical work', a point that is quoted

11 Brick (2009: 5) explains this fact about Lakṣmīdhara, Hemādri, Ballālasena and Madanasiṃha: 'Significantly, each of these *dānanibandhas* consists primarily of citations from earlier scriptures, which their authors draw together, arrange in some order, and comment upon as they see fit.'

12 Kāṇe (1962: vol. 5, part II, 885) says about the editor of the *Kṛtyakalpataru*, Aiyangar: 'He has been assiduous in pointing out how Hemādri, Caṇḍeśvara and Mitramiśra have copied wholesale from the *Kalpataru*. It is not impossible that even the *Kalpataru* might have done the same to some extent as regards its predecessors such as the Pārijāta, Prakāśa, Smrtimañjarī, and Kāmadhenu. But as those works are not yet available, no positive conclusion can be drawn about its borrowing for the present.'

13 Chapters 48 and 49 of Ballālasena's *Dānasāgara*, titled *Vanaspatidaivatāramadānāvartaḥ* and *Vanaspatidaivatavṛkṣadānāvartaḥ*, cite two verses from the *Ādityapurāṇa*, two verses from the *Mahābhārata*, 12 *pādas* from the *Nandipurāṇa* and five verses from the *Viṣṇudharmottara*. While *Matsyapurāṇa*, *Padmapurāṇa* and *Skandapurāṇa* contain material about tree rituals and Ballālasena quotes these sources in other parts of his work, he does not use these works for the tree topic.

by Lakṣmīdhara and Hemādri in their chapter dedicated to tree rituals. Ballālasena quoted the *Skandapurāṇa*[14] and *Nandipurāṇa* in other parts of his DS, so these *Purāṇas* are considered as authoritative sources for him. However, while these two *purāṇas* contain evidences of tree adoption, Ballālasena skips this topic. If we take this remark into account and the fact that Ballālasena quoted the SP, the MP, the NP† and the PP elsewhere in his *Dānasāgara* as authoritative sources, his silence on tree adoption is not due to neglect but could be a purposeful rejection. Several hypotheses can be suggested: Ballālasena may have considered tree adoption a heterodox ritual showing a kind of heretical feature, because trees are said to be superior to real sons or because of the female gender of the adopter in the SP's evidence. One last hypothesis could be that tree adoption may not have been practised in his region, but this seems to be less convincing. In any case, Ballālasena's silence on tree adoption highlights the fact that this kind of ritual does not elicit unanimity amongst the compilers.

As Brick noted,[15] Hemādri copies Lakṣmīdhara, quoting the same works and even including his glosses and comments. A thorough review of the tree chapters of these two authors, Lakṣmīdhara and Hemādri, throws some new light on Hemadri's quotations.[16]

Lakṣmīdhara gathers all his sources on trees in the 21st chapter, titled *vṛkṣapratiṣṭhā* 'The establishment of trees'. As is often the case, it is up to the reader to find an order in the layout of quotations. In the 20th chapter, Lakṣmīdhara compiles the prescribed rules on the establishment of ponds, wells, tanks, etc. and closes it with a long quotation of the *Devīpurāṇa*. The next chapter, the one dedicated to tree rituals, begins with the same *Devīpurāṇa*[17] and seems to be a transition from the previous chapter by presenting a quotation about the plantation of a tree park

14 Adriaensen, Bakker and Isaacson (1998: 8–9), in particular note 26, which gives the detail of the SPBh quotations in the DS.

15 Brick 2009: 74–76. From the fact that Lakṣmīdhara is quoted by name in other *Dharmanibandha* works, Brick concludes that 'at one time, the text enjoyed a rather wide circulation despite the absence of extant South Indian manuscripts'. He adds that 'Lakṣmīdhara's work was one literary source with which these later texts on gifting were familiar'. Then he gives a table in which he compares the glosses of Hemādri to his predecessor, Lakṣmīdhara, and he concludes: 'The clear similarities between these passages, especially in the commentarial sections, can hardly be a coincidence and strongly suggest the underlying influence of the *Dānakāṇḍa* upon the later *Dānakhaṇḍa* of Hemādri.'

16 The study of De Simini (2015: 609) shows examples in which Lakṣmīdhara is more accurate in his choices of sources than Hemādri. She observes that Lakṣmīdhara is 'more in accordance with our knowledge of the extant texts' (2015: 610). She gives also several examples in which Hemādri copied Lakṣmīdhara, including his glosses (2015: 612–613). Nevertheless, she concludes this observation with the following remark: 'What seems to emerge from these brief examples, though, is a dynamic in which the clear reliance on the predecessors is contrasted with the attempt to differentiate their own works even just by rearranging passages that were already cited in the earlier *Nibandhas*' (2015: 613).

17 *Devīpurāṇa* KKT21.1–23.

in watery place.[18] Then, the next four quotations[19] are on the same topic and also discuss the benefits obtained by planting a tree. Since the last four explain how a tree can be a substitute for a son, these four really concern tree-adoption ritual.[20]

It is an undeniable fact that Hemādri quotes the same *Purāṇas* as Lakṣmīdhara, including the latter's glosses and comments, but it must also be pointed out that Hemādri is selective in his borrowing. For example, he quotes a shorter passage from the SPBh111 and repeatedly uses longer passages or verses than those cited by Lakṣmīdhara.[21] He also refers to other works not used by Lakṣmīdhara.[22] Finally,

---

18 As for the other compilers, one could argue that the chapter titles are later additions and the result of scribal task. But, given that the aim of these compilations is to order the quotations in thematic order, it is very unlikely that it can be the case.

19 *Nandipurāṇa* KKT21.24–6; *Skandapurāṇa* KKT21.27–8; *Mahābhārata* KKT21.29–31; *Matsyapurāṇa* KKT21.32–49.

20 *Padmapurāṇa* KKT21.50–60, in particular KKT21.50:

aputrasya ca putratvaṃ pādapā iha kurvate |
yacchanti ropakebhyas te sattīrthe tarpaṇādikam

In this world, trees perform the role of sons for a sonless man. To their planters they offer refreshments, etc. at an illustrious pilgrimage site. (Brick's translation)

Nandipurāṇa KKT21.61:

taruputraṃ tu yaḥ kuryād vidhivad vahnisaṃnidhau |
sa mahāpātakair yuktaḥ samuddhṛtya kulatrayam |
narakebhyo naro yāti prajāpatipuraṃ śubham ||

When a man plants a tree as a son, following the prescribed rules, in the presence of fire, even if he is guilty of great sins, he saves three of his family- members from hells and goes to the auspicious city of Prajāpati. (Brick's translation);

Skandapurāṇa KKT21.62–73 in particular KKT21.62 and 71:

śṛṇuṣva yena vidhinā gṛhyate 'vanijaḥ sutaḥ [...]
tatas tair apy anujñātaṃ taṃ taruṃ taruṇāyuṣi |
bhūmidevasamakṣaṃ vai gṛhṇīyāt tanayaṃ priye ||

'Now hear the rules through which a tree is accepted as son!' [...] Then, permitted by them, O beloved, she should accept that tree in its youthful state as her son in the presence of the gods on earth. (Brick's translation)

Matsyapurāṇa KKT21.74:

daśakūpasamā vāpī daśavāpīsamo hradaḥ |
daśahradasamaḥ putro daśaputrasamo drumaḥ ||

A pond is equal to ten wells, a lake is equal to ten ponds, a son is equal to ten lakes, and a tree is equal to ten sons. (Brick's translation)

21 We can find about 20 *ślokas* of the *Mahābhārata* not cited in KKT, two additional verses from the *Matsyapurāṇa* and about 15 additional lines of the *Skandapurāṇa*. Brick's edition of Lakṣmīdhara's *Dānakāṇḍa* makes the question of the loss of verses in the transmission mostly improbable. (See the list of the manuscripts collected by him and his philological principles, 2009: 276–284). Nevertheless, the absence of critical edition of the CVC leaves the question open.

22 In his chapters on tree rituals, Hemādri cites about ten verses of the *Bhaviṣyapurāṇa*, about 30 verses of the *Brahmavaivartapurāṇa*, about 40 verses of the *Vāyupurāṇa* and about 30 of the *Viṣṇudharmottarapurāṇa*, giving a total of more than 100 verses not borrowed.

he organises his quotations in a different, thematic and structured sequence. Thus, contrary to Brick's view and first impression, I claim that Hemādri is not a poor copycat, but composes an original work by introducing a new layout of quotations and by adding some other relevant texts. While Lakṣmīdhara devotes only one chapter to tree rituals, Hemādri deals with this topic by identifying five main subjects:

(i) the benefit to be enjoyed from planting a tree;[23]
(ii) the gift of a tree;[24]
(iii) how to plant trees in a garden;[25]
(iv) the consecration of a tree;[26]
(v) tree adoption.[27]

These five sections are detailed in the following five tables. One can compare Hemādri's quotations in front of those of his predecessor, Lakṣmīdhara, and their location in the KKT.

A quick look at these tables (6.1, 6.2, 6.3, 6.4 and 6.5) immediately shows that, while Hemādri quotes almost all of KKT's sources, he completely shakes their order up and gives them a new layout. Moreover, he regularly quotes longer passages,[28]

Table 6.1: vṛkṣāropanikaphalam by Hemādri

CVC vṛkṣāropanikaphalam	*KKT*
Mahābhārata 13.99.23–4 and 26	21.29–31
Mahābhārata 13.99.28–31	not quoted
Viṣṇusmṛti 91.5–8	20.8–12
Padmapurāṇa 28.22–32	21.50–60
Bhaviṣyatpurāṇa not identified but the first two *pādas* match SPBh158.4cd	not quoted

Table 6.2: vṛkṣadānavidhiḥ by Hemādri

CVC vṛkṣadānavidhiḥ	*KKT*
Skandapurāṇa SPBh111.38	21.27
not quoted	21.28 *Skandapurāṇa* SPBh111.39ab–40
Nandipurāṇa†	21.25–6
Mahābhārata not identified except Mbh13.57.36	not quoted
Vayūpurāṇa not identified	not quoted

23 The introductory title is *vṛkṣāropaṇam*, p. 1029, and the final title *vṛkṣāropanikaphalam*, p. 1033.

24 The introductory title is *vṛkṣadānam*, p. 1033 and the final title *vṛkṣadānavidhiḥ*, p. 1041.

25 The introductory title is *vṛkṣārāmaropaṇam*, p. 1041 and the final title *ārāmaropaṇam*, p. 1047.

26 The introductory title is *vṛkṣapratiṣṭhā*, p. 1047 and the final title *vṛkṣapratiṣṭhāvidhiḥ*, p. 1049.

27 The introductory title is *taruputradānavidhiḥ*, p. 1049, and the final title *taruputravidhiḥ*, p. 1056.

28 For examples, see four additional verses from *Mahābhārata* in the *vṛkṣāropanikaphalam* part, two additional verses from *Matsyapurāṇa* in the *vṛkṣapratiṣṭhāvidhiḥ* part or ten additional *pādas* and ten *ślokas* from *Skandapurāṇa* in the *taruputravidhiḥ* part.

Table 6.3: *ārāmaropaṇam* by Hemādri

CVC ārāmaropaṇam	*KKT*
Nandipurāṇa†	21.24
Viṣṇudharmottarapurāṇa (= *Vṛkṣāyurveda* 14, *khaṇḍa* II, chapter 300, 1–33)	not quoted
Devīpurāṇa	21.1–23

Table 6.4: *vṛkṣapratiṣṭhāvidhiḥ* by Hemādri

CVC vṛkṣapratiṣṭhāvidhiḥ	*KKT*
Matsyapurāṇa 59.1–2	not quoted
Matsyapurāṇa 59.3–19	21.32–49

Table 6.5: *taruputravidhiḥ* by Hemādri

CVC taruputravidhiḥ	*KKT*
Matsyapurāṇa 154.512	21.73
Nandipurāṇa†	21.61
Skandapurāṇa 10 *pādas* not identified	not quoted
Skandapurāṇa 2 *pādas* not identified	21.62ab
Skandapurāṇa SPBh158.45–7, 48cd and 58–68	21.62cd–73
Skandapurāṇa SPBh162.57–64ab and 67–8	not quoted
Brahmavaivartapurāṇa† (does not match the printed edition)	not quoted

on one occasions cuts a quotation and moves it according to his point of view[29] and frequently uses sources not quoted by Lakṣmīdhara.[30]

Concerning the last part titled *taruputravidhiḥ*, whose subject is the concern of this paper, the adjacent table (6.6) shows that the consistency of each compiler varies.

Lakṣmīdhara begins with two quotations (*Padmapurāṇa* and *Nandipurāṇa*) that claim trees can substitute sons when they are planted by prescribed rules as sons, then he quotes the *Skandapurāṇa*, which details the adoption ceremony and finally he uses the proverb of the *Matsyapurāṇa*, whose substance emphasises the tree-adoption merit, in order to close his chapter. As for Hemādri, he chooses the latter sentence to introduce his part devoted to adoption and, in this way, establishes the

29 In KKT, one of the quotations of the *Nandipurāṇa* is composed by three *ślokas* (KKT21.24, 25 and 26). In the CVC, the first *śloka* is quoted in the *ārāmaropaṇam* part, while the other two are cited together earlier in the *vṛkṣadānavidhiḥ* part. Given that *Nandipurāṇa* is a lost source, it is not possible to determine wether these three *ślokas* form continuous text or not.

30 *Bhaviṣyatpurāṇa* (maybe understand *Bhaviṣyapurāṇa*?), *Vayūpurāṇa*, *Viṣṇudharmottarapurāṇa* and *Brahmavaivartapurāṇa*.

Table 6.6: comparison between Lakṣmīdhara's and Hemādri's layouts

KKT	*CVC taruputravidhiḥ*
Padmapurāṇa 28.22–32, in particular verse 22: *aputrasya ca putratvaṃ pādapā iha kurvate* | *yacchanti ropakebhyas te sattīrthe tarpaṇādikam* In this world, trees perform the role of sons for a sonless man. To their planters they offer refreshments, etc. at an illustrious pilgrimage site. (Brick's translation)	*Matsyapurāṇa* 154.512: *daśakūpasamā vāpī daśavāpīsamo hradaḥ* | *daśahradasamaḥ putro daśaputrasamo drumaḥ* || A pond is equal to ten wells, a lake is equal to ten ponds, a son is equal to ten lakes, and a tree is equal to ten sons. (Brick's translation)
Nandipurāṇa KKT21.61: *taruputraṃ tu yaḥ kuryād vidhivad vahnisaṃnidhau* | *sa mahāpātakair yuktaḥ samuddhṛtya kulatrayam* | *narakebhyo naro yāti prajāpatipuraṃ śubham* || When a man plants a tree as a son, following the prescribed rules, in the presence of fire, even if he is guilty of great sins, he saves three of his family- members from hells and goes to the auspicious city of Prajāpati. (Brick's translation);	*Nandipurāṇa*†: almost the same *taruputraṃ tu yaḥ kuryād vidhivad vahnisaṃnidhau* | *sa mahāpātakair muktaḥ samuddhṛtya kulatrayam* | *narakebhyo naro yāti prajāpatipuraṃ śubham* || When a man adopts a tree as a son, following the prescribed rules, in the presence of fire, free from his great sins, he saves three of his family members from hell and goes to the auspicious city of Prajāpati. (All translations are mine unless stated otherwise)
Skandapurāṇa KKT21.62–73, in particular KKT21.62 and 71: *śṛṇuṣva yena vidhinā gṛhyate 'vanijaḥ sutaḥ [...]* *tatas tair apy anujñātaṃ taṃ taruṃ taruṇāyuṣi* | *bhūmidevasamakṣaṃ vai gṛhṇīyāt tanayaṃ priye* || 'Now hear the rules through which a tree is accepted as son!' [...] Then, permitted by them, O beloved, she should accept that tree in its youthful state as her son in the presence of the gods on earth. (Brick's translation)	*Skandapurāṇa*: the same passage to which nearly 10 *ślokas* are added
Matsyapurāṇa KKT21.74: *daśakūpasamā vāpī daśavāpīsamo hradaḥ* | *daśahradasamaḥ putro daśaputrasamo drumaḥ* || A pond is equal to ten wells, a lake is equal to ten ponds, a son is equal to ten lakes, and a tree is equal to ten sons. (Brick's translation)	*Brahmavaivartapurāṇa*† 32 verses beginning: *ataḥ praraṃ* (read *paraṃ*?) *pravakṣyāmi vṛkṣasyodyāpane vidhim* | *sarvapāpapraśamanaṃ sarvāśubhavināśanaṃ* | *aputrayā purā pārtha pārvatyā mandarācale* | *aśokaḥ śokaśomanaḥ putratve parikalpitaḥ* || Henceforth I will expose the supreme rule to bring tree to accomplishment, rule which protects from all sins and which destroys all bad acts. Once Pārvatī adopted on Mandara mountain, an *aśoka* tree, which softens the sorrow, O son of Pṛtha.

relevance of the following quotations. Then, quoting the *Nandipurāṇa*,[31] he explains the general purpose of adopting a tree by means of a *vidhi*. Finally, he gives two examples of the latter *vidhi* using two long extracts of *purāṇas* (*Skandapurāṇa* and *Brahmavaivartapurāṇa*†), which describe two different *vidhi* to adopt a tree. Hemādri's part on tree adoption *taruputravidhiḥ* is more comprehensive than that of Lakṣmīdhara and provides his reader with two ways to perform the ritual, one when it is performed by a woman (*Skandapurāṇa*) and the other by a man (*Brahmavaivartapurāṇa*†).

Comparing quotations of these two compilers on the same topic offers us a new perspective on Hemādri's work and shows us that, to appreciate the relevance of a compiler, a more thorough analysis is often required. The compilers clearly chose their quotations and arranged them according a rigorous plan.

Turning to the *Dānavivekoddyota*, its appendix states that Madanasiṃha knew and used the compilations of Lakṣmīdhara and Hemādri, but not that of Ballālasena. Now the question of how he handles his sources arises. First, it is interesting to note that he only deals with tree adoption and not with the other tree rituals, and that his chapter is called *taruputrakavidhiḥ*, as is Hemādri's. His point of view seems to be the opposite of Ballālasena's. All the texts quoted by Madanasiṃha had already been used by his predecessors. By studying the different readings contained in MRP,[32] it seems that MRP used both KKT and CVC, while introducing its own layout and selection of sources. To sum up, Madanasiṃha selects only three sources, but clearly claims that they testify to a tree-adoption ritual: the first (*Nandipurāṇa*) tells the reader about the general merit of adopting and about the requirement to perform a *vidhi*; the second (*Padmapurāṇa*) develops the topic of

31 I suggest a new translation of the expression *taruputraṃ kṛ* for the *Nandipurāṇa*'s quotation. Indeed, Brick (2009: 258) translates it as the act of planting a tree as a son. His choice is influenced by the earlier quotation (*Padmapurāṇa* 28.22–32), which prescribes plantation in PP 28. 23 (pippalāropaṇaṃ kuru). But given that the CVC and the MPR both consider the NP† passage as an evidence of tree adoption and given that another verb could be used than *kṛ* for meaning the plantation, I suggest to translate it by 'a man adopts a tree as a son'.

32 Among the 57 lines of its chapter, MRP agrees entirely with KKT's readings ten times, with CVC's readings eight times, with the common readings of both KKT and CVC 19 times and finally gives its own readings 20 times. In the absence of a critical edition of CVC, this observation cannot lead to a meaningful conclusion. Nevertheless, it should be noted what MRP omits or adds. In this matter, MRP shows us that it chooses the verses it quotes and its comments (for example, among the common references used by the three authors, MRP reproduces two of Lakṣmīdhara's comments that had been deleted by Hemādri; it omits one of Lakṣmīdhara's comments and two *pādas* of the PP (PP28.23cd), as does Hemādri; it quotes six *pādas* of the SP (SPBh158.47cd,65ab,65cd) found in CVC, but not in KKT; and finally no verses of the SPBh162 quoted by Hemādri). Moreover, it arranges the sources in a different layout and does not quote all the testimonies of the ritual of tree adoption. This brief overview of the MRP's manner of quoting seems to match De Simini's conclusion in her article (De Simini 2015: 621): 'From this sketch, it emerges that the authors' approach to the quoted sources was less rigid and more dynamic than expected. The text of the authorities was from time to time rearranged, juxtaposed with that of other sources, reduced in size when not almost completely omitted, paraphrased.'

Table 6.7: Madanasiṃha's layout

MRP taruputrakavidhiḥ	*KKT*	*CVC taruputravidhiḥ*
Nandipurāṇa† = KKT21.61	*Padmapurāṇa* 28.22–32	*Matsyapurāṇa* 154.512
Padmapurāṇa 28.22–32	*Nandipurāṇa*† KKT21.61	*Nandipurāṇa*† = KKT21.61
Skandapurāṇa 2 *pādas* non identified + SPBh158.45–7, 48cd and 58–68	*Skandapurāṇa* 2 *pādas* non identified + SPBh158.45–7, 48cd and 58–68	*Skandapurāṇa* 12 *pādas* non identified + SPBh158.45–7, 48cd and 58–68 + SPBh162.57–64ab and 67–8
	Matsyapurāṇa 154.512	*Brahmavaivartapurāṇa*† (does not match the printed edition)

the merit obtained by a tree adoption depending on the tree species, while the third details how one can adopt a tree. Madanasiṃha's chapter is more concise, follows a rigorous plan and features the essence of the topic (see Table 6.7).

Amongst our four compilers, three of them (Lakṣmīdhara, Hemādri and Madanasiṃha) emphasise the merit of having a tree son, two of them (Hemādri and Madanasiṃha) certify four sources as evidence of tree adoption by calling their chapter *taruputravidhiḥ*, while one of them, Ballālasena, seems to pass over this ritual in silence and another, Madanasiṃha, only deals with this tree ritual without mentioning the planting or donation of a tree. Could this discrepancy between these perspectives be explained by the purpose of adopting a tree? How is the merit of tree adoption different from planting or giving a tree?

The Purpose of Adopting a Tree

By cross-checking the quotations of KKT, CVC and MRP, at least five *purāṇas* talk about a tree adoption:[33] the *Padmapurāṇa* (PP28.22–32); six *pādas* of the *Nandipurāṇa* (NP), a lost *Purāṇa*; the *Skandapurāṇa* (verses from the chapters SPBh158 and SPBh162); one single verse of the *Matsyapurāṇa* (MP154.512); and about 30 verses of the *Brahmavaivartapurāṇa* (BVP), which does not agree with anything in the text of the current edition. To understand as much as possible the tree-adoption ritual, I have consulted the context of the quotations whenever possible, for the PP, MP and SP.

The different presentations of the topic of tree rituals by the four selected *Nibandha* authors raise the question whether there is a difference between planting, giving and adopting a tree: is the adoption of a tree a specific ritual or one

33 The details of the quotations in each *Nibandha* author are given in the Table 6.A1 in the Appendix.

equivalent to a donation or a plantation? Does one of these rituals have more merit than the others?

The sources agree that the purpose of the tree adoption is the same as that of the gift of a tree: one who adopts a tree makes a very pious act and thus ensures a favourable situation in the afterlife, which is also the usual benefit of a gift in general. The argument of the NP†, although a lost source, can be reconstructed through the KKT's quotations:

> KKT21.61 *Nandipurāṇa* (CVC1059)
> *taruputraṃ tu yaḥ kuryād vidhivad vahnisaṃnidhau*
> *sa mahāpātakair yuktaḥ samuddhṛtya kulatrayam*
> *narakebhyo naro yāti prajāpatipuraṃ śubham* /61/
>
> 'When a man adopts a tree as a son, following the prescribed rules, in the presence of fire, free from his great sins, he saves three of his family members from hell and goes to the auspicious city of Prajāpati.'
>
> KKT20.19 *Nandipurāṇa* (not quoted in CVC nor in MRP):
> *Vāpyās tīre yaḥ kuryāt sacchāyaṃ taruputrakam* |
> *tarudānād daśaguṇaṃ vāpīdānāc caturguṇam* |
> *saṃyogadānena phalaṃ labhate puruśaḥ sa vai* ||
>
> 'In addition, if a man then adopts a shady tree as a son on the bank of that pond, he obtains a reward ten times greater than the gift of a tree and four times greater than the gift of a pond, by giving the combination of both.'[34]

According to the NP†, the merit of adopting a tree is clearly superior to offering a tree, and the tree son substitutes a real son by freeing his father from his sins and by saving his ancestors. MP154.106–112 also expresses these two ideas: first, the tree adoption is presented as the safest way to reach paradise;[35] second, it is a

34 Here I change the translation of the expression *taruputrakam kṛ* as before and disagree on Brick's translation (2009: 242): 'In addition, if man then *plants* a shady tree as a son on the bank of that pond, he obtains a reward ten times greater than the gift of a tree and four times greater than the gift of a pond by giving the combination of both.' See my argument above.

35 MP154.111–12cd:

evaṃ nirudake deśe yaḥ kūpaṃ kārayed budhaḥ
bindau bindau ca toyasya vaset saṃvatsaraṃ divi || *111* ||
daśakūpasamā vāpī daśavāpīsamo hradaḥ
daśahradasamaḥ putro daśaputrasamo drumaḥ

fundamental injunction made by Pārvatī.[36] The dialogue between Pārvatī and the assembly of wise men suggests that this ritual is a way to heaven for sonless people (MP154.109cd). The PP affirms this very clearly in the first verse quoted by the three *Nibandha* authors:

aputrasya ca putratvaṃ pādapā iha kurvate

'In this world, trees perform the role of sons for a sonless man.'[37]

The remaining part of the PP's quotation comprises a long list of tree species and the benefit they provide to those who plant and adopt one of them.[38] It ends with this following sentence:[39]

ity ādayas tathānye ca ye noktās te'pi dāyakāḥ
pratiṣṭhāṃ te gamiṣyanti ye narā vṛkṣadāyakāḥ

'These trees and also the others that have not been mentioned are heirs. Men who possess a tree-heir will attain accomplishment.'

As for the BVP†, the tree adoption destroys all the sins and provides the fulfilment of all desires now and hereafter.[40] The SP's passage offers the longest explanation

So a wise man who orders the digging of a well in an arid area, will live in heaven for as many years as there are drops of water in it. One pond is equal to ten wells, one lake is equal to ten ponds, one son is equal to ten lakes and one tree is equal to ten sons.

36 MP154.112ef: *eṣaiva mama maryādā niyatā lokabhāvinī*

This is really the law existing in the world, the law established by me.

37 PP28.22 (KKT21.50, CVC1030, MRP293) Brick's translation (2009: 536).

38 Brick (2009: 258) translates as follows: 'These and other trees that have not been mentioned are givers. Men who give such trees will become very established.' Here Brick's translation is not clear, maybe because he does not take this quotation to refer to the practice of tree adoption. According to Apte (1998: 810), the word *dāyakaḥ* means first 'an heir, inheritor' and secondly 'a donor'. My translation considers *vṛkṣadāyakāḥ* a Bahuvrīhi compound, 'men who possess a tree-heir', which makes a better sense in the context. Indeed, the function of the tree is to replace the son, as it has been said in the beginning of the quotation : *aputrasya ca putratvaṃ pādapā iha kurvate.* Madanasiṃha who quotes this text as evidence of tree adoption has chosen the reading *vṛkṣadāyakāḥ*, while Hemādri's text shows a different reading for *vṛkṣadāyakāḥ*: *vṛkṣaropakāḥ* 'those who plant trees', which really explains why Hemādri does not quote the PP in his chapter devoted to tree adoption.

39 This sentence concludes chapter 28 in the current edition of the PP. The translation of Deshpande, Shastri and Bhatt (1988: 359–362) understands *dāyakaḥ* as givers. They seem to have the same reading as Hemādri.

40 BVP† (CVC1052):

ataḥ paraṃ pravakṣyāmi vṛkṣasyodyāpane vidhiḥ
sarvapāpapraśamanaṃ sarvāśubhavināśanaṃ

on the aims of tree adoption.[41] The superiority of this ritual is demonstrated in a dialogue between Śiva and Pārvatī. Śiva explains to his wife that only a tree is able to save ancestors from hell and one tree is worth more than 100 sons. The superiority of the trees is based on a traditional and philosophical idea: they are provided with obscurity/inertia (*tamas*)[42] and are deprived of sensory organs (*karaṇa*).[43] Because of this, they cannot commit sins and therefore are more virtuous than human sons. Here the tree adoption is not something one makes in addition to having sons and doing other virtuous things; rather, it is a special way to be saved from hell. For the adopted tree is the only true son, the only one guaranteed to be virtuous, a *satputra*:

pitṝṃs tathāśubhair ghorair veṣṭitān rākṣasārditān
satputras trāyate devi netaraḥ pāpaniścayaḥ || *10* ||
narasya na ca satputrāḥ sarva eva bhavanty uta
eka evātra bhavati yaḥ pitṝṃs trāyate bhayāt || *11* || ...
indriyāṇāṃ tu prābalyāt tatputreṣv api pārvati
pāpakāny api kurvanti te'satputrā bhavanty uta || *15* ||
ime hi taravo devi dakṣaśāpād hatendriyāḥ
pāpakāni na kurvanti saṃvṛtaiḥ karaṇaiś ca ha || *16* ||
etasmāt kāraṇād devi koṣṭhajānāṃ śatād api
eko bhūmiruhaḥ putraḥ śasyate na tu koṣṭhajaḥ || *17* ||[44]

10. O Devī, only a true son can save these ancestors, covered with their terrible inauspicious [karmas] and tormented by Rākṣasas. No other, evil-minded person can do so.

Henceforth I will expose the supreme rule to bring tree to accomplishment, rule which protects from all sins and which destroys all bad acts.

BVP† (CVC1055)

etat te kathitaṃ pārtha vṛkṣāṇāṃ sumahotsavaṃ
sarvān kāmān avapnoti iha loke paratra ca

I told you the very great festival of trees, O son of Pṛtha; one (who performs it) obtains all his desires here and hereafter.

41 On the originality of the theoretical basis of the tree adoption according to the SP, see Wattelier-Bricout (2018) 'Adopter un arbre: un rite unique décrit dans les chapitres 158 et 162 du *Skanda-purāṇa*', Actes du colloque international 'L'arbre en Asie' des 8 et 9 décembre 2016 organisé par la Société Asiatique et l'Académie des Inscriptions et Belles-Lettres, Paris.

42 *Manusmṛti* 1.49ab expresses the idea according to which plants are covered by darkness due to the result of former acts:

tamasā bahurūpeṇa veṣṭitāḥ karmahetunā

43 SPBh158.16 and SPBh158.21ab.

44 SPBh158.10–1 and SPBh158.15–17.

> 11. All of the sons of a man are not virtuous sons; among these sons, there is only one who is able to save the fathers from calamity. [...][45]
> 15. But some of these sons commit sins because of the predominance of the senses and they are not true sons, O Pārvatī.
> 16. In fact, the trees have lost their senses due to Dakṣa's curse, O Goddess. Having their sense organs blocked, they do not commit any sins.
> 17. For this reason, O Goddess, it is taught that one son born from the earth is [better] than even a hundred sons born from the womb, but not an uterine son.[46]

Among the other presentations on this topic, the SP is unique. First, it is only the SP that gives a theoretical justification for the superiority of tree adoption above having a natural son. Second, tree adoption appears in the SP as almost the only guarantee, or at least the ideal way, to be saved from hell. Contrarily, the NP† and BVP† stress the value of the ritual to prove that this act is really auspicious, but without any real justification; the MP merely describes tree adoption as a possibility for sonless people and affirms the value of this act; and the PP presents this rite as a way to ensure heaven for sonless men by comparing fruits, leaves and refreshments offered by a tree to the duties of a son.

In conclusion, the *Nibandha*'s quotations simply state the superiority of a tree son[47] and do not give explanations.

Now, although the sources agree on the major benefits of a tree adoption, the question arises as to whether they describe the same practicalities involved in adopting a tree.

The Procedure to Adopt a Tree: A Standard Adoption?

On the basis of the *Nibandha* quotations, three of the five *Purāṇas* that mention tree adoption describe the ritual of adopting a tree as a son. If one checks the current editions of these *Purāṇas*, it turns out that chapter 59 of the current MP constitutes the first 20 verses of chapter 28 of the current PP; and that this passage

45 SPBh158.12–14 depict some of these bad sons and explain the meaning of the word *putra* in the same way as *Manusmṛti* 9.138:

puṃnāmno narakād yasmāt trāyate pitaraṃ sutaḥ
tasmāt putra iti proktaḥ svayam eva svayaṃbhuvā

The son is called '*pu-tra*' by the Self-existent himself because the son saves his father from the hell called *Puṃs*.

46 A critical edition of chapters 158 and 162 is in preparation and will be a part of my doctoral thesis. In this article I refer to the text established by Bhaṭṭarāī (1988).

47 PP28.32; NP† KKT21.61ef; SPBh158.67; MP154.512cd; BVP† CVC1055.

of MP59–PP28.1–21 describes a tree ritual titled 'consecration of a tree'[48] by CVC. Kāṇe (1962: vol. 2, 893) already observed the fact that the MP and the PP share some verses,[49] raising some questions concerning the history of the transmission of these two *Purāṇas*. He concludes that the PP borrows from the MP and approximately dates this borrowing[50] before 1000 CE. The KKT quotes MP59 as *Matsyapurāṇa* and immediately after the passage PP28.22–32 as *Padmapurāṇa*. Although the title *Padmapurāṇa* separated the text, it seems to make a whole in the KKT.[51] The CVC quotes chapter MP59 as *Matsyapurāṇa* and the passage PP28.22–32 as *Padmapurāṇa*, but the two texts are clearly regarded as different due to Hemādri's reading of PP28.32. The MRP only cites the passage PP28.22–32 as *Padmapurāṇa* in his chapter titled *taruputrakavidhiḥ*, whereas he quotes about 80 times the MP in all other chapters. So it seems that in the period between the composition of the CVC and the MRP, MP59 was separated from PP28.22–32, while the situation is not clear in the KKT.

However, if the ritual described in MP59/PP28.1–21 is read as forming a whole with the remaining part PP28.22–32, it can be considered a testimony of tree adoption and included in the comparison of the procedure to adopt a tree. Consequently, we have four descriptions of the ritual of tree adoption to compare.

Among these four descriptions, one of them, the NP†, is very short and belongs to a lost *Purāṇa*. Nevertheless, it provides us with some interesting information: adoption in general follows prescribed rules, including a fire sacrifice,[52] but it is not stated what rules are prescribed in order to adopt a tree.

To answer this question, I first compared the tree adoption in the three other testimonies (PP28, SPBh158–62, BVP†) to the standard procedure[53] of adoption. The practicalities of the standard adoption require a donor, a son, an adopter, auspicious time and space, the pouring of water, which symbolises the giving up of property rights, *mantra*, fees for Brahmins, the declaration of the auspicious day *puṇyāha*, an

48 Hemādri only quotes the MP59 in his part titled *vṛkṣapratiṣṭhāvidhiḥ*.

49 Kāṇe (1962: vol. 2, 893): 'one remarkable fact is that hundreds of verses are common to *Matsyapurāṇa* and *Padmapurāṇa* and some writers like Hemādri quote long extracts from the *Padmapurāṇa*, which other quote from the *Matsyapurāṇa*'.

50 Kāṇe (1962: vol. 2, 893): 'there are no materials to assign a definite date for the borrowing, but it is likely that it was before 1000 AD'.

51 If we take a look at the critical apparatus of Brick's edition, we can see that in one of the four main recensions (the U manuscripts), the KKT quotes MP59.3, then omits the remaining part of MP59 till the end and continues from PP28.23cd to PP28.32 without a title-insertion. So in this recension MP59 and PP28 are a single text attributed to the MP. We cannot affirm that chapters MP59 and PP28 were formerly a single text, but U recension shows that it will be one of several possible scenarios of transmission.

52 NP† (KKT21.61ab; CVC1050; MRP293): *taruputraṃ tu yaḥ kuryād vidhivad vahnisaṃnidhau.*

53 The standard procedure of adoption is described by Kāṇe (1946: vol. 3, 687–689). I applied this methodology to the sole SP in a previous article titled 'Adopter un arbre: un rite unique décrit dans les chapitres 158 et 162 du *Skandapurāṇa*' (forthcoming).

optional fire oblation and gifts for the adopted son, including clothes, golden rings and earrings.

As Table 6.A2 in the Appendix shows, most of these practicalities can be found in the four testimonies, except the donor, which is not mentioned in PP28, SPBh158–162 or BVP†. This could be explained by the fact that the son to be adopted is a tree, so it has no previous family. The fire oblation is not mentioned in the SP, but Kāṇe (1946: vol. 3, 687) states 'it is not necessary that the *dattahoma* must be performed immediately after the giving and the taking, but it may be performed later and its performance may be delegated to others when the giver or the taker is a widow or a *śūdra* or is ill etc [...]'. The tree adoption clearly follows the ceremony of adoption, but adds some details.

A minor addition is the mention of the appropriate dress that the person performing the sacrifice must wear: the three excerpts (SP, BVP†, MP–PP) prescribe a white cloth. The lack of donor seems to be offset by the requirement to perform the *saṃskāras* for the tree as if it were a real son.[54] Indeed, in a standard adoption, the donor, that is to say the father who gives his natural son to another, have already performed the *saṃskāras* of his natural son. Here the adoptive son is replaced by a tree already born, but not recognised by sacraments. In the SP, the husband of the woman who adopts the tree performs all the *saṃskāras*, while in the BVP†, the *saṃskāras* seem to be done by the Brahmins.[55] For the SP and the BVP†, all the *saṃskāras* have to be celebrated,[56] while the MP–PP only prescribes the *karṇavedha*. Performing one or all *saṃskāras* ensures the regular status of the tree. By this way, the presence of the donor, which guarantees the initiated state of the son, is useless. Finally, we can observe a major addition: the performance of a great festival called *aśokatarukotsavam* (SPBh162.74), *tarukotsavam* (SP162.107),

54 As discussed above, the NP† prescribes an adoption and not the planting of a tree by the expression *taruputraṃ kṛ*, but the quotation only mentions that it will be done according to the prescribed rules, *vidhivad*. As for SP and BVP†, the tree is an already existing one, already planted. The BVP† (CVC 1053.5–6) specifies that the tree will be young and healthy and then that all the trees around the chosen tree must be decorated with banners (CVC1053.12ab: *patākālaṅkṛtāḥ sarve kāryās tatsaṃnidhau drumāḥ*). In the SP, Pārvatī chooses an *aśoka* tree seen on the Mandara mountain and the ceremony takes place where the tree is located:

SPBh158.70: *proṣite tvayi deveśa bhramantyā mandare mayā |*

aśokataruko dṛṣṭaḥ komalaḥ sumanoramaḥ ||

In your absence, O Lord of the Gods, when I was walking on Mount Mandara, I saw a tender and charming *Aśoka* tree.

SPBh162.41cd: *umāmāha prayāmeti yatrāśokaḥ sutaḥ ||*

He (*i.e.* Śiva) said Umā: Let's go where the aśoka [will be taken as] a son.

55 All verbs are in the third person of the singular of the optative. So this impersonal structure seems to refer to Brahmin(s) performing the whole ceremony.

56 BVP†–CVC1054 details the names of the *saṃskāras* to perform and adds that a wedding of the tree with a creeper can be performed: *vivāhaṃ kecid icchanti mādhavīlatayā taroḥ.*

mahotsavaṃ (BVP†-CVC1055.28), *vṛkṣāṇāṃ sumahotsavaṃ* (BVP†--CVC1055.31), *utsavaḥ* and *vṛkṣotsavaḥ* (MP59.15–17–PP28.15–17). A last point to be noticed is the gender of the adopter. The ceremony of tree adoption has to be performed by a man in the NP†, the BVP† and MP59–PP28, whereas the SP suggests an adoption in two steps: the sonless man performs the *saṃskāras* of the tree (SPBh158.40), while the ceremony of adoption is celebrated by a sonless woman (SPBh158.45–64 and SPBh162.57–69). As already noted earlier, the SP slightly differs from other attestations: on the one hand, the authors logically demonstrate that tree is superior to a real son, and, on the other hand, the main part of the ritual is performed by a woman.

The Detailed Ceremony: Agreement or Disagreement Between the Texts Dealing with the Tree Adoption Ritual?

Comparing the performance of the tree adoption in each *Purāṇa* will help us to determine the relationships between our three rituals. By focusing especially on the following aspects – the preparation of the tree and that of the sacrificer, the objects required, including offerings and gifts, the timings to perform the whole ritual and finally what must be said during the ceremony – a relative chronology between our descriptions of tree adoption can be established. To obtain a synoptic view of each aspect, the reader can refer to the following detailed tables in the Appendix: Table 6.A3, The preparation of the tree; Table 6.A4, The preparation of the sacrificer; Table 6.A5, Objects, offerings and gifts; Table 6.A6, The time of the ceremony; Table 6.A7, Ritual formulas.[57]

Concerning the preparation of the tree, in all rituals, the tree must wear clothing, be decorated by ribbons, banners or garlands, be anointed and sprinkled. Parasols are required by the SP and the BVP†, but not by MP59–PP28. As for the adopter, he must be clean and in a peaceful state of mind. The way to obtain this purification differs slightly: the SP suggests a fast and a night on the ground in the *añjali* posture, whereas the BVP† and the MP59–PP28 prescribe a bath. In the BVP†, the sacrificer makes the *añjali* posture in front of the tree just before the statement of a ritual sentence. Thus, here the BVP† shares common features with both the SP and MP59–PP28. All in all, the testimonies sketch almost the same preparations of the tree and the adopter.

In contrast, the disagreements concerning the objects are more numerous. All agree on *bali* offerings and food offerings. On this last point, the SP again offers a theoretical explanation, arguing that food offerings to Brahmins are the best gift (SPBh158.49–50) and justifying this by a semantic etymology linking the suffix

57 Tables 6.A3, 6.A4, 6.A5, 6.A6 and 6.A7 are in the Appendix.

-*aṇa* of the word *brāhmaṇa* with the word *anna*- 'food' (SPBh158.52). *Bali*, food offerings and incense are the only objects required by the SP ritual. The two other rituals require more objects and resources: to adopt a tree, a man needs golden or silver fruits, pots and jars, a milk-yielding cow and the payment of the fees of the Brahmins, including gold. In MP59–PP28, the pots should contain gold, the cow should be adorned with ornaments made of gold and having horns covered with gold, the Brahmins' fees include cows, golden threads, bracelets, rings and other valuable items. Here there is a striking contrast between the testimonies: the SP ritual seems to be very simple to perform and accessible to everyone, while to adopt a tree requires substantial funds in the BVP† and even more in MP59–PP28. The prescribed duration of the ritual corresponds to this contrast of funds: in the SP–BVP†, two days are enough to perform the ritual, while MP59–PP28 requires at least four days.

Concerning the ritual formulas to declare, the SP's ritual is again very plain. The *mantras* are only those of the *saṃskāras* and they are not included in the tree adoption performed by the sonless woman. A Brahmin or the adopting woman herself has to declare the day auspicious, *puṇyāha*[58] and then she has to state:[59]

> *aputrā bhagavanto'haṃ putraprakṛtakaṃ tarum*
> *grahīṣye tadanujñāṃ vai kartum arhata me'naghāḥ* || *63* ||
>
> 'I am a sonless woman, O Lords, I shall take this tree as my son, may you deign to accept my demand, O sinless beings!'

The role played by Brahmins in the SP is only to be witnesses of the adoption and to authenticate it. Apart from the mantras for the *saṃskāra* rituals, the formulas to pronounce in the BVP† are also non-vedic *mantras* and they must be muttered by the adopter, whereas there is no non-vedic sentence in MP59–PP28. Nevertheless, the Brahmins play a more important role in the BVP† than in the SP: they have to make an oblation to Indra, the Lokapālas, Vanaspati and others. The latter is a strong common feature between the BVP† and MP59–PP28. If we consider this detail and the other previously common features, we can assert a close relationship between the testimonies of the MP and the BVP†. In view of this, it does not seem too far-fetched to say that MP59 makes a whole with PP28.22, and that they both offer an evidence of the tree adoption.

To summarise the results of the detailed comparison of the three excerpts: they agree on the goal of the ritual, follow a standard procedure of adoption and share numerous details in their ceremonies. It can now be asserted that the SP shows

58 SPBh158.61.
59 SPBh158.63.

some special features that distinguish it from the others: it furnishes a theoretical explanation to justify the tree adoption and describes a very plain ceremony involving limited time and funds. The most important discrepancy is perhaps that the leading role is played by a woman in the ceremony, while no other document gives such a prominent role to a woman.

On this point, it must be added that the ritual prescription is introduced in a very didactic manner in SPBh158 and SPBh162. In SPBh158, Śiva himself explains the rite to Pārvatī, and in SPBh162, Pārvatī herself performs the ritual adoption of an *aśoka* tree.[60] Thus, the SP offers an additional explanation of the origin of the ritual, and a model for its performance provided by the goddess herself. All this forms a cohesive whole in the SP.

The myth of *aśoka* adoption by Pārvatī is clearly known by BVP†:[61]

> *aputrayā purā pārtha pārvatyā mandarācale*
> *aśokaḥ śokaśamanaḥ putratve parikalpitaḥ*
>
> At the top of Mount Mandara, O son of Pṛthā, the *aśoka*, which softens sorrow, was once adopted by the sonless goddess Pārvatī.[62]

There is no mention of it in MP59–PP28, but in chapter 154 of the current edition whose verse 512 is quoted by Lakṣmīdhara and Hemādri, Pārvatī rears a sprout of *aśoka* before stating that 'a tree is equal to ten sons'. So, the cohesive whole found in the SP seems to disintegrate in the MP: the ritual is transformed into a consecration of trees found in MP59, while the myth ends in a proverb without explanation in MP154. Hence it is possible to conceive that a cohesive whole prevailed in a previous state of the MP text, but in the current edition it is clearly not the case. It is also conceivable that the MP borrowed[63] the tree ritual and the myth of the *aśoka* as Pārvatī's son from the SP.

Among these versions, the SP's testimony of tree adoption seems to be the oldest one. The mention of the *aśoka* myth by the BVP† and other common features shared with the SP suggest that the BVP†'s testimony might be placed before the disintegration of the MP's version, if (but that remains highly hypothetic) MP59, PP28 and MP154 once constituted a whole. The increase in ritual objects and required funds (even more conspicuously in MP59–PP28), the *mantras* to be recited

60 On the parallels of this myth in earlier Sanskrit literature, see Wattelier-Bricout (2017) and (2018).

61 BVP†–CVC1053.2.

62 By this way, here, as described in Kālidāsa's *Kumārasaṃbhava* V.14 and the SPBh158–162, the *aśoka* tree is Pārvatī's first-born son.

63 Adriaensen, Bakker and Isaacson (1998: 22) and Bisschop (2002: 239) also consider the borrowing of SP by MP as possible.

by Brahmins and the addition of the fire sacrifice complicate the ritual[64] and give Brahmins a more prominent role.

Conclusion

Taking into account several *Dharmanibandha* authors and their entire chapters dedicated to trees allowed us to sketch an array of types and instances of tree adoption and to understand that each *Nibandha* author suggests his own vision of the subject, including a kind of rejection of this heterodox ritual.[65] Their analyses shows that the study of *Nibandha* literature is crucial for us in order to understand the history of text transmission and the evolution of ritual practices. On this subject it can now be affirmed that tree adoption was a ritual prescription performed at least from the 6th–7th century CE (the date of the SP's composition) to the 15th century (the date of its quotation by Madanasiṃha), but which probably did not always enjoyed the same popularity or obey the same rules.

Applying a systematic comparison of the described rituals reveals the relationships between them and outlines their chronological order as much as possible in the absence of critical editions of some *Purāṇas*. It appears that the SP seems to be the oldest text, not only because of its relatively early date, but also because of its consistency and the ease with which it can be performed. The comparison between the *Nibandha* quotations and the current editions of the MP and the PP points to the compelling need to critically edit these.

Further Development of Tree Adoption

Finally, I would like to add some remarks on the spread of tree adoption from parts of the current edition of the PP, which are not quoted by *Nibandha* authors. Chapter I.43.432ss of the PP in its current edition tells the same story as that of

64 Pradhan (2002: 113–14) talks about the purāṇic testimonies of *vṛkṣotsava* in his article. He refers to MP59.1–20 and PP5.24.192–211 (a passage at which I could not look because he does not mention the edition consulted) and states that 'the requirement of *homa* in all these texts is an attempt to vedicise an original Dāsa ritual which does not involve *homa*. [...] Invoking gods like Indra and the Lokapālas too along with the trees in the *Vṛkṣotsava* is also part of the vedicisation of a Dāsa ritual'. For my part, I have no decisive element that would enable me to argue that tree adoption was originally a Dāsa ritual. SP testimony is a cohesive and constructed whole, but it is also possible that it was based on a ritual that previously existed. In all the cases, it does not include *homa* and suggests a very plain procedure in which Brahmins played a minor role against MP59–PP28 and BVP†.

65 See above the development on the interpretation of the lack of tree adoption in Ballālasena's *Dānasāgara*.

chapter 154 of the MP, except for the following point: Pārvatī says that a tree is equal to ten girls and not ten sons. Thus we may remark that this discrepancy in Pārvatī's story introduces a version that points out some evolutions of the purpose of the ritual. In the same way, PP.II.102 relates the story of Aśokasundarī, which is very close to the myth of *aśoka* adoption by Pārvatī: during a walk in *Nandanavana* with Śiva, Pārvatī sees a shining tree, a *kalpadruma*. Śiva says to her that the tree can give her everything she wants. She wishes a child and, with Śiva's consent, she obtains a daughter called Aśokasundarī. The vision of a tree during a walk, Śiva's consent and Pārvatī's delight are three common features shared by this story and that of the SP, but not by that of MP154. Thus, this seems to be a new story based on the older topic of the *aśoka* tree adoption. Finally, in the current edition of the PP, an entire chapter, PP.I.58, is dedicated to tree planting. Verses 3 to 11 explained the benefits of planting a tree on the bank of a lake or a pond: the leaves falling in the water are like *Bali* offerings and the fruits eaten by birds (*dvija*) are like food offerings presented to Brahmins (*dvija*). Planting a tree is therefore better than having 100 sons. Then (PP.I.58.12–28) the passage describes how to worship the holy fig tree, which is conceived of as a *trimūrti* representation.[66] This chapter may be a regional development on the topic of tree rituals, a later development or a ritual discarded by the *Nibandha* authors consulted.

As for the BVP†, it has already been pointed out that the BVP† passage quoted by Hemādri is not found in the current edition and must therefore refer to a lost text[67] already titled *Brahmavaivarta purāṇa*. In order to clarify the history of this *Purāṇa*, manuscripts 3820 and 3821 mentioned by Shastri (1928: 490–493) should be consulted and compared with the numerous quotations of this *Purāṇa* in *Nibandha* literature.

To conclude on the development of tree adoption, a rather fascinating parallel to the story of *aśoka* adoption by Pārvatī may be cited, which relates the birth of Gaṇeśa. The story is found in the current BVP, in chapters 2–9 of the *Gaṇeśa Khaṇḍa*: Pārvatī is sad (*śoka*) because she is a barren woman. She really wants a son and complains to her husband. Śiva then teaches her a vow, a *vrata*, to perform in order to obtain a son who will eliminate her pain (she will become without pain: *aśoka*). This *puṇyakavrata* is then explained in many details, Pārvatī accomplishes it and ends up discovering an infant on her bed. Chapter 9 closes with Pārvatī nursing her child. He is none other than Gaṇeśa, the eldest son of Pārvatī and Śiva. In this story, the *aśoka*, the first-born son of Pārvatī, gives its place away to the elephant-headed god.

66 In the root resides Viṣṇu, in the middle stays Śiva, while Brahmā lives at the top.
67 On this matter, see Rocher (1986: 160–164).

Abbreviations

BVP *Brahmavaivartapurāṇa* (see Śrīkṛṣṇadā, K. 1951; Sen 1992; Bhatt 2016)
BVP† the *Brahmavaivartapurāṇa*, which is quoted by the Nibandha and is not the text of the current edition of the *Brahmavaivartapurāṇa*
CVC Hemādri: (*dānakhaṇḍa* part of the) *Caturvargacintāmaṇi* (see *Śiromaṇi* 1873)
DS *Dānasāgara*: Ballāla Sena (see Bhattacharya 1953)
KKT Lakṣmīdhara: (*dānakāṇḍa* part of) *Kṛtyakalpataru* (see Rangaswami Aiyangar 1941; Brick 2009)
MP *Matsyapurāṇa* (see Singh *et al.* 1983)
MRP Madanasiṃha: (*dānavivekoddyota* part of) *Madanaratnapradīpa* (see Deśapāṇḍe 1964–1967)
NP† refers to *Nandipurāṇa*, a lost *purāṇa* quoted by the *Nibandha*
PP *Padmapurāṇa* (see Mandlik 1894; Deshpande, Shastri and Bhatt 1988; Vedavyas 2007)
SP *Skandapurāṇa* (see Adriaensen, Bakker and Isaacson 1998; Adriaensen and Bakker 2004; Bakker, Bisschop and Yokochi 2014; Kṛṣṇadāsa *et al.* 1989)
SPBh *Skandapurāṇa* (see Bhaṭṭarāī 1988)

References

Adriaensen, R. and Bakker, H.T. (eds) (2004) *The Skandapurāṇa: Critically edited with prolegomena and English synopsis*, vol. 2A. Groningen: Egbert Forsten.

Adriaensen, R., Bakker, H.T. and Isaacson, H. (eds) (1998) *The Skandapurāṇa. Adhyāyas 1–25: Critically edited with prolegomena and English synopsis*, vol. 1. Groningen: Egbert Forsten.

Bakker, H.T. (2014) *The World of the Skandapurāṇa: Northern India in the sixth and seventh centuries*. Leiden: Brill.

Bakker, H.T. (2004) *Origin and Growth of the Purāṇic Text Corpus: With special reference to the Skandapurāṇa*. Delhi: Motilal Banarsidass.

Bakker, H.T., Bisschop, P.C. and Yokochi, Y. (eds) (2014) *The Skandapurāṇa. Adhyāyas 31–52: The Vāhana and Naraka cycles*, vol. 2B. Groningen: Egbert Forsten

Bhatt, G.P. (ed.) (2016) *Brahmavaivarta Purāṇa*. Delhi: Motilal Banarsidass Publishers.

Bhattacharya, B. (ed.) (1953) *Dānasāgara of Ballāla Sena*. Calcutta: Asiatic Society.

Bhaṭṭarāī (ed.) (1988) *Skandapurāṇasya Ambikākhaṇḍa*. Śrīmahendrasaṃskṛtaviśvavidyālayagranthamālā. Mahendra Saṃskṛta Viśvavidyālaya, Velajhuṇḍī.

Bisschop, P.C. (2002) On a Quotation of the *Skandapurāṇa* in the *Tīrthavivecanakāṇḍa* of Lakṣmīdhara's *Kṛtyakalpataru*. Studies in the *Skandapurāṇa* V. *Indo-Iranian Journal* 45(3), 231–243.

BISSCHOP, P.C. (2006) *Early Śaivism and the Skandapurāṇa: Sects and centres.* Groningen: Forsten.

BRICK, D. (ed. and trans.) (2009) *Brahmanical Theories of the Gift: A critical edition and annotated translation of the Dānakāṇḍa of the Kṛtyakalpataru.* Cambridge: Harvard University Press.

DEŚAPĀṆḌE, K. (ed.) (1964–1967) *Śrīmadanasiṃhadevaviracite Madanaratnapradīpe Dānavivekoddyotaḥ.* Sanskrit Academy Series 10, 15–16, 3 vols. Hyderabad: Sanskrit Academy, Ousmania University.

DESHPANDE, N.A., SHASTRI, J.L. AND BHATT, G.P. (eds) (1988) *The Padma-Purāṇa.* Delhi: Motilal Banarsidass Publishers.

DE SIMINI, F. (2015) Observations on the Use of Quotations in Sanskrit *Dharmanibandhas. Journal of Indian Philosophy* 43, 601–624.

HARIMOTO, K. (2006) The Original *Skandapurāṇa,* Lakṣmīdhara and Caṇḍeśvara. Studies in the *Skandapurāṇa* VIII. *Indo-Iranian Journal* 49(1/2), 23–38.

KĀṆE, P.V. (1930, 1946, 1962) *History of Dharmaśāstra.* (Ancient and mediaeval religious and civil law), vol. 1, 3, 5 (part II). Poona: Bhandarkar Oriental research Institute.

KHERA, K.L. (1997) *Index to History of Dharmaśāstra by Pandurang Vaman Kane: Comprehensive guide to Hindu rites and rituals.* New Delhi: Munshiram Manoharlal Publishers.

KṚṢṆADĀSA, K., ŚARMĀ, R. and SIṂHA, N. (eds) (1989) *The Skandamahāpurāṇam aṣṭam bhāga bhūmikā evaṃ ślokānukramaṇī.* Delhi: Nag Publishers.

MANDLIK, V.N. (ed.) (1894) *Padmapurāṇa.* Pune: Anandashram Press.

NARAYANAN, V. (1997) 'One Tree Is Equal to Ten Sons': Hindu Responses to the Problems of Ecology, Population and Consumption. *Journal of the American Academy of Religion* 65(2), 291–332. Oxford: Oxford University Press. Available online at: http://www.jstor.org/stable/1465767.

PRADHAN, S. (2002) The Biography of Caitya. *Annals of the Bhandarkar Oriental Research Institute* 83, 91–120.

RANGASWAMI AIYANGAR, K.V. (ed.) (1941) *Kṛtyakalpataru of Bhaṭṭa Lakṣmīdhara,* vol. 5. Baroda: Oriental Institute.

ROCHER, L. (1986) *The Puranas.* Wiesbaden: Otto Harrassowitz.

SEN, R.N. (ed.) (1992) *Brahmavaivarta Puranam, Part 2 Ganesa and Krisna Janma Khandas.* Sudhindra Nath Vasu, Bahadurganj, Allahabad.

SHASTRI, H.P. (1928) *A Descriptive Catalogue of Sanskrit Manuscripts in the Government Collection Under the Care of the Asiatic Society of Bengal,* vol. 5. Calcutta: Baptist Mission Press.

SINGH, N.S. (1983) *The Matsyamahāpurāṇam text in Devanagari, translation & notes in English part I and part II.* Delhi: Nag Publishers.

ŚIROMAṆI, B. (ed.) (1873) *Chaturvarga Chintámani* 1. Calcutta: Asiatic Society of Bengal.

SRĪDATTA, U. AND ŚĀSTRĪ, A.C. (1972) *Pitṛbhakti of Śrīdattopādhyāya.* Vārāṇasī: Chowkhamba Sanskrit Series Office.

ŚRĪKṚṢṆADĀ, K. (1951) *Brahmavaivarta Mahāpurāṇa.* Muṃbayī: Śrī Veṅkaṭeśvara Yantrālaya.

VEDAVYAS, K.D. (ed.) (2007) *Padma Purāṇam by Shrimanmaharshi Krishna Dwaipayan Vedavyas part VI containing śloka index.* Varanasi: Chowkhamba Sanskrit Series Office.

WATTELIER-BRICOUT, A. (2017) Les fonctions du stéréotype d'adoption par l'allaitement dans le *Skandapurāṇa* chap. 158 et 162. *Traits-d'Union*, Le stéréotype: fabrique d'identité. Available online at: https://hal.archives-ouvertes.fr/hal-01630307.

WATTELIER-BRICOUT, A. (2018) Adopter un arbre: un rite unique décrit dans les chapitres 158 et 162 du *Skandapurāṇa*. In Filliozat, P.-S. and Zink, M. (eds) (2018) *L'arbre en Asie*. Actes du colloque international organisé par l'Académie des Inscriptions et des Belles-Lettres, la Société Asiatique et l'INALCO. Paris: Académie des Inscriptions et des Belles-Lettres.

Appendix

Table 6A.1: Details of the references quoted as taruputravidhiḥ in Lakṣmīdhara's Dānakāṇḍa of his Kṛtyakalpataru (KKT),[1] Hemādri's Dānakhaṇḍa of his Caturvargacintāmaṇi (CVC) and Madanasiṃha's Dānavivekoddyota of his Madanaratnapradīpa (MRP)[2]

Purāṇa	*KKT*	*CVC*	*MRP*
PP28.22–23ab	21.50	1030 (part titled *vṛkṣaropaṇam*)	293
PP28.23cd	21.51ab	1030 (part titled *vṛkṣaropaṇam*)	not quoted
PP28.24ab	21.51cd	1030 (part titled *vṛkṣaropaṇam*)	293
PP28.24cd–25ab	21.52	1031 (part titled *vṛkṣaropaṇam*)	293
PP28.25cd	21.53	1031 (part titled *vṛkṣaropaṇam*)	293
PP28.26ab	21.54	1031 (part titled *vṛkṣaropaṇam*)	293
PP28.26cd–27ab	21.55	1031 (part titled *vṛkṣaropaṇam*)	293
PP28.27cd–28ab	21.56	1031 (part titled *vṛkṣaropaṇam*)	294
PP28.28cd–29ab	21.57	1031 (part titled *vṛkṣaropaṇam*)	294
PP28.29cd–30ab	21.58	1031 (part titled *vṛkṣaropaṇam*)	294
PP28.30cd–31	21.59	1031 (part titled *vṛkṣaropaṇam*)	294
PP28.32	21.60	1031 (part titled *vṛkṣaropaṇam*)	294
NP†	21.61	1050 (part titled *taruputravidhiḥ*)	293
Skandapurāṇa	not quoted	four *pādas* not found in the SPBh	not quoted
SPBh158.44cd–45cd	21.62	1050 (part titled *taruputravidhiḥ*)	294
SPBh158.45ab	not quoted	1050 (part titled *taruputravidhiḥ*)	not quoted
SPBh158.46ab	21.63ab	1050 (part titled *taruputravidhiḥ*)	295
SPBh158.46cd	21.63cd	1050 (part titled *taruputravidhiḥ*)	295

(continued)

Table 6A.1 (continued)

Purāṇa	*KKT*	*CVC*	*MRP*
SPBh158.47ab	21.64ab	1050 (part titled *taruputravidhiḥ*)	295
SPBh158.47cd	not quoted	1050 (part titled *taruputravidhiḥ*)	295
SPBh158.48cd	21.64cd	1050 (part titled *taruputravidhiḥ*)	295
SPBh158.58	21.65	1051 (part titled *taruputravidhiḥ*)	295
SPBh158.59	21.66	1051 (part titled *taruputravidhiḥ*)	295
SPBh158.60	21.67	1051 (part titled *taruputravidhiḥ*)	295
SPBh158.61	21.68	1051 (part titled *taruputravidhiḥ*)	295
SPBh158.62	21.69	1051 (part titled *taruputravidhiḥ*)	295
SPBh158.63	21.70	1051 (part titled *taruputravidhiḥ*)	295
SPBh158.64	21.71	1051 (part titled *taruputravidhiḥ*)	296
SPBh158.65	not quoted	1051 (part titled *taruputravidhiḥ*)	296
SPBh158.66	21.72	1051 (part titled *taruputravidhiḥ*)	296
SPBh158.67	21.73	1051 (part titled *taruputravidhiḥ*)	296
SPBh158.68	not quoted	1051 (part titled *taruputravidhiḥ*)	not quoted
SPBh162.57	not quoted	1052 (part titled *taruputravidhiḥ*)	not quoted
SPBh162.58	not quoted	1052 (part titled *taruputravidhiḥ*)	not quoted
SPBh162.59	not quoted	1052 (part titled *taruputravidhiḥ*)	not quoted
SPBh162.60	not quoted	1052 (part titled *taruputravidhiḥ*)	not quoted
SPBh162.61	not quoted	1052 (part titled *taruputravidhiḥ*)	not quoted
SPBh162.62	not quoted	1052 (part titled *taruputravidhiḥ*)	not quoted
SPBh162.63	not quoted	1052 (part titled *taruputravidhiḥ*)	not quoted
SPBh162.64ab	not quoted	1052 (part titled *taruputravidhiḥ*)	not quoted
SPBh162.67	not quoted	1052 (part titled *taruputravidhiḥ*)	not quoted
SPBh162.68	not quoted	1052 (part titled *taruputravidhiḥ*)	not quoted
MP154.512	21.74	1050 (part titled *taruputravidhiḥ*)	not quoted
BVP† (32 ślokas)	not quoted	1052–6 (part titled *taruputravidhiḥ*)	not quoted

1 I used the numbering established by Brick (2009) in his edition.

2 In the absence of numbering in the current editions of CVC and MRP, only the page number is given. Nevertheless one can clearly observe the verses quoted by comparison with the KKT's references.

Table 6A.2 The standard procedure of adoption applied to tree adoption

Standard practicalities	*SPBh158 and 162*	*BVP† (CVC1052–6)*	*PP28.1–22 = MP59*
Donor	none	none	none
Object to give	young tree/a tender *aśoka*	CVC1053.5: a young tree covered with buds	MP59.4: trees
Time	SPBh 158.46: to make a fast the day before the day of adoption	CVC1053.9: preparation of the tree the day before the adoption	MP59.3 refers to MP58.4–5 which indicates the proper time
Space	SPBh 158.59: the place where the tree is to be found (158 and 162: on Mandara mountain)	CVC1053.7: purification of the place where the tree is to be found	MP59.3 refers to MP58.4–5 which indicates the choice of the place
Watering	SPBh158.72 and SPBh162.62: Pārvatī sprinkles the tree by the milk of her breasts	CVC1053.10 and 11: watering with jugs	MP59.5: to sprinkle the trees with water mixed with All-Herb
Mantra	SPBh158.41: *mantravad vidhitaś caiva*	CVC1054.19 *mantras* belonging to the *saṃskāras* ceremonies CVC1055.24 and 25: quotation of a non-vedic *mantra*	MP59.12: different kind of *mantras*
Fees	SPBh 158.59: food for Brahmins	CVC1055.28: food but also a milk-yielding cow, clothes, *dakṣiṇā*	MP59.4: gold, clothes and ointments MP59.13–14: cows, golden threads, bracelets, rings, sacred clothes, beds household utensils and sandals
Auspicious day	SPBh 158.61: *puṇyāha* declared by the woman or the Brahmins	CVC1053.8: auspicious day declared by the *vipras*	MP59.3 refers to MP58.4–5 in which there is a declaration of auspicious day
Oblation	SPBh 162.64: *Bali* offerings	CVC1054.14, 18: *Bali* and *caru* offerings	MP59.9: Bali offering MP59.14: oblations of ghee, barley and black sesame seeds
State of mind: sacrificer	SPBh158.46 and 61–2	CVC1054.23: bathed, purified and wearing a white cloth	MP59.17: free from envy

(continued)

Table 6A.2 (continued)

Standard practicalities	*SPBh158 and 162*	*BVP† (CVC1052–6)*	*PP28.1–22 = MP59*
Preparation of the tree	SPBh158.60: ribbons, parasol, ornaments	CVC1053.9: banners, red clothes and red string	MP59.5: to adorn the trees with perfumed powder, decorate them with garlands and cover them with cloth
Fire sacrifice	none	CVC1054.17 *homa*	MP59.16: kindling of *Palāśa* is prescribed
Gifts for the son	SPBh162.62: white clothes	CVC1053.9: red clothes and CVC1053.13: 15 golden fruits	MP59.7: seven or eight golden fruits
Additions			
Utsava/Festival	SPBh162.74 and 107	CVC1055.28: *mahotsavaṃ* and CVC1055.31: *vṛkṣāṇāṃ sumahotsavaṃ*	MP59.16 and MP59.18: a Tree Festival
Sa59.16 a made as if the tree was a real son	SPBh158.41–2: all the *saṃskāras* made by the sonless man; not detailed	CVC1052.3 and CVC1054,18–22: all the *saṃskāras* made by the man who wants to adopt the tree, they are detailed (including ear piercing)	MP59.5 (KKT21.34–CVC1048) *karṇavedha*
Sacrificer	SPBh158.58: the sacrificer is purified and wears white clothes, *añjali* posture with *darbha* grass in the hands	CVC1054.23: bathed and wearing white clothes, *añjali* posture with flowers in the hands	MP59.13: bathed sacrificer should don white garments
Adopter	man and woman	Man	man

Table 6.A3: The detailed ritual: the preparation of the tree

Preparation of the tree	*SPBh158 and SPBh162*	*BVP†*	*MP59*	*PP28.1–32*
Number of trees	one *aśoka*	one tree but surrounded by other trees decorated for the occasion CVC1053.12	MP59.5 several trees MP59.5 all decorated MP59.18 a single tree	PPI.28.5 several trees PPI.28.5 all decorated PPI.28.18 a single tree
saṃskāra	SPBh158.41–42 *garbhādhāna* till the end	CVC1053.3 *Jātakarmādikās* CVC1054.18–22 *jātaka nāmakaraṇa annapraśanna cuḍakarma godana vivāha* (optional)	MP59.5 (KKT21.34–CVC1048) *karṇavedha*	PPI.28.5 *karṇavedha*
Ointments	SPBh162.59 (CVC1052) santal	CVC1053.7 CVC1053.11 santal ointment	MP59.5 & 8 (KKT21.34 and 37–CVC1048) perfumed powders MP59.6 *añjana*	PPI.28.5 and 8 PPI.28.6
'Watering' the tree	SPBh158.72 SPBh162.65 Pārvatī sprinkles the tree by the milk of her breasts	CVC1053.10 *snāpita* CVC1054.19 *pādapaṃ snapayitvā*	MP59.5 (KKT21.34–CVC1048) with water mixed herbs	PPI.28.5
Clothes for the tree	SPBh162.62 (CVC1052) white clothes	CVC1053.9 red clothes and red thread	MP59.5 and 8 (KKT21.34 and 37–CVC1048) on the branches and at the tree stump	PPI.28.5 and 8
Ribbons/banners on the tree	SP158.60 (KKT21.67–CVC1051) SP162.60 (CVC1052) ribbons adorned with gems	CVC1053.9 banners	MP59.5 (KKT21.34–CVC1048) garlands	PPI.28.5
Parasol	SP158.60 (KKT21.67–CVC1051) SP162.58 (CVC1052) made with peacock feathers	CVC1053.11 with gems	None	none

Table 6.A4: The detailed ritual: the preparation of the sacrificer

Preparation of the sacrificer	*SPBh158 and SPBh162*	*BVP†*	*MP59*	*PP28.1–32*
Añjali posture	SP158.58 (KKT21.65–CVC1051) *darbha* grass	CVC1054.23 *puṣpa*	none	none
State of mind and purification of the sacrificer	SP158.46 (KKT21.63–CVC1050) SP158.61–2 (KKT21.68–9–CVC1051)	CVC1054.23	MP59.13 (KKT21.42–CVC1049)	PPI.28
A white cloth for the sacrificer	SP158.58 (KKT21.65–CVC1051)	CVC1054.23	MP59.13 (KKT21.42–CVC1049)	PPI.28
Bathed	none	CVC1054.23	MP59.12–13	PPI.28.12–13
Fast	SPBh158.46	none	none	none
Spend a night on the ground	SPBh158.58 SPBh162.40	none	none	none

Table 6.A5: The detailed ritual: objects, offerings and gifts

Objects, offerings, gifts	*SPBh158 and SPBh162*	*BVP†*	*MP59*	*PP28.1–32*
Incense	SP162.63 (CVC1052) *guggula*	none	MP59.8 (KKT21.37–CVC1048) *guggula*	PPI.28.8
Golden or silver fruits	none	CVC1053.13 15 fruits	MP59.7(KKT21.36–CVC1048) seven or eight fruits	PPI.28.7
Food offerings	SP158.59 (KKT21.66–CVC1051) SP158.61 (KKT21.68–CVC1051) SP162.4	CVC1055.29–30	MP59.14–15 (KKT21.43–4–CVC1049) during four days	PPI.28.14–5
Cup/jar or bawl	none	CVC1053.10–12	MP59.8 (KKT21.37–CVC1048)	PPI.28.8
A cow given to Brahmins	none	CVC1055.28	MP59.11(KKT21.40–CVC1048)	PPI.28.11
Bali offering	SP162.64cd	CVC1054.14 *bali* and CVC1054.18: *caru*–offering	MP59.9 (KKT21.38–CVC1048) *balinivedana*	PPI.28.9
Fees	none	CVC1054.16 and CVC1055.28	MP59.15	PPI.28.15

Table 6.A6: The detailed ritual: ritual formulas

Time	*SPBh158 and SPBh162*	*BVP†*	*MP59*	*PP28.1–32*
The day before	SPBh158.46 (KKT21. 63–CVC1050) SPBh162.5 preparation of the sacrificer	CVC1053.9: preparation of the tree the day before	none	none
Time of the tree preparation	SPBh158.60 the same day than the adoption	CVC1053.9: preparation of the tree the day before	MP59.5–9 the first day of the ceremony	PPI.28.5–9
Time for music	SPBh162.64ab (CVC1052) with *bali* offerings	CVC1054.14 music with *bali* offerings	MP59.12 (KKT21.41–CVC1049) without *bali* offerings, with the bath of the sacrificer	PPI.28.12 without *bali* offerings, with the bath of the sacrificer
Festival time	SPBh162.38 and 71–4: the festival begins the night before the adoption and closes just after the adoption	CVC1055.31 the same day than the adoption	MP59.15 the fourth day	PPI.28.15 the fourth day

Table 6.A7: The detailed ritual: ritual formulas

Ritual formulas	*SPBh158 and SPBh162*	*BVP†*	*MP59*	*PP28.1–32*
Day declared auspicious	SPBh158.61 (KKT21.68–CVC1051) SPBh162.67–68 (CVC1052)	CVC1053.8	none	none
Mantras	SPBh158.41–2 those of the *saṃskāras* ceremonies	CVC1054.19 *mantras* belonging to *saṃskāras* rituals	MP59.12 (KKT21.41–CVC1049) *abhiṣekamantreṇa ṛgyajuḥsāmamantrais*	PPI.28.12 *abhiṣekamantreṇa ṛgyajuḥsāmamantrais*
Ritual request	SPBh158.63 (KKT21.70–CVC1051) SP162.69	CVC1055.24–5 and 27: specific and non-vedic *mantras* quoted and said after the *saṃskāras'* ceremonies	none	none
Offerings made to Indra Lokapāla Vanaspati by Brahmins	none	CVC1054.15 Lokapālas beginning with Indra as during the *grahayajña*	MP59.10(KKT21.39–CVC1048) Lokapālas beginning with Indra and Vanaspati	PPI.28.10

The Vedic *Idáṃ Bhū*-Construction as a Precursor of the Compound Type *X-Bhūta**

Yūto Kawamura

Bhartṛhari analyses the compound *āttvabhūta* given by Patañjali as *āttvaṃ bhūtāḥ* 'those [items] which have reached (acquired) a property of the long vowel *ā*' or *āttvena bhūtāḥ* 'those [items] which have been reached by a property of the long vowel *ā*' (= those verbs which end in the long vowel *ā*). In the analysis of compounds of the type x-*bhūta*, such as *āttvabhūta*, native grammarians usually adduce dhātupāṭha X.300: *bhū prāptau* to substantiate that the verb *bhū* can be used in the meaning of reaching (*prāpti*) and thereby that this verb can take an object, as in *āttvaṃ bhūtāḥ*. Bhartṛhari shows, on the other hand, that actual Vedic usages such as *sá rāṣṭrám abhavat* 'he came to gain dominion' and *rāṣṭráṁ ha bhavati* '[he] comes to gain dominion' (*idáṃ bhū*-construction) in the Maitrāyaṇī-Saṁhitā do serve as testimonies to the sense of reaching. Put differently, in his view it is these usages that enable us to assign this meaning to the verb *bhū*. This meaning assignment is necessarily presupposed to form a compound of the type x-*bhūta*. Bhartṛhari's point of view thus implies a historical link between the Vedic *idáṃ bhū*-construction and this type of compound.

Introduction

The so-called Vedic *idáṃ bhū*/*as*-construction has the structure {neuter singular form + finite verb form of *bhū* or *as*} meaning 'come to control/rule/possess something, control/rule/possess something'.[1] For example:

* This paper, a short version of which was presented at the 9th International Indology Graduate Research Symposium (IIGRS) held at Ghent University, 22–23 September 2017, is a revised and enlarged version of Kawamura (2017). The speakers at this conference were invited by the organising committee to submit their papers for this volume of *Puṣpikā*. Although the basic structure and conclusion of the present paper are almost the same as Kawamura (2017), I would like to welcome and use this

> *rāṣṭrám̐ ha bhavati* 'He comes to gain dominion' (*rāṣṭrá* 'dominion'; *bhū* 'become, be, come into being', see below for the source of this expression).

It is Hoffmann (1976) who first discussed this *idáṃ bhū/as*-construction. As Hoffmann argues, this construction is surely of Indo-Iranian date, since a similar expression is found in Young Avestan: *yaθa azəm upəməm xšaθrəm bauuāni* 'that I may come to gain the highest dominion'.[2] Recently, Weiss (2017) has argued that a reflex of the construction at issue is also observed in a Middle Irish text (*bid uadib nert for Herind* 'A power will be from them over Erin'), which suggests that one can reconstruct the phrase *rāṣṭráṃ bhū* as an archaic formula *h_3rḗĝ-s *b^huh_x- 'become the power' > 'become king' for Inner Indo-European.

Whereas Hoffmann (1976) assumes the initial part of the *idáṃ bhū/as*-construction as a predicative nominative (prädikativer Nominativ),[3] Gotō (2007 and 2008) opens up the possibility that in most occurrences the part in question can be explained as a content accusative (Inhaltsakkusativ) used to characterise the meaning of the verb.[4] The literal translation of the utterance *rāṣṭráṃ bhavati* would be 'so werden, da eines Dasein mit der Herrschaft charakterisiert wird' (Gotō 2008).[5] On the construction, Witzel and Gotō (2007) explicitly say:

> Die Konstruktion von *idám bhū/as* (Hoffmann, *Aufsätze*, S. 557–559): 'für etwas zuständig werden/sein; über etwas herrschen, etwas innehaben/haben werden', die nichts anderes als eine Konstruktion mit dem Inhaltsakkusativ des Verbs *as/bhū* darstellt. (Witzel and Gotō 2007: 652)[6]

How do indigenous Indian grammarians (*vaiyākaraṇa*) treat this construction? As for the combination *idám as*, worthy of attention is Sāyaṇa's (*c.* 14th century CE) comment on ṚV I.109.7d. The whole verse runs as follows:

opportunity to correct some disastrous mistakes in the previous work, to clarify the points that may have not been clear therein and to add new, helpful information. It is my hope that readers may benefit from this improved version. I am profoundly indebted to Adam Catt (Kyoto University) and Yiming Shen (University of Oxford) for offering constructive comments on earlier drafts. I am also grateful to the two anonymous reviewers for a number of helpful suggestions.

1 Gotō (2008: § 4 [117–118]): '"diese [Herrschaft] hier erlangen/werden/innehaben"; eine allgemein gültige Formulierung wäre: *idám as/bhū* "für etw. zuständig sein/werden; über etw. herrschen/herrschen werden, etw. innehaben/innehaben werden"'. See also Gotō (1999: § 2.12 [137–138]) and Gotō (2002: 31).

2 Hoffmann (1976: 558).

3 Hoffmann (1976: 558).

4 Gotō (2007: § 4 [807–808]) and Gotō 2008: (§ 5 [121–122]). For details on the Inhaltsakkusativ, see Gotō (2002: § 9 [32–35]).

5 Gotō (2008: 121–122): 'Es gibt aber Aussicht, da die Mehrheit der Beispiele unmittelbar aus Sätzen von *as* und *bhav^i/bhū* mit dem Inhaltsakkusativ erklärt wird: *rāṣṭrám as/bhū* "so sein/werden, da eines Dasein mit der Herrschaft charakterisiert wird", *ṛṇám as* "in beschuldetem/n Zustand sein/geraten"'.

6 For a more extended discussion of the Vedic *idáṃ bhū/as*-construction, see Amano (2009: § 2.1.5 [39–43]). No further details need be discussed in this paper.

R̥V I.109.7: *ā́ bharataṃ śíkṣataṃ vajrabāhū*
asmā́m̐ indrāgnī avataṃ śácībhiḥ |
imé nú té raśmáyaḥ sū́ryasya
yébhiḥ sapitvā́ṃ pitáro na ā́san ||

'Bring it to the fore, ready your skill, you two with the mace in your arms. Help us, O Indra and Agni, with your skills. Here are the very rays of the sun with which our forefathers were in communion.' (Jamison and Brereton 2014: 257)

Sāyaṇa accounts for the expression *sapitvám ... ā́san* by taking *sapitvám* as an accusative form and *āsan* as an imperfect form of the verb *as*, which denotes the action of going (*gati*), registered in dhātupāṭha I.934: *ásÁ gatidīptyādāneṣu*. This *as*, unlike the well-known verb *as* 'be' listed in dhātupāṭha II.56: *ásÁ bhuvi*, can take an object (*sakarmaka*).[7]

In his Mahābhāṣyadīpikā, Bhartr̥hari (c. 5th century CE) deals with the combination *idáṃ bhū* in a similar manner: the verb *bhū* in this combination signifies the act of reaching (*prāpti*) and not its usual meaning 'become, be, come into being'. The important point is that the *idáṃ bhū*-construction serves for Bhartr̥hari to explain a compound of the type x-*bhūta*. His discussion indicates that this Vedic construction is a source for this type of compound. This paper aims to demonstrate this point in order to give a fresh angle on the compound type, which is highly productive in classical Sanskrit literature.[8]

Bhartr̥hrari's Discourse

Concerning the compound *āttvabhūta* 'that [item] which has reached (acquired) a property of the long vowel *ā* (= that verb which ends in the long vowel *ā* [*ākārānta*])' mentioned by Patañjali,[9] Bhartr̥hari brings forward the following argument:

MBhD (II.21.19–25): [a] *āttvaṃ bhūtā āttvabhūtāḥ* | [b] *nanu ca bhavater akarmakatvāt āttvaṃ bhūtā ity etan nopapadyate* | *na cāsya bhavateḥ*

7 R̥VS on R̥V I.109.7 (I.479.3–5): ... *sthānam āsan brahmalokam agacchan* | ... *asa gatidīptyādāneṣu* | *laṅy āḍāgama udāttaḥ* | See A 3.2.111: *anadyatane laṅ* and A 6.4.72: *āḍ ajādīnām*. The former provides for *lAṄ* (suffix to derive imperfect forms) to occur after verbs if they denote actions performed at a time in the past that excludes the day on which the speaker referring to it utters the sentence (*anadyatane*); the latter teaches that stems beginning with vowels (*ajādi*) receives a high-pitched (*udātta*) vowel *ā́* as the initial augment (*āṭ*) when *lAṄ* follows.

8 For a list of compounds of this type found in Sanskrit works, see Böhtlingk and Roth (1855–1875: V.335). According to this comprehensive dictionary, the oldest example of the compound type is seen in the R̥gveda-Prātiśākhya, which is believed to postdate Pāṇini's Aṣṭādhyāyī (Sakamoto-Gotō 2018: 6 with note 7).

9 MBh on vt. 1 to A 1.1.20 (I.73.22): *āttvabhūtānām iyaṃ sañjñā kriyate* | ('This class name [*ghu*] is applied to those [items] which have reached (acquired) a property of the long vowel *ā* [=those verbs which end in the long vowel *ā*].') See note 19 for Kaiyaṭa's comment on the expression *āttvabhūta*.

> *prāptivacanatvāt sakarmakopapattiḥ* [read: *sakarmakatvopapattiḥ*][10] | *asti punar ayaṃ bhavatiḥ kva cit prāptivacane* | *astīty āha* | [c] *tad yathā* | *etena vai bharadvājaḥ pratardanaṃ daivodāsiṃ sam anahyat* | *sa rāṣṭram abhavat* | *yaṃ kāmayeta rāṣṭriyam ayaṁ rāṣṭraṃ syād iti tam etena saṃ nahyed rāṣṭraṁ ha bhavati* | [d] *tathā mahadbhūtaś candramā mahattvaṃ prāpta ity ucyate* | [e] *āttvena vā bhūtā āttvabhūtāḥ* | *āttvena prāptā ity arthaḥ* |
>
> '[a] The compound *āttvabhūta* is analysed *as āttvaṃ bhūtāḥ* 'those [items] which have reached (acquired) a property of the long vowel *ā* (=those verbs which end in the long vowel *ā*)'.
> [b] [Objection] However, since the verb *bhū* is objectless (*akarmaka*), it is not reasonable to give this [analysis], *āttvaṃ bhūtāḥ*. [Objection] However, since the verb *bhū* [in this case] denotes the act of reaching (*prāpti*), is it not reasonable that this verb takes an object (*sakarmaka*)? [Question] However, does this verb *bhū* at times denote the act of reaching? [Answer] 'Yes', people say.
> [c] For example: quotation from the *Maitrāyaṇī Saṁhitā* (see below).
> [d] Such being the case, it is said that [the expression] *mahadbhūtaś candramāḥ* is equal to *mahattvaṃ prāptaḥ* [*candramāḥ*] 'The moon has become full' (lit., 'The moon has reached [acquired] greatness').
> [e] Alternatively, the compound *āttvabhūta* is analysed *as āttvena bhūtāḥ*. What is meant is: 'those [items] which have been reached by a property of the long vowel *ā*' (=those verbs which end in the long vowel *ā*).'

Let us inquire closely into [a]–[e] in the following.

Āttvaṃ Bhūtāḥ and Prāptivacana

The points in [a] and [b] are as follows. First, Bhartṛhari gives an analysis of the compound *āttvabhūta*: *āttvaṃ bhūtāḥ*. This analysis presupposes that the verb *bhū* takes an object (*karman*), since otherwise the second-triplet ending (accusative ending) *am* in *āttvaṃ* cannot be accounted for in Pāṇini's grammatical system. Second-triplet endings are introduced by A 2.3.2: *karmaṇi dvitīyā* to denote an object if it is not otherwise denoted (A 2.3.1: *anabhihite*). Then an opponent argues that the verb *bhū* cannot take an object (*akarmaka*) and hence it is inappropriate to analyse the compound *āttvabhūta* as above. It is evident that the opponent says this on the presumption that *bhū*, as an intransitive verb, usually signifies the act of becoming, being (*sattā*) or coming into being (*jāta*), which does not involve an object.[11]

10 See Limaye, Palsule and Bhagavat (1985: 136).

11 On the latter two meanings of the verb *bhū*, see Ogawa (2005: § 4.6.2.1 [129–132]).

To this the reply is that this verb is occasionally employed in the sense 'reach' (*prāpti*), and it is this meaning that is to be assumed in the sentence *āttvaṃ bhūtāḥ*. One has to note in this context that, under this view, the affix *Kta* (affix to derive past participle forms) introduced after the verb *bhū* in *bhūtāḥ* signifies an agent (*kartṛ*) according to A 3.4.72: *gatyarthākarmakaśliṣaśīṅsthāsavasajanaruhajīryatibhyaś ca.* This rule provides for this affix to follow verbs signifying movement (*gatyartha*), on condition that an agent is to be denoted. Needless to say, the act of reaching entails movement.

Here a question naturally arises. What is an actual example in which the verb is used in the sense of reaching?

Vedic Passage

In [c], Bhartṛhari adduces a passage from the Maitrāyaṇī Saṁhitā. The original accentuated text goes as follows:

> MS 3.3.7 (40.6–8): *eténa vaí bharádvājaḥ pratárdanaṃ daívodāsiṁ sám anahyat sá rāṣṭrám abhavad yáṃ kāmáyeta rāṣṭríyam ayáṁ rāṣṭráṁ syād íti tám eténa sáṃ nahyed rāṣṭráṁ ha bhavaty* ... ||
>
> 'Bharadvāja did arm Pratardana Daivodāsi with this [hymn]. Then he (Pratardana Daivodāsi) came to gain dominion (*sá rāṣṭrám abhavat*).[12] If one has a wish for an heir to the throne that this person will come to gain dominion (*rāṣṭráṁ syāt*),[13] he should arm him with this [hymn]. [He] comes to gain dominion (*rāṣṭráṁ ha bhavati*).'

---

12 von Schroeder (1881–1886) reads *ábhavat*. But this udātta is not justified at all; it may be a mere misprint. As Mittwede (1986: 114) notes, the correct reading is given in Sātavalekar (1941–1942: 236). I would like to thank Werner Knobl (Kyoto University) and Kyōko Amano (Kyoto University) for valuable advice about this issue.

13 In the Vedic language, *syāt* can function as an optative form of the verbal root *bhū* (Gotō 2007: 222; 2008: 121). In Pāṇini's system of grammar, however, this type of suppletion is not provided for. It is therefore uncertain how Bhartṛhari himself, as a vaiyākaraṇa, sees the construction *rāṣṭráṁ syāt* in our passage. See Cardona (1997: §§ 379–381 [263–265]) and Ozono (2016: § 2 [267–271]) on verb suppletion taught in the Aṣṭādhyāyī.

Note in passing that the verb *bhū* replaces the verb *as* when a wish (*āśis*) is expressed by the L-suffix *lIṄ* (suffix to derive optative forms) introduced after the latter: A 3.4.116: *liṅ āśiṣi* provides that verb endings which substitute for *lIṄ* (A 3.4.78: *tiptas...*) introduced on condition that a wish is expressed (A 3.3.173: *āśiṣi liṅloṭau*) are called *ārdhadhātuka* (class name assigned to the items that meet the condition given by A 3.4.114: *ārdhadhātukaṁ śeṣaḥ*); and A 2.4.52: *aster bhūḥ* provides that *bhū* is used in place of *as* when an ārdhadhātuka affix is to occur. Accordingly, *lIṄ* in *syāt* of the utterance *rāṣṭráṁ syāt* cannot be taken to express a wish as far as Pāṇini's grammatical system is concerned, since otherwise the form at hand should be *bhūyāt* on account of the two rules mentioned. In Pāṇini's grammar the optative form *syāt* under consideration could be explained by A 3.3.157:

The Vedic usages [1] *sá rāṣṭrám abhavat* 'Then he (Pratardana Daivodāsi) came to gain dominion' and [2] *rāṣṭrám ha bhavati* '[He] comes to gain dominion' can be explained in Pāṇini's system of grammar only if one considers that the form *rāṣṭrám* is an accusative denoting an object (*karman*) and that *bhū* is employed here as a transitive verb (*sakarmaka*). That is to say, the usual senses of the verb *bhū* ('become, be, come into being') cannot be applied to these usages; instead, one has to assign this verb a special meaning. Clearly, meanings such as 'reaching' and 'obtaining' fit within the context.[14] Thus, for Bhartṛhari, who is an orthodox vaiyākaraṇa, the Vedic usages in the Maitrāyaṇī Saṁhitā offer evidence to prove that the verb *bhū* at times denotes the act of reaching/obtaining, hence can take an object.[15]

Mahadbhūtaś Candramāḥ

If the verb *bhū* could signify the action of reaching, which requires an object, then one can account for the compound *āttvabhūta* by analysing it as *āttvaṃ bhūtāḥ*.

At this point, Bhartṛhari supplies a further example of this type of compound ([d]): *mahadbhūtaś candramāḥ* 'The moon has become full', which is equal in meaning to *mahattvaṃ prāptaḥ candramāḥ* 'The moon has acquired greatness'.[16] As [d] shows, in the analysis of the compound type x-*bhūta*, the part x is generally paraphrased with an item ending in a bhāvapratyaya (*tva*, *taL* [= *tā*], and so

icchārtheṣu liṅloṭau, which teaches that *lIṄ* and *lOṬ* (suffix to form imperative forms) alternately follow verbs used with other verbs meaning 'wish, desire' (*kāmáyeta* in our case).

14 It is worth mentioning in this connection that the use of verb forms of *pra-āp* 'reach, obtain' with an accusative denoting an object is fairly common in Sanskrit. Such a use might have influenced Bhartṛhari's assignment of the meaning of reaching (*prāpti*) to the verb *bhū*.

15 One might ask why Bhartṛhari cites examples of the *idáṃ bhū*-construction from Maitrāyaṇī Saṁhitā when other instances of this construction are seen in other Vedic texts as well. A simple answer to this is that Bhartṛhari may have belonged to the Maitrāyaṇīya school and therefore have had an intimate acquaintance with and a preference for works of this school. On Bhartṛhari's Vedic affiliation, see Rau (1980) and Bronkhorst (1981; 1987; 2009).

Incidentally, the affix *ṆiC* [affix usually introduced to derive (1) causative forms and (2) verbal forms of the 10th present class (*curādi*)] is said to have the sense of *pra-āp* 'reach, obtain' when expressing a remarkable event (vt. 10 on A 3.1.26: *citrīkaraṇe prāpi*). The example sentence given by Patañjali is *ujjayinyāḥ prasthito māhiṣmatyāṃ sūryodgamanaṃ sambhāvayate* 'Departing from Ujjayinī, he reaches [the time of] the sunrise in Māhiṣmatī' (MBh [II.35.10–11]). Notice that in *sambhāvayate* (*sam* + *bhū* + *ṆiC* + *ŚaP* [affix to derive present stems] + *ta* [→ *te*]) it is *ṆiC* and not *bhū* that conveys the sense of *pra-āp*. The instance cited by Patañjali thus cannot testify that the verb *bhū* is employed in the sense of reaching.

16 The expression *mahadbhūtaś candramāḥ* is already found in the Mahābhāṣya: MBh on A 6.3.46 (III.160.2): *iha kasmān na bhavati | amahān mahān sampanno mahadbhūtaś candramā iti*; MBh on vt. 1 to A 6.3.46 (III.160.14): *yady evam āttvam api prāpnoti | mahadbhūtaś candramāḥ*. Here Patañjali develops arguments concerning the replacement of the final sound of the item *mahat* 'great' by *ā* (**mahābhūtaś candramāḥ*). The details of the arguments are not crucial to the purpose of this paper.

forth), unless x already terminates in this affix. This is also indicated in Kaiyaṭa's explanation of the compound *pramāṇabhūta* '[The teacher (Pāṇini) who] has achieved authority', which he paraphrases with *prāmāṇyaṃ prāptaḥ*.[17] This supply of a bhāvapratyaya, by grammarians, in a paraphrase of the compound type x-*bhūta* is a sign that, to interpret this type of compound, they apply to the part x *guṇa*- or *bhāva-pradhānanirdeśa*, a grammatical device by which one is sanctioned to see that a given word is presented (*nirdeśa*) as denoting a quality (*guṇa/bhāva*) as its principal meaning (*pradhāna*).[18] According to this device, for example, the item *mahat* itself can be taken to mean 'greatness' (*mahattva*), without a bhāvapratyaya. Greatness (*mahattva*) is a quality (*guṇa/bhāva*) of what is great (*mahat*). Thus, the phrase *mahadbhūtaś candramāḥ* is interpreted as meaning 'the moon has acquired greatness' (= the moon has become full). The compound *pramāṇabhūta* '[The teacher (Pāṇini) who] has achieved authority' is accounted for in the same way. Authority (*prāmāṇya*) is a quality of an authoritative person (*pramāṇa*).

Āttvena Bhūtāḥ

In [e], Bhartṛhari proceeds to present a different interpretation of the compound *āttvabhūta*: *āttvena bhūtāḥ* equivalent in meaning to *āttvena prāptāḥ* 'those [items] which have been reached by a property of the long vowel *ā*' (= those verbs which end in the long vowel *ā*). Under this analysis, the suffix *Kta* in *bhūtāḥ* and *prāptāḥ* signifies an object (*karman*) in accordance with A 3.4.70: *tayor eva kṛtyaktakhalarthāḥ*. This rule lets *Kta* occur if an object or an act (*bhāva*) is to be signified.[19]

---

17 MBh on vt. 7 to A 1.1.1 (I.39.10–12): *pramāṇabhūta ācāryo darbhapavitrapāṇiḥ śucāv avakāśe prāṅmukha upaviśya mahatā yatnena sūtraṃ praṇayati sma tatrāśakyaṃ varṇenāpy anarthakena bhavitum ...* | ('The teacher (Pāṇini) who has achieved authority sat facing east in a pure place, with a ring of kuśa grass around his [fourth] finger, and composed sūtras with great care. Such being the case, it is impossible that even a single sound could be meaningless [in his sūtras]'). Pradīpa on MBh to vt. 7 ad A 1.1.1 (I.128.14–15): *pramāṇabhūta iti* | *prāmāṇyaṃ prāpta ity arthaḥ* | *bhū prāptāv ity asyā dhṛṣād veti ṇijabhāve rūpam* | *vṛttiviṣaye ca pramāṇaśabdaḥ prāmāṇye vartate* | One may note that here Kaiyaṭa alludes to dhātupāṭha X.300 with the meaning entry *prāptau*, as evidence that the verb *bhū* is permitted to be used in the meaning of reaching. See the penultimate section of this paper for Kaiyaṭa's way of grammatical explanation of the form *bhūta* derived from the verb *bhū*, listed in dhātupāṭha X.300.

18 This grammatical device is adopted by Patañjali in explicating some Pāṇinian rules. See Ogawa (1988) for details.

19 It may be added that Kaiyaṭa follows Bhartṛhari's interpretation in commenting upon the compound *āttvabhūta*, although he does not invoke the Vedic passage cited in the Mahābhāṣyadīpikā. See the penultimate section of this paper for Kaiyaṭa's way of grammatical explanation of the form *bhūta* used in the sense of reaching. Pradīpa on MBh to vt. 1 ad A 1.1.20 (I.239.12–14): *āttvabhūtānām iti* | *bhavateḥ prāptyarthād ā dhṛṣād veti vibhāṣitaṇicaḥ kartari karmaṇi vā ktapratyayaḥ* | *tatra āttvaṃ bhūtā āttvena vā bhūtā ākārāntā ity arthaḥ* |

Bhartṛhari and Meaning Entries in the Dhātupāṭha

To the best of my knowledge, Bhartṛhari is the first among the indigenous grammarians to state that the verb *bhū* is sometimes used in the sense of reaching (*prāpti*). What is of great importance is that he justifies this use by resorting to the actual Vedic usages cited above.[20] This fact brings up an additional point to be taken into account.

There are two types of *bhū* in the dhātupāṭha as handed down to us:

> [*bhū* 1] dhātupāṭha I.1: *bhū́ sattāyām* ||
> [*bhū* 2] dhātupāṭha X.300: *bhū prāptau* [*ātmanepadī*] ||

bhū 1 belongs to the first present class (*bhvādi*) and mostly means 'be, exist' (*sattā*); *bhū* 2 belongs to the 10th present class (*curādi*) and mostly means 'reach' (*prāpti*).[21] The former is viewed as a parasmaipadin (*bhavati*, A 1.3.78: *śeṣāt kartari parasmaipadam*) and the latter as an ātmanepadin (*bhāvayate/bhavate*). It must be noted here that there is no such rule in the Aṣṭādhyāyī as provides that *bhū* 2 takes ātmanepada affixes; the introduction of them after this verb is accomplished by the direct statement *ātmanepadī* in dhātupāṭha X.300.[22] It cannot be sure, however, whether dhātupāṭha X.300 already contained this direct statement in Bhartṛhari's time. If not, both *bhū* 1 and *bhū* 2 fall under the domain of A 1.3.78, so that the finite verb forms *abhavat* and *bhavati* in [1]–[2] can be derived from *bhū* 2 as well as *bhū* 1.[23] Consequently, one cannot tell which *bhū* Bhartṛhari considered to be the base for the verbal forms.[24]

---

20 One might consider that Bhartṛhari could have more easily given an explanation of the use at issue by resorting to Patañjali's view that verbs are observed to have more than a single meaning (MBh on vt. 7 to A 1.3.1 [I.256.11]: *bahvarthā api dhātavo bhavanti*; MBh on vt. 3 to A 8.2.48 [III.408.22]: *anekārthā api dhātavo bhavanti*); at the same time, however, one should not overlook that the assignment of meanings to a verb must not be made freely but has to be made in harmony with usage (*tac ca prayogānusāreṇaiva, na tv amaryādam*, see Ogawa [2005: § 4.2.6.4.2 (97–100)]). This would be the reason why Bhartṛhari had to refer to actual examples wherein the verb *bhū* expresses the sense of reaching.

21 I said 'mostly' because, according to later vaiyākaraṇas, meaning entries in the dhātupāṭha just serve to offer illustrative examples (*upalakṣaṇa*). See Ogawa (2005: 99, note 46 and 4.6.2.1) on this matter.

22 MDhV (396.18): *bhū prāptāv ātmanepadī vā*; DhP (146.21–147.2): *bhū prāptātmanepadī* | ... *bhāvayate bhavate*; KT (190.8–9): *bhū prāptāv ātmanepadī* | *sambhāvayate* | *sambhavate* | *itthambhūtaḥ* | On the two forms [*sam-*]*bhāvayate* (*bhū* + *ṆiC* + *ŚaP* + *te*) and [*sam-*]*bhavate* (*bhū* + *ŚaP* + *te*), see the penultimate section of this paper.

23 The introduction of the affix *ṆiC* is optional with respect to *bhū* 2. See the penultimate section of the present paper.

24 In Kawamura (2017: 63, note 15), I wrote:

> 'Even if dhātupāṭha X.300 did not contain this statement (=*ātmanepadī*) in Bhartṛhari's time, that *bhū* 2 is an ātmanepadin is easily deduced: Since *bhū* 1 is a parasmaipadin, dhātupāṭha X.300 would become purposeless if *bhū* 2 also were a parasmaipadin.'

Suppose that dhātupāṭha X.300 as known to Bhartr̥hari contained the meaning entry *prāptau*. This being the case, in order to verify that the verb *bhū* signifies 'reach', hence takes an object, he could have simply referred to dhātupāṭha X.300, as later grammarians such as Jinendrabuddhi (*c*. 700 CE) and Kaiyaṭa (*c*. 11th century CE) do in elucidating the structure of the compound type x-*bhūta*.[25] Nevertheless, Bhartr̥hari does not touch on it at all during the discourse of the compound *āttvabhūta*. The dhātupāṭha as transmitted to early grammarians like Kātyāyana (*c*. 3rd century BCE) and Patañjali (*c*. 2nd century BCE) did not have meaning entries (*arthapāṭha*).[26] It is probable that the same was also true of Bhartr̥hari.

Later Grammarians on Compounds of the Type X-*Bhūta*

According to later grammarians such as Jinendrabuddhi and Kaiyaṭa, the structure of the compound type x-*bhūta* can be explained in the following manner. In principle, the affix *ṆiC* (affix usually introduced to derive (1) causative forms and (2) verbal forms of the 10th present class) is redundantly introduced after verbs of the 10th present class registered in the dhātupāṭha (A 3.1.25: *satyāpapāśarūpavīṇātūlaślokasenālomatvacavarmavarṇacūrṇacurādibhyo ṇic*),

---

This was an error: even if dhātupāṭha X.300 did not contain the statement *ātmanepadī* in Bhartr̥hari's time and as a result of which A 1.3.78 applies to *bhū* 2, dhātupāṭha X.300 still serves a purpose in deriving forms such as *bhāvayati* without a causative meaning, so that *bhū* 2 cannot be determined as an ātmanepadin unless the direct statement *ātmanepadī* is made in dhātupāṭha X.300. It follows from this that the arguments built up in Kawamura (2017 § 4 [60–61]) does not make any sense:

> 'Furthermore, one should not overlook that it must be *bhū* 1 and not *bhū* 2 which Bhartr̥hari considers to denote the action of reaching. *bhū* 2 is an ātmanepadin, so it is not compatible with usages [1] and [2], where parasmaipada forms of the verb *bhū* are given (*abhavat, bhavati*). This also buttresses the view that the dhātupāṭha Bhartr̥hari was familiar with did not contain meaning entries. Otherwise, he would not have been able to quote [1]–[2] as examples where the verb occurs in the sense of reaching.
>
> To be sure, there is interchange among parasmaipada and ātmanepada endings (*parasmaipadavyatyaya, ātmanepadavyatyaya*) in the domain of Vedic usage (*chandas*), as Patañjali points out. According to him, all grammatical operations apply variously in this domain (MBh on A 3.1.85 [II.64.19]: *bahulaṃ chandasi viṣaye sarve vidhayo bhavanti*). Therefore it cannot be absolutely denied that this principle allowed Bhartr̥hari to conceive of both *abhavat* and *bhavati* in [1] and [2] as derivates from *bhū* 2. If so, however, it is rather strange that he says nothing about this matter of interchange of verb endings in the course of his discussion. On the other hand, this is not strange, given that the dhātupāṭha handed down to Bhartr̥hari did not contain meaning entries: for him, there was no problem about regarding the two verbal forms as derivates of *bhū* 1.'

I withdraw this.

25 See notes 17 and 28.

26 Cardona (1984) convincingly demonstrates that 'Pāṇini's dhātupāṭha originally listed verbs separately, without sandhi substitutions and also without meaning entries'. See more recently Ogawa (2005: § 4.2.6.3 [95–100]) for the full details of the issue.

but this introduction is optional with respect to *bhū* 2 (dhātupāṭha X.300), by the following gaṇasūtra (dhātupāṭha [73.4]):

> *ā dhr̥ṣād vā* ||

This sūtra states that *ṆiC* optionally occurs with verbs of the set beginning with *yuj* (dhātupāṭha X.264: *yujA saṁyamane*), through *dhr̥ṣ* (dhātupāṭha X.306: *dhr̥ṣÀ prasahane*); and *bhū* 2 belongs to this set. Where *ṆiC* does not occur, the form *bhūta* is derived from this verb with the suffix *Kta* signifying an agent or an object (*bhū* 2 + *Kta* [A 3.4.72 or A 3.4.70]).[27] When the item *bhūta* terminating in a nominative ending is combined with a syntactically related item terminating in an accusative or an instrumental ending, a compound of the type x-*bhūta* is obtained (A 2.1.4: *saha supā* or A 2.1.32: *kartr̥karaṇe kr̥tā bahulam*).[28]

Conclusion

In the explanation of the compound type x-*bhūta*, dhātupāṭha X.300 with the meaning entry *prāptau* is generally provided by native grammarians as evidence to demonstrate that the verb *bhū* is used in the sense of reaching.[29] According to Bhartr̥hari, however, actual Vedic usages [1]–[2] do serve as testimonies to this meaning. Put differently, in his view it is these usages that enable us to assign the meaning to the verb *bhū*.[30] As the grammatical analysis of a compound of the type x-*bhūta* described above amply indicates, this meaning assignment is necessarily presupposed to form this type of compound. Bhartr̥hari's viewpoint thus implies a historical link between the *idáṃ bhū*-construction and the compound type.

27 Where *ṆiC* occurs, we have *bhāvita* (*bhū* 2 + *ṆiC* + *Kta*).

28 Nyāsa on KV to A 2.3.21 (II.178.32–179.27): *kañ cit prakāram ity anena ittham ity asyārtham ācaṣṭe | tathā hi prakāravacane idamas thamv iti thumpratyaye vihita ittham ity etad rūpaṃ bhavati | sāmānyasya bhedako viśeṣaḥ prakāra ucyate | āpanna ity anena bhūtaśabdasyārtham ācaṣṭe | tathā hi—bhū prāptāv ātmanepadīty asya caurādikasyā dhr̥ṣād veti yadā ṇij nāsti tadā ktapratyaye bhūta iti rūpaṃ bhavati* | For Kaiyaṭa's explanation, see note 17.

29 This meaning entry, *prāptau*, is already known to Jinendrabuddhi (see note 28). Notice that here I am not saying that we, modern scholars, can consider dhātupāṭha X.300 with the meaning entry to be evidence for a particular usage. What I am saying is that indigenous grammarians make use of it to explain compounds of the type x-*bhūta*.

30 Pāṇini (*c.* 5th–4th century BCE), who knows of the Maitrāyaṇī Saṁhitā (see Thieme 1935), also might have been cognisant of such usages when he employed the same type of compound in his work, *itthambhūta* 'that which has come to a particular status': A 1.4.90: *lakṣanetthambhūtākhyānabhāgavīpsāsu pratiparyanavaḥ*; A 2.3.21: *itthambhūtalakṣaṇe*; A 6.2.149: *itthambhūtena kr̥tam iti ca*. KV on A 2.3.21 (I.137.18): *kañ cit prakāraṃ prāptaḥ itthambhūtaḥ* | This is a topic for a future paper that focuses on a more detailed discussion of Pāṇini's wording.

Whichever interpretation is put on the construction, all this makes it licit to suggest that this Vedic construction is a forerunner of the compound type x-*bhūta*.

Abbreviations

A	Pāṇini: *Aṣṭādhyāyī* (see Cardona 1997)
dhātupāṭha	Pāṇini: *dhātupāṭha* (see Katre 1967)
DhP	Maitreyarakṣita: *Dhātupradīpa* (see Chakravarti 1919)
KT	Kṣīrasvāmin: *Kṣīrataraṅgiṇī* (see Liebich 1930)
KV	Jayāditya and Vāmana: *Kāśikāvṛtti* (see Sharma, Deshpande and Padhye 1969–1970)
MBh	Patañjali: *Mahābhāṣya* (see Abhyankar 1962–1972)
MBhD	Bhartṛhari: *Mahābhāṣyadīpikā* (see Limaye, Palsule and Bhagavat 1985)
MDhV	Sāyaṇa: *Mādhavīyadhātuvṛtti* (see Shastri 1964)
MS	*Maitrāyaṇī Saṁhitā* (see von Schroeder 1881–1886)
Nyāsa	Jinendrabuddhi: *Nyāsa* (see Miśra 1985)
Pradīpa	Kaiyaṭa: *Pradīpa* (see Vedavrata 1962–1963)
ṚV	*Ṛgveda* (see Aufrecht 1877)

ṚVS = Sāyaṇa's commentary on the *Ṛgveda* (see Müller 1890–1892)
vt = Kātyāyana: *Vārttika*. See MBh

References

Abhyankar, K.V. and Kielhorn, F. (eds) (1880–1885) *The Vyākaraṇa-mahābhāṣya of Patañjali.* 3 vols. Bombay Sanskrit and Prakrit Series 18–22, 28–33. Bombay: Government Central Press.

Amano, K. (2009) *Maitrāyaṇī Saṁhitā I–II: Übersetzung der Prosapartien mit Kommentar zur Lexik und Syntax der älteren vedischen Prosa.* Bremen: Hempen Verlag.

Aufrecht, T. (ed.) (1877) *Die Hymnen des Ṛigveda.* 2 vols. Bonn: Adolph Marcus.

Böthlingk, O. and Rudolph, R. (1855–1875) *Sanskrit-Wörterbuch.* 7 bde. St Petersburg: Kaiserliche Akademie der Wissenschaften.

Bronkhorst, J. (1981) On Some Vedic Quotations in Bhartṛhari's Works. *Studien zur Indologie und Iranistik* 7, 173–175.

— (1987) Further Remarks on Bhartṛhari's Vedic Affiliation. In *Studies in Indian Culture: S. Ramachandra Rao Felicitation Volume*, 216–223. Bangalore: Professor S. Ramachandra Rao Felicitation Committee.

— (2009) Studies on Bhartṛhari, 9: Bhartṛhari and His Vedic Tradition. In Chaturvedi, M (ed.), *Bhartṛhari: Language, thought and reality (Proceedings of the International Seminar, Delhi, December 12–14, 2003)*, 99–117. Delhi: Motilal Banarsidass.

CARDONA, G. (1984) On the Mahābhāṣya Evidence for a Pāṇinīya dhātupāṭha without Meaning Entries. In Joshi, S.D. (ed.), *Amṛtadhārā: Professor R.N. Dandekar Felicitation Volume*, 79–84. Delhi: Ajanta Publications.

CARDONA, G. (1997) *Pāṇini: His work and its traditions. Volume one. Background and introduction.* Delhi: Motilal Banarsidass (second edition, revised and enlarged; first edition 1988).

CHAKRAVARTI, S.C. (ed.) (1919) *The Dhatu-Pradeepa by Maitreya-Rakshita: Edited with Annotations.* Rajshahi: The Varendra Research Society.

GOTŌ, T. (1999) Notizen zur altindischen und avestischen Syntax. In Eichner, H., Luschützky, H.C., Sadovski, V. and Schindler, J. (eds), *Compositiones Indogermanicae: In Memoriam Jochem Schindler*, 127–142. Praha: Enigma Corporation.

— (2002) Funktionen des Akkusativs und Rektionsarten des Verbums: anhand des Altindoarischen. In Hettrich, H (ed.), *Indogermanische Syntax: Fragen und Perspektiven*, 21–42. Wiesbaden: Dr Ludwig Reichert Verlag.

— (2007) Cart and Hut: *śālám as* 'to live in the hut' in the Śatapathabrāhmaṇa. *Journal of Indian and Buddhist Studies* 55(2), 805–809. [In Japanese.]

— (2008) Reisekarren und das Wohnen in der Hütte: *śālám as im Śatapatha-Brāhmaṇa.* In Kulikov, L. and Rusanov, M. (eds), *Indologica: T. Ya. Elizarenkova Memorial Volume, Book 1*, 115–125. Orientalia et Classica. Papers of the Institute of Oriental and Classical Studies, Issue XX. Moscow: Izdatelstvo RGGU.

HOFFMAN, K. (1976) Ved. *idám bhū.* In Narten, J. (ed.), *Aufsätze zur Indoiranistik band 2*, 557–559. Wiesbaden: Dr. Ludwig Reichert Verlag.

JAMISON, S. W. and BRERETON, J. P. (2014) *The Rigveda: The earliest religious poetry of India.* 3 vols. New York: Oxford University Press.

KATRE, S.M. (ed.) (1967) *Pāṇinian Studies I.* Deccan College Building Centenary and Silver Jubilee Series 52. Poona: Deccan College Postgraduate and Research Institute.

KAWAMURA, Y. (2017) Bhartṛhari's Interpretation of the Vedic *idáṃ bhū*-Construction. *Tetsugaku* (Hiroshima Philosophical Society) 69, 57–65.

LIEBICH, B. (ed.) (1930) *Kṣīrataraṅgiṇī, Kṣīrasvāmin's Kommentar zu Panini's Dhātupāṭha, zum ersten Mal herausgegeben; mit fünf Anhängen.* Indische Forschungen, Doppelheft 8(9). Breslau: Verlag von M. & H. Marcus.

LIMAYE, V.P., PALSULE, G.B. AND BHAGAVAT, V.B. (eds) (1985) *Mahābhāṣyadīpikā of Bhartṛhari.* Fascicule II: Āhnika V. Bhandarkar Oriental Research Institute, Post-Graduate and Research Department Series 23. Poona: Bhandarkar Oriental Research Institute.

MIŚRA, N. (ed.) (1985) *Kāśikāvṛtti of Jayāditya-Vāmana (Along with Commentaries Vivaraṇapañcikā–Nyāsa of Jinendrabuddhi and Padamañjarī of Haradatta Miśra).* 6 vols. Ratnabharati Series 5–10. Varanasi: Ratna Publications.

MITTEWEDE, M. (1986) *Textkritische Bemerkungen zur Maitrāyaṇī Saṁhitā: Sammlung und Auswertung der in der Sekundärliteratur bereits geäußerten Vorschläge.* Alt- und Neu-Indische Studien 31, Stuttgart: Franz Steiner Verlag Wiesbaden GmbH.

MÜLLER, M.F. (ed.) (1890–1892) *Rig-Veda-Samhitâ: The Sacred Hymns of the Brâhmans Together with the Commentary of Sâyanâkârya.* 4 vols. London: Frowde.

Ogawa, H. (1988) On *bhāvapradhāna-nirdeśa*. *Journal of Indian and Buddhist Studies* 37(1), 443–446. [In Japanese.]

— (2005) *Process and Language: A Study of the Mahābhāṣya ad A 1.3.1 bhūvādayo dhātavaḥ*. Delhi: Motilal Banarsidass.

Ozono, J. (2016) Verb Suppletion and Pāṇini's Grammar: On the alternation between *ad* and *ghas*. In Cardona, G. and Ogawa, H. (eds) *Vyākaraṇaparipṛcchā: Proceedings of the Vyākaraṇa Section of the 16th World Sanskrit Conference*, 265–289. New Delhi: DK Publishers Distributors.

Rau, W. (1980) Bhartṛhari und der Veda. *Studien zur Indologie und Iranistik* 5(6) (Festschrift Paul Thieme), 167–180.

Sakamoto-Gotō, J. (2018) Syllable and Mātrā: Basic concepts of Indian metres observed in indigenous metrics, phonology, and grammar. *Journal of South Asian Languages and Cultures* 9, 1–55. [In Japanese.]

Sātavalekara, Ś.D. (1941–1942) *Yajurvedīya Maitrāyaṇī-Saṁhitā*. Aundh: Svādhyāyamaṇḍala.

Sharma, A., Deshpande, K., and Padhye, D.G. (eds) (1969–1970) *Kāśikā: A Commentary on Pāṇini's Grammar by Vāmana & Jayāditya*. 2 vols, Sanskrit Academy Series 17, 20. Hyderabad: Sanskrit Academy.

Swami, D.S. (ed.) (1964) *The Mādhavīyā Dhātuvṛtti (A Treatise on Sanskrit Roots Based on the Dhātupāṭha of Pāṇini) by Sāyaṇācārya*. Prāchya Bhāratī Series 1. Varanasi: Prāchya Bhāratī Prakāshana.

Thieme, P. (1935) *Pāṇini and the Veda: Studies in the early history of linguistic science in India*. Allahabad: Globe Press.

Vedavrata (ed.) (1962–1963) *Śrībhagavat-patañjali-viracitam Vyākaraṇa-Mahābhāṣyam (Śrī-kaiyaṭakrta-pradīpena nāgojībhaṭṭa-kṛtena-bhāṣyapradīpoddyotena ca vibhūṣitam)*. 5 vols. Gurukul Jhajjar (Rohatak), Hairyāṇā Sāhitya Saṃsthāna.

von Schroeder, L. (ed.) (1881–1886) *Maitrâyaṇî Saṁhitâ*. 4 Bde. Leipzig: Brockhaus.

Weiss, M. (2017) King: Some observations on an East-West archaism. In Simmelkjær Sandgaard Hansen, B., Hyllested, A., Jørgensen, A. R., Kroonen, G., Larsson, J. H., Nielsen Whitehead, B., Olander, T. and Mosbæk Søborg, T. (eds), *Usque ad Radices: Indo-European Studies in Honour of Birgit Anette Olsen*, 793–800. Copenhagen: Museum Tusculanum Press.

Witzel, M. and Gotō, T. (2007) *Rig-Veda: Das heilige Wissen*. Erster und zweiter Liederkreis. Aus dem vedischen Sanskrit übersetzt und herausgegeben von Michael Witzel und Toshifumi Gotō unter Mitarbeit von Eijirō Dōyama und Mislav Ježić. Frankfurt am Main und Leipzig: Verlag von Weltreligionen.

The *Paribhāṣā – Yadāgamās Tadguṇībhūtās Tadgrahaṇena Gṛhyante* in the *Paribhāṣāvṛtti* of Nīlakaṇṭha Dīkṣita*

Yiming Shen

This article sheds light on a metalinguistic rule (*paribhāṣā*) in the Sanskrit grammatical tradition (*vyākaraṇa*) – *yadāgamās tadguṇībhūtās tadgrahaṇena gṛhyante* 'Āgamas added to [*āgamins*], being subordinate to [these *āgamins*], are [also] referred to by that which refers to [these *āgamins*]', as commented upon by Nīlakaṇṭha Dīkṣita in his work *Paribhāṣāvṛtti*. The text of the commentary is given, translated and explained in a detailed manner.

Introduction

In the Pāṇinian system, *paribhāṣās* (metalinguistic rules) are general interpretative rules that help in such issues as the interpretation of a particular *sūtra* or the determination of the order of application of different *sūtras*. Some of the *paribhāṣās* are explicitly stated by Pāṇini in his *sūtrapaṭha*, *e.g.* *sūtra* 1.1.66,[1] and others are found stated for the first time in the *Mahābhāṣya* (Bh), *e.g.* the *yadāgamaparibhāṣā* (ypbh) in issue.[2] For a detailed discussion on *paribhāṣā*, one may see Abhyankar (1967: 1–64) or Kielhorn (1960: i–xxv).

* I would like to express my gratitude to James Benson, John Lowe and Christopher Minkowski for their generous help during the writing process.

1 A 1.1.66 *tasminn iti nirdiṣṭe pūrvasya*. This *paribhāṣāsūtra* explains how a form ending in the locative case (*saptamī*) should be understood in the *Aṣṭādhyāyī*: it refers to the right context of an operation.

2 ypbh = the *yadāgamaparibhāṣā* = the *paribhāṣā* – *yadāgamās tadguṇībhūtās tadgrahaṇena gṛhyante*. The ypbh is found, for example, in 1.1.20 vt 5 *na vārthavato hy āgamas tadguṇībhūtas tadgrahaṇena gṛhyate yathānyatra* (Kielhorn 1880: 75).

The ypbh is a *paribhāṣā* that deals with *āgamas* (see below). It is found in all of the nine Pāṇinian *paribhāṣā* texts included in Abhyankar 1967,[3] a fact that may point to its popularity or controversial nature. In the current article, I wish to focus on the ypbh in one of these *paribhāṣā* texts, *i.e.* Nīlakaṇṭha Dīkṣita's *Paribhāṣāvṛtti*, translating and explaining the commentary on the ypbh therein, with the hope that I may shed some light on Nīlakaṇṭha Dīkṣita's *paribhāṣā* treatise, a little-studied one, as well as on the ypbh and its functioning in the Pāṇinian system.

Nīlakaṇṭha Dīkṣita and his Paribhāṣāvṛtti

Nīlakaṇṭha Dīkṣita is dated to the 17th century, perhaps earlier than Nāgeśa Bhaṭṭa (also see fn. 25). He is said to be the student of Jñānendra Sarasvatī, the author of *Tattvabodhinī* on *Siddhāntakaumudī*. He wrote other works on grammar, including commentaries on the *Aṣṭādhyāyī*, *Mahābhāṣya* and *Siddhāntakaumudī*. The relation between this Nīlakaṇṭha Dīkṣita and the Nīlakaṇṭha Dīkṣita connected with Appayya Dīkṣita should be clarified by further research.

The *Paribhāṣāvṛtti*, presumably following the Pāṇinian tradition, contains the commentary on 140 *paribhāṣās*. The commentary on each *paribhāṣā* is generally short. As far as I know, two editions of this work are available: Sāstrī (1915) (based on two manuscripts in Malayalam script, marked as क and ख) and Abhyankar (1967) (#14; based on presumably Sāstrī (1915)[4] and one manuscript, further information of which I did not manage to find out).[5]

3

# of the text in Abhyankar 1967	*Title of the text*	*Author*	*# of ypbh in the text*
1	*Paribhāṣāsūcana*	Vyāḍi	17
2	*Vyāḍiparibhāṣāpāṭha*	Vyāḍi	20
12	*Laghuparibhāṣāvṛtti*	Puruṣottamadeva	18
12a	*Paribhāṣāpāṭha*	Puruṣottamadeva	12
13	*Bṛhatparibhāṣāvṛtti*	Sīradeva	4
14	*Paribhāṣāvṛtti*	Nīlakaṇṭha Dīkṣita	4
15	*Paribhāṣābhāskara*	Haribhāskara Agnihotrin	4
16	*Paribhāṣenduśekhara*	Nāgeśa Bhaṭṭa	11
17	*Paribhāṣābhāskara*	Śeṣādrisudhī	11

4 Abhyankar (1967: 4 in the 'prefatory note') writes that 'the text of this *vṛtti* [= *Paribhāṣāvṛtti*] has been based upon the printed edition, now rare, and one manuscript'. I have not managed to find out in Abhyankar 1967 what this 'printed edition' exactly refers to, and I presume the referent is Sāstrī 1915.

5 The sources of the information I give in the current section are the following: Sāstrī 1915: 'preface' and '*nivedanā*'; Abhyankar 1967: 4 in the 'prefatory note' and 30–31 section 48; Abhyankar 1986: 226

Āgama and Sūtras 1.1.46–47

In the Pāṇinian system, an *āgama* (augment) is a meaningless sound added to a stem or suffix. For example, to derive *gajānām* 'of the elephants', we first add the suffix *ām* to the stem *gaja*, and then modify both: first, we add the *āgama nUṬ*, that is a meaningless sound *n*,[6] to the suffix *ām*; then, we replace the final sound of the stem with a long vowel:

1. *gaja* ām	
2. *gaja nām*	*hrasvanadyāpo nuṭ* 7.1.54
3. *gajā nām*	*nāmi* 6.4.3

In this way, we arrive at the final form *gajānām*.

In his *Aṣṭādhyāyī* (A), Pāṇini has given many items similar to *nUṬ*, for example *nUM* in forms like *kulāni* by A 7.1.72,[7] and *pUK* in forms like *dāpayati* by A 7.3.36.[8] Nevertheless, he has never given the name *āgama* to these items. Probably he has not felt the need to do so due to the lack of any functional purpose of such a name within his system. In the Pāṇinian tradition, it is Kātyāyana, in his *vārttikas*, that first used the name *āgama* to refer to these items,[9] and the tradition followed him in this practice. The tradition[10] also uses the name *āgamin* to refer to that to which an *āgama* is added, *e.g*. the suffix *ām* in *gajānām*. In the *Aṣṭādhyāyī*, an *āgamin* is usually put in the genitive case (*ṣaṣṭhī*), and the *āgama* in the nominative case (*prathamā*). For example, in A 7.2.35 *ārdhadhātukasyeḍ valādeḥ*, the *āgamin ārdhadhātuka* is put in the genitive case (together with its qualifier *valādi*), and the *āgama iṬ* in the nominative case.[11]

The *āgamas* are taught together with various *its* (markers). In the *āgama nUṬ*, there are two *its*. The *it U* is for facilitating pronunciation. The *it Ṭ* is for indicating where the *āgama* should be added in the *āgamin:* for when we add the *āgama nUṬ* to the *āgamin ām*, we could have three different results depending on where *nUṬ* is added: *nām*, *ānm* and *āmn*. Pāṇini clarifies this issue in *sūtras* 1.1.46 and 1.1.47:

---

entries 'nīlakaṇṭha', 'nīlakaṇṭhadīkṣita or vājapeyin' and 'nīlakaṇṭhamakhin'. See these for more information.

6 *U* and *Ṭ* are both *its* (markers) – see below. In this article, the *its* are presented in the capital letter. Any *it* is elided by A 1.3.9 *tasya lopaḥ*.

7 A 7.1.72 *napuṃsakasya jhalacaḥ*.

8 A 7.3.36 *artihrīvlīrīknūyīkṣmāyyātāṃ puṅ ṇau*.

9 For example, in 1.1.20 vt 5 *na vārthavato hy āgamas tadguṇībhūtas tadgrahaṇena gṛhyate yathānyatra* (Kielhorn 1880: 75).

10 For example, Patañjali in his *Mahābhāṣya* on *Śivasūtra* 7–8 (Kielhorn 1880: 36 line 2).

11 A 7.2.35 is translated and explained below.

1.1.46 *ādyantau ṭakitau*
anuvṛtti:[12] None
translation: Those [items] which are marked with *Ṭ* and *K* [become] the beginning and the end [respectively].

1.1.47 *mid aco 'ntyāt paraḥ*
anuvṛtti: None
translation: That which is marked with *M* [occurs] after the final *aC* (= vowel).
explanation of 1.1.46–47: That which is marked with *Ṭ*, *K* or *M* is added to the beginning, end or after the final vowel, respectively, of a form presented in the genitive case.

Accordingly, here *nUṬ* is added to the beginning of *ām*, and so we get *nām*.

Text and Translation

The texts of the ypbh with the commentary in Sāstrī (1915: 2–3) and Abhyankar (1967: 293) are identical in most places. Below is the reproduction of the text from these two sources together with the translation.

IV *yadāgamās*[13] *tadguṇībhūtās tadgrahaṇena gṛhyante*

IV *Āgamas* added to [*āgamins* (= yad = tad)], being subordinate to [these *āgamins*], are [also] referred to by that which refers to [these *āgamins*].

1. *pradhānasyāvayavabhūtā āgamā avayavigrahaṇena gṛhyanta ity arthaḥ.*

1. The meaning is: *āgamas*, being parts of a predominant [item], are [also] referred to by that which refers to the whole.

2. *iyaṃ ca lokanyāyasiddhety ādyantau ṭakitāv iti sūtre bhāṣyam.*

2. And [according to] *Bhāṣya* on the *sūtra ādyantau ṭakitau* (1.1.46), this [*paribhāṣā*] is established through principles of ordinary life.

3. *neṭīti niṣedho 'pi jñāpakaḥ. anyatheḍvati sici sici vṛddhiḥ parasmaipadeṣv ity asya prāpter evābhāvāt kiṃ tanniṣedhārthena neṭīti sūtreṇeti spaṣṭam evākare.*[14]

12 In this article, in giving *anuvṛtti*, I have made reference to the *Kāśikā* (Rānaḍe 1898) and Sharma 1999–2003.

13 Ms. ख in Sāstrī 1915 has *tadāgamās*.

14 *spaṣṭam evākare* is the reading in Abhyankar 1967 and ms. ख in Sāstrī 1915 (the latter found in a footnote). Sāstrī has adopted and presented in his edition rather the reading *spaṣṭam ākare*, presumably the reading in ms. क.

3. Also the prohibition *neṭi* (A 7.2.4) is a *jñāpaka* (= a clue in a *sūtra* intimating the existence of a *paribhāṣā*). Otherwise (= if the ypbh does not exist), since before [the suffix] *sIC* with [the *āgama*] *iṬ* [the *sūtra*] *sici vṛddhiḥ parasmaipadeṣu* (A 7.2.1) will not apply in the first place, what is the use of the *sūtra neṭi*, which aims at prohibiting it (= *sūtra* 7.2.1)? This is indeed clear in the source (= *Bhāṣya*).

4. *iyaṃ ca varṇagrahaṇe na pravartata āne muko vidhānād iti ur aṇ rapara*[15] *iti sūtre bhāṣye spaṣṭam.*

4. And [the following] is clear in *Bhāṣya* on the *sūtra ur aṇ raparaḥ* (1.1.51): this [*paribhāṣā*] does not apply when a [single] sound is mentioned [as the *āgamin*], because [the *sūtra*] *āne muk* (7.2.82) has been taught.

Explanation

An Example of the Application of the Ypbh

To derive the stem *lavitṛ* 'he who cuts',[16] we start with the verbal root *lū*, and add the agent suffix *tṛ* to it. Then, we add the *āgama iṬ* to the suffix *tṛ* by A 7.2.35:

1. *lū*	*tṛ*	
2. *lū*	*itṛ*	*ārdhadhātukasyeḍ valādeḥ* 7.2.35

7.2.35 *ārdhadhātukasyeḍ valādeḥ*
anuvṛtti: *aṅgasya* 6.4.1
translation: To an *ārdhadhātuka* [suffix] beginning with *vAL* and following an *aṅga*, *iṬ* is added.
explanation:
1. On *ārdhadhātuka* suffix. Any suffix added to a verbal root is either *ārdhadhātuka* or *sārvadhātuka*. Roughly speaking, among such post-verbal(-root) suffixes, all except the verbal endings (*tiṄ*) and those marked with the letter *Ś* (*śit*) are *ārdhadhātuka*. See A 3.4.113–117.[17]
2. *vAL* = all the consonants except *y*.
3. The *āgama* is *iṬ*; the *āgamin* is the *ārdhadhātuka* suffix in issue (in the current case, *tṛ*).

15 I have adopted the reading in Sāstrī 1915. Abhyankar 1967 has, perhaps erroneously, *ur aṇ pare*.
16 This example is found under Bh 1.1.20 vt 5 (Kielhorn 1880: 75 line 8).
17 3.4.113 *tiṅśit sārvadhātukam*; 3.4.114 *ārdhadhātukaṃ śeṣaḥ;* 3.4.115 *liṭ ca*; 3.4.116 *liṅ āśiṣi;* 3.4.117 *chandasy ubhayathā.*

At this stage, in order to obtain the desired form, we need the *guṇa* replacement of *ū* by A 7.3.84.

> 7.3.84 *sārvadhātukārdhadhātukayoḥ*
> anuvṛtti: *aṅgasya* 6.4.1; *guṇaḥ* 7.3.82
> translation: [The final *iK*] of an *aṅga* that is followed by a *sārvadhātuka* or *ārdhadhātuka* [suffix is replaced by] *guṇa*.
>
> explanation:
> 1. The substituend (*sthānin*), *i.e.* the supplied 'final *iK*', is not explicitly given in the *sūtra* or the *anuvṛtti*. It is identified with the help of the two *paribhāṣāsūtras* 1.1.52 *alo 'ntyasya* and 1.1.3 *iko guṇavṛddhī*. According to the former *sūtra*, it must be a final sound; according to the latter, this sound is *iK*. I understand the genitive case (*ṣaṣṭhī*) in *aṅgasya* in the *anuvṛtti* as one expressing part-whole relation (*avayavaṣaṣṭhī*). The genitive case added to the substituend (*sthāniṣaṣṭhī*) necessary for the substitution operation is also understood from these two *paribhāṣāsūtras*.
> 2. *iK* = *i*, *ī*, *u*, *ū*, *ṛ*, *ṝ*, *ḷ*.

Although here we do have an *ārdhadhātuka* suffix, *i.e. tṛ*, and an *aṅga* ending with *iK*, *i.e. lū*, A 7.3.84 still cannot apply, for the *ārdhadhātuka* suffix is not immediately following the *aṅga* – the *āgama iṬ* is intervening between them. There is a problem.

This problem can be solved with the help of the ypbh. The *āgama iṬ*, added to the *āgamin tṛ*, being subordinate to it, is also referred to by that which refers to *tṛ*, that is, in our case, the technical name *ārdhadhātuka*. It follows then that the technical name *ārdhadhātuka* can now refer to *itṛ*, or in other words, *itṛ* can now have the name *ārdhadhātuka*. Therefore, we do have an *aṅga* that is immediately followed by an *ārdhadhātuka* suffix, and thus A 7.3.84 can now apply.[18]

1. *lū*	*tṛ*	
2. *lū*	*itṛ*	*ārdhadhātukasyeḍ valādeḥ* 7.2.35
3. *lo*	*itṛ*	*sārvadhātukārdhadhātukayoḥ* 7.3.84[19]

18 It appears to me that by applying the *sūtras* in a different order, *i.e.* A 7.3.84 before A 7.2.35 (*lū* + *tṛ* ⟶ *lo* + *tṛ* ⟶ *lo* + *itṛ* ⟶ *lav* + *itṛ*), we would no longer have the problem in issue and could smoothly derive the desired form *lavitṛ* without resorting to the ypbh at all. Under Bh 1.1.20 vt 5 (Kielhorn 1880: 75) or in *Pradīpa* and *Uddyota* thereon (Shastri 1938: 294–295), I did not find this alternative discussed. I think this issue needs to be clarified by further research.

19 With one more step, *i.e.* the replacement of *o* by *av* by A 6.1.78 *eco 'yavāyāvaḥ*, we arrive at the desired form *lavitṛ*.

On the Source of Text Paragraph 2 in the Bh

I cannot find any relevant passage in Bh on A 1.1.46 or by using Lahiri's concordance 1935 (1.1.46 is on p. 2).

On the Source of Text Paragraph 3 in the Bh

I cannot find any relevant passage in Bh on A 7.2.1 and A 7.2.3 (there is no *Bhāṣya* on A 7.2.4) or by using Lahiri 1935 (A 7.2.1, 3 and 4 are on p. 94).

On the Working of the Argument in Text Paragraph 3

7.2.1 *sici vṛddhiḥ parasmaipadeṣu*
<u>*anuvṛtti*</u>: *aṅgasya* 6.4.1
<u>translation</u>: [The final *iK*] of an *aṅga* that is followed by *sIC* which is [itself] followed by *parasmaipadas* [is replaced by] *vṛddhi.*
<u>explanation</u>:
1. On A 1.1.52 and A 1.1.3. The two *paribhāṣāsūtras* 1.1.52 *alo 'ntyasya* and 1.1.3 *iko guṇavṛddhī* work here and give 'final', '*iK*' and 'is replaced by' in my translation (in square brackets) – see explanation 1 on 7.3.84 above.
2. On *sIC*. *sIC* is a suffix added to the verbal root when the aorist suffix *lUṄ* (or its verbal ending substitutes) follows. It is one of the most common suffixes or signs of the aorist, found in forms like *a-nai-ṣ-am* '[I] led' and *a-lāv-iṣ-am* '[I] cut'. (In both cases, A 7.2.1 is applied and *sIC* is replaced by the retroflex *ṣ*.[20])

7.2.3 *vadavrajahalantasyācaḥ*
<u>anuvṛtti</u>: *aṅgasya* 6.4.1; *sici vṛddhiḥ parasmaipadeṣu* 7.2.1
<u>translation</u>: The *aC* (= vowel) [of an *aṅga* that is (1) the verbal root] *vad, vraj,* or ends with *hAL* (= consonant) [and (2) followed by *sIC* which is itself followed by *parasmaipadas*] is replaced by [*vṛddhi*].

7.2.4 *neṭi*
<u>anuvṛtti</u>: *aṅgasya* 6.4.1; *vadavrajahalantasyācaḥ* 7.2.3; *sici vṛddhiḥ parasmaipadeṣu* 7.2.1
<u>translation</u>: [The *aC* (= vowel) of an *aṅga* that is (1) the verbal root *vad, vraj,* or ends with *hAL* (= consonant) and (2) followed by *sIC* that itself begins with] *iṬ* [and is followed by *parasmaipadas* is] not [replaced by *vṛddhi*].

---

20 By 8.3.59 *ādeśapratyayayoḥ*.

Table 8.1

<table>
<tr><th colspan="2">Shape of the verbal root/aṅga</th><th>Vowel of the verbal root is replaced by</th><th>Sūtra</th><th>Example</th></tr>
<tr><td colspan="2">Ending with iK (iganta)[1]</td><td>vṛddhi</td><td>7.2.1</td><td>anai-ṣ-am '[I] led'</td></tr>
<tr><td rowspan="2">Ending with a consonant (halanta)</td><td>aniṭ verbal root</td><td>vṛddhi</td><td>7.2.3</td><td>abhait-s-am '[I] split'</td></tr>
<tr><td>seṭ verbal root (so iṭi sici)</td><td>no vṛddhi</td><td>7.2.4</td><td>adev-iṣ-am '[I] played' (guṇa substitute by A 7.3.86[2])</td></tr>
</table>

[1] It can be inferred (*e.g.* from the above translation of A 7.2.1) that the *aṅga* in A 7.2.1 must be one ending with *iK* (*iganta*).

[2] A 7.3.86 *pugantalaghūpadhasya ca.*

explanation:
1. On *iṭi sici*. *iṭi sici* is interpreted as *iḍādau sici* 'before *sIC* which begins with *iṬ*' with the help of the following *paribhāṣā*:

   yasmin vidhis tadādāv algrahaṇe. (*Paribhāṣenduśekhara* 33 [Kielhorn 1868: 31])

   translation: When a term referring to [a single] *aL* (= any sound) [is in such a form as] '*yasmin*' (*i.e.* in the locative case), an operation [takes place] with [an item] that begins with that (= *aL*) serving as the right context.[21]
2. For convenience and ease of understanding, here is a rough summary of the working of A 7.2.1, 7.2.3 and 7.2.4 (Table 8.1). With the verbal root/*aṅga* followed by *sIC* which is itself followed by a *parasmaipada* (*sici parasmaipadeṣu*; *e.g.* -*s-am*), the vowel of the verbal root/*aṅga* is modified differently depending on the different shapes of the verbal root/*aṅga*.

As is clear from the above clarification of the three *sūtras* 7.2.1, 3 and 4, the target of the prohibition in A 7.2.4 is not, as presented here by Nīlakaṇṭha Dīkṣita, the *vṛddhi* resulting from A 7.2.1, but rather the *vṛddhi* resulting from A 7.2.3. Despite this imprecise identification of the source of the *vṛddhi*, the actual working of the argument is not influenced. My explanation here builds upon this correction.

21 The translation here is tentative in nature. I wish to mention the following interpretational decisions that I made during my translation: 1) *algrahaṇe*: the locative case here is interpreted as a locative absolute (*satisaptamī*), the predicate here being *yasminn* [*iti*]; 2) *yasmin*: as *yasminn* [*iti*], so 'in such a form as "*yasmin*"' (*i.e.* in the locative case). See, for example, Sīradeva on this *paribhāṣā* in his *Bṛhatparibhāṣāvṛtti* (Abhyankar 1967: 174): *yasminn iti saptamīnirdiṣṭe 'lgrahaṇe* ... It then follows that *yasmin* here does not need to pair with *tad* in *tadādau*.

It may be possible to interpret this *paribhāṣā* in other ways, and I am not sure about the best way to take it. In addition, I think the word order of this *paribhāṣā* is remarkable: if *yasmin* really goes with *algrahaṇe*, why are they not put next to each other? (Incidentally, *yasmin vidhis tadādāv al* forms an odd *pāda* in the *anuṣṭubh* metre – is this only a coincidence?)

In deriving, for example, the aorist finite form *adeviṣam* '[I] played' from the verbal root *div*, we have the following stages of *prakriyā* that are relevant:

1. *div*	*s*	*am*	
2. *div*	*is*	*am*	*ārdhadhātukasyeḍ valādeḥ* 7.2.35
3. *dev*	*is*	*am*	*pugantalaghūpadhasya ca* 7.3.86

7.3.86 *pugantalaghūpadhasya ca*
<u>*anuvṛtti*</u>: *aṅgasya* 6.4.1; *sārvadhātukārdhadhātukayoḥ* 7.3.84; *guṇaḥ* 7.3.82
<u>translation</u>: And *guṇa* [replaces the *iK*] of an *aṅga* that (1) is followed by a *sārvadhātuka* or *ārdhadhātuka* [suffix] and (2) ends with *pUK* or has a *laghu* as its penultimate sound.
<u>explanation:</u>
1. On '[replaces the *iK*]' in my translation. The substituend is not specified in the *sūtra* or the *anuvṛtti*. It is identified with the help of the *paribhāṣāsūtra* 1.1.3 *iko guṇavṛddhī*. Accordingly, I supply *ikaḥ* and thus have '[replaces the *iK*]' in my translation.
2. On *laghu*. *Laghu* is a short vowel that is not followed by a consonant cluster. See 1.4.10–12.[22]
3. *iK* = *i, ī, u, ū, ṛ, ṝ, ḷ*.

If the ypbh exists and applies here, then under *sic* in *sici* in A 7.2.3 (carried forth from A 7.2.1) one would understand also *is*, *i.e.* the suffix *sIC* with the *iṬ āgama* added, and hence we will have an undesired *vṛddhi* substitution for the vowel in *div* by A 7.2.3:

*3. *daiv*	*is*	*am*	*vadavrajahalantasyācaḥ* 7.2.3

leading finally to **adaiviṣam*.[23]

With A 7.2.4, this undesired *vṛddhi* substitution is prohibited. **Hence if the ypbh exists and applies, A 7.2.4 has a purpose and is not redundant.**

If the ypbh does not exist, *sic* in *sici* in 7.2.3 can only refer to *s* and not *is*, and as in *div-is-am* the *aṅga div* is not followed by *sIC* due to the intervention of *iṬ*, A 7.2.3 will not be able to apply, and there will not be *vṛddhi* substitution in *div-is-am* in the first place. Hence it does not make sense to prohibit it as in A 7.2.4. The same applies in all the parallel cases. **Therefore, if the ypbh does not exist, A 7.2.4 becomes redundant.**

Since no *sūtra* is redundant, the ypbh must exist.

22 A 1.4.10 *hrasvaṃ laghu*; A 1.4.11 *saṃyoge guru*; A 1.4.12 *dīrghaṃ ca*.
23 The first *a* results from A 6.4.71 *luṅlaṅlṛṅkṣv aḍ udāttaḥ*, and the sound *ṣ* in the place of *s* from A 8.3.59 *ādeśapratyayayoḥ*.

On the Source of Text Paragraph 4 in the Bh and the Identification of Bh Sources in the Current Text

I cannot find any relevant passage in Bh on 1.1.51 or by using Lahiri 1935 looking for 7.2.82 (7.2.82 is on p. 97).

It is remarkable that none of the three Bh sources mentioned in the text can be identified (see above). Did Nīlakaṇṭha Dīkṣita know a *Bhāṣya* the text of which is different from that in Kielhorn 1880–1885?

On the Working of the Argument in Text Paragraph 4

Text paragraph 4 has not appeared clear to me. In what follows I try to bring to light how the argument may run. For this purpose, I first explain *sūtra* 7.2.82.

> 7.2.82 *āne muk*
> <u>*anuvṛtti*</u>: *aṅgasya* 6.4.1; *ataḥ* 7.2.80
> <u>translation</u>: The [*āgama*] *m*UK is added to [the sound] *a* that is a part of an *aṅga* that is followed by *āna*.
> <u>explanation</u>:
> This *sūtra* accounts for the sound *m* in the middle and passive present participles ending with *māna* – for example, *pac-am-āna* 'cooking for oneself', from the verbal root *pac*:
> 1. *pac* *a* *āna*
> 2. *pac* *am* *āna* *āne muk* 7.2.82
> The *āgama* here is *m*, and the *āgamin* is the second *a* in *pac-a*.[24]

Now, **if the ypbh also applies in cases where the *āgamin* consists of a single sound (*varṇagrahaṇa*)**, then it will also apply in the context of *pac-am-āna*, where the *āgamin* is the single sound *a*. As a result, *am*, the combination of the *āgama m* plus the *āgamin a*, will be treated like the *āgamin a*, and so A 6.1.101 will come into

24 My interpretation of A 7.2.82 here follows that of the *Kāśikā* (Rānaḍe 1898: 687). A problem with this interpretation may be the unspecifiedness of *a* – in forms like *pac-a*, it would also be possible to add *mUK* to the first *a*, which would then lead to undesired forms. Indeed, in Bh on 7.2.82 (Kielhorn 1885: 303), we find discussions touching on the interpretation of the *sūtra* and the identity of the *āgamin*. If we interpret the *sūtra* in another way, translated as 'The [*āgama*] *mUK* is added to an *aṅga* that ends with [the sound] *a* and is followed by *āna*', the *āgamin* would then be *pac-a* rather than *a*. But this interpretation is also not completely unproblematic, as discussed, *e.g.*, under Bh 7.2.82 vt 1 (Kielhorn 1885: 303). Thus the interpretation of the *sūtra* and the identity of the *āgamin* here seems to me an issue that cannot be immediately solved in a satisfactory way, and for the current context I think a temporary interpretation following the *Kāśikā* would suffice.

play, by which one would substitute *ā* for *am-ā* (treated like *a-ā*), and then arrive at the undesired form *pacāna.*

1. *pac*	*a*	*āna*	
2. *pac*	*am*	*āna*	*āna muk* 7.2.82
*3. *pac*		*āna*	*akas savarṇe dīrghaḥ* 6.1.101

6.1.101 akas savarṇe dīrghaḥ
anuvṛtti: *saṃhitāyām* 6.1.72; *ekaḥ pūrvaparayoḥ* 6.1.84
translation: In close junction of sounds, a single [substitute] being a long vowel replaces both [the *aK*] that precedes its homogeneous sound and [the homogeneous sound] that follows the *aK* (= *a, ā, i, ī, u, ū, ṛ, ṝ, ḷ*).

Consequently, *sūtra* 7.2.82 becomes redundant, because the *m* it teaches will invariably drop in such a way. Since no *sūtra* is redundant, the ypbh does not apply in cases where the *āgamin* consists of a single sound (*varṇagrahaṇa*).[25]

Conclusion

To the above statement that the ypbh does not apply in cases where the *āgamin* consists of a single sound, we can already find a counterexample in *adeviṣam* discussed above. Here, at stage 2 of the *prakriyā* (p. 151), in order that A 7.3.86 applies, it seems that we cannot but resort to the ypbh, so that the *āgama iṬ* plus the *āgamin ārdhadhātuka* suffix *sIC* is taken together as having the technical name *ārdhadhātuka.* Otherwise, due to the intervention of *iṬ*, 7.3.86 would not be able to apply. Thus, the ypbh does apply here in a case where the *āgamin* consists of a single sound, *i.e. s* (also compare fn. 25). This issue, joined by others such as that discussed in fn. 18, shows that the ypbh requires further exploration and elucidation. A careful study, where, *e.g.*, the various commentaries on the ypbh in Abhyankar 1967 and the relevant discussions in the *Bhāṣya* are treated in detail, would help to clarify the various issues, so that a more comprehensive and precise understanding

25 This argument here has been employed by Nāgeśa in his *Paribhāṣenduśekhara* on the ypbh to argue for a different point – that the ypbh is not universally applicable (*anitya*). See the following in *Paribhāṣenduśekhara* (Kielhorn 1868: 9 lines 10–12): *āne mug iti mugvidhānasāmarthyād eṣā* [= ypbh] *anityā. anyathā pacamāna ity* ādāv *akārasya muky anayā paribhāṣayā* [= ypbh] *viśiṣṭasya savarṇadīrghe tadvaiyarthyaṃ spaṣṭam eva.*

Moreover, Nāgeśa may have had Nīlakaṇṭha's position in text paragraph 4 in mind when he, a little bit further down from the above quotation, argued the following (Kielhorn 1868: 9 lines 15–16): *na coktajñāpakād* [= A 7.2.82 *āne muk*] *varṇagrahaṇe 'syā* [= ypbh] *apravṛttir iti vācyam* ..., where he seems to be directly refuting Nīlakaṇṭha's position in text paragraph 4.

not only of the ypbh itself, but also of the notion of *āgama* and the working of the Pāṇinian system, could be achieved.

References

ABHYANKAR, K.V. (1986) *A dictionary of Sanskrit grammar,* 3rd edition, Oriental Institute, Baroda.

ABHYANKAR, K.V. (ed.) (1967) *Paribhāṣāsaṃgraha: A collection of original works on vyākaraṇa paribhāṣās.* Pune: Bhandarkar Oriental Research Institute.

KIELHORN, F. (ed.) (1868) *The Paribhāṣenduśekhara of Nāgojībhaṭṭa Part I The Sanskrit text and various readings.* Bombay: Indu-Prakash Press

KIELHORN, F. (ed.) (1880/1883/1885) *The Vyākaraṇa-Mahābhāṣya of Patanjali Vol. I/II/III.* Bombay: Government Central Book Depot.

KIELHORN, F. (ed.) (1960) *The Paribhāṣenduśekhara of Nāgojībhaṭṭa Part II Translation and notes,* 2nd edition by K.V. Abhyankar. Pune: Bhandarkar Oriental Research Institute.

LAHIRI, P.C. (1935) *Concordance Panini-Patañjali (Mahābhāṣya).* Breslau: Verlag von M. & H. Marcus.

RĀNAḌE, B. (ed.) (1898) *Kāśikā,* 2nd edition. Varanasi: Medical Hall Press.

SĀSTRĪ, T.G. (ed.) (1915) *The Paribhāṣāvṛitti of Nīlakaṇṭha Dīkshita.* Trivandrum: Travancore Government Press.

SHARMA, R.N. (trans.) (1999–2003) *The Aṣṭādhyāyī of Pāṇini vol. 1–6.* Delhi: Munshiram Manoharlal.

SHASTRI, N.K. (ed.) (1938) *Patañjali's Vyākaraṇamahābhāṣya with Kaiyaṭa's Pradīpa and Bhaṭṭoji Dīkṣita's Śabdakaustubha and Nāgojibhaṭṭa's Uddyota with the commentary Rājalakṣmī by Pt. Guruprasad Shastri (Navāhnika vol. 1).* Delhi: Pratibha Prakashan.

Reconsidering the *Sarva-Siddhānta-Saṅgraha*

Authorship, Doxography and Pedagogy*

Karl-Stéphan Bouthillette

The first and only critical edition of the *Sarvasiddhāntasaṅgraha* (SSS) was produced over a century ago, in 1909, by Professor M. Raṅgācārya. Since then, besides being mentioned as one of the many spurious literary attributions of the famous theologian Śaṅkara, the text received little attention. My purpose here will be to summarise what has been said concerning both the authorship and the possible dates of the SSS, and to contribute my own observations on the subject in tune with what we know so far in regard to Śaṅkara's work in particular and the genre of doxography in general. I begin by aligning the several arguments in favour of and against the authorship of Śaṅkara, so as to identify and localise the problematic passages. I argue that these passages are found within precise locations of the text that could potentially be later additions. I explain how doxographies are, by nature, composite texts, and that new content can easily be added onto them without breaking their continuity. I then explain that doxography is in tune with Śaṅkara's pedagogy and is a logical development of his work as an embattled religious teacher. In this regard, the SSS even appears to support a form of spiritual exercise essential for the soteriological project of the Advaita. Taking all these matters into consideration, I suggest that the core of the SSS might have been assembled between the eighth and tenth centuries, still allowing for later additions until the 14th century.

* I would like to express my gratitude to Christophe Vielle for his insightful remarks and recommendations; to the reviewers at Puṣpikā, who did outstanding work to improve on my initial draft; and especially to Agnieszka Rostalska, for her attentive reading and sound advice.

Introduction

The first and only critical edition of the *Compendium of Tenets of All Views*, commonly known in Sanskrit as the *Sarvasiddhāntasaṅgraha* (SSS),[1] was produced over a century ago, in 1909, by Professor M. Raṅgācārya,[2] on the basis of five manuscripts.[3] The scholar mentions that the colophons at the end of each chapter of the SSS give the longer title *Sarvadarśanasiddhāntasaṅgraha.*[4] The reason for this difference in titles is unclear. However, it is known that, at this period, the term *darśana* (view, doctrine, opinion) had become a generic appellation for speculative systems and was commonly used to designate similar doctrinal compendia. The term *siddhānta* (established end, conclusion, tenet) serves to specify that the text deals with the main tenets of these systems, as in an epitome. Relatively less common in similar doxographical titles than the term *darśana*, it is possible that the word *siddhānta* was kept as a more useful designator when the title was shortened. In brief, the SSS counts 12 chapters (*prakaraṇa*-s)[5] summarising 11 doctrines, if we list the two

1 A partial edition of the SSS had previously been given in Poussin (1902). Other non-critical editions of the text (*i.e.* editions without any critical apparatus to determine which manuscript version most closely approximates the original version) can be found in Bose (1929), Gokulbhai (2009) and Śukla (approx. 1930).

2 Regarding the learned Indian scholar, Catherine Morice-Singh (2017: 1) noted that 'M. Raṅgācārya had been appointed in 1901 as Professor of Sanskrit and Comparative Philosophy, as well as Curator of the Library of Oriental Manuscripts (GOML). Even before the recognition he received for this work on the GSS [*Gaṇita-sāra-saṃgraha*], he had already been awarded the prestigious "Rao Bahadur" medal and title in 1903, in recognition of his profound scholarship.'

3 Raṅgācārya (2006: v–vi) observes that the two best-preserved manuscripts of SSS were kept in Madras, at the GOML and in Mysore, at the Oriental Research Library (ORI). He mentions that GOML possesses the transcript of another original, which contains the only available commentary composed by Śeṣa Govinda (*c.* 16th century) and indicates that a partial palm-leaf manuscript is preserved in Cochin, at the Palace Library of H.H. the Maharaja of Cochin, while the Palace Library of Travancore is in possession of another.

However, the recension of Raṅgācārya needs to be updated in the light of the new manuscript catalogues available. Based on *the Online Library of Digitized Sanskrit and Prakrit Manuscript Catalogues*, maintained by Dominik Wujastyk, at http://catalogues.indology.info/, I could trace a number of manuscripts of the SSS from the locations indicated by Raṅgācārya. I will give the list in the bibliography, as recensions of the manuscripts of the SSS. A quick look at the list will serve to demonstrate that a serious review of the available manuscripts needs to be done, and perhaps a new critical edition.

4 Raṅgācārya (2006) also indicates that the shorter title *Sarva-siddhānta-saṅgraha* appears in the Tamil *Pramāṇattiraṭṭu* of Maṇavālamāmuni, the renowned South Indian Vaiṣṇava teacher. It is also known as such in the catalogue of the Sanskrit Manuscripts of the India Office Library, in London.

5 The 12 chapters are: 1. Introduction (*upodghāta-prakaraṇa*); 2. The thesis of the Lokāyatas (*lokāyatika-pakṣa-prakaraṇa*); 3. The thesis of the Ārhatas (*ārhata-pakṣa-prakaraṇa*), Jains; 4. The thesis of the Bauddhas (*bauddha-pakṣa-prakaraṇa*); 4a. The opinion of the Mādhyamikas (*mādhyamika-mata*); 4b. The opinion of the Yogācāras (*yogācāra-mata*); 4c. The opinion of the Sautrāntikas (*sautrāntika-mata*); 4d. The opinion of the Vaibhāṣikas (*vaibhāṣika-mata*); 5. The thesis of the Vaiśeṣikas

types of Mīmāṃsā treated separately as independent systems. The text stands at 537 concise verses of simple form. No explicit refutation of each doctrine is formulated, but an implicit hierarchical progression suggests that each following system stands closer to truth, as conceived by the Advaitins, than the preceding one. In comparison, the famous *Ṣaḍ-darśana-samuccaya* (ṢDS) by the 7th-century Jaina author Haribhadra Sūri consists of 87 verses describing six (in fact, six plus one – the materialists) *darśana*-s, whereas the 14th-century Mādhava-Vidhyāraṇya's *Sarvadarśanasaṅgraha* (SDS) deals with 16 *darśana*-s in prose. Haribhadra's ṢDS provides no explicit refutation and applies a flat hierarchical structure in tune with the Jaina *anekānta-vāda* methodology. Mādhava's text follows a hierarchical presentation of competing views similar to that of the SSS.

Since Raṅgācārya, although the text has been briefly debated in the early 1920s (Jacobi 1921; Liebich 1923) and subsequently classified as one of the many spurious literary attributions of the famous theologian Śaṅkara, it received little attention. The exception to the rule is Paul Hacker who, by dedicating a whole three and half pages to the subject, reprinted in *Kleine Schriften* (Hacker 1978: 55–58),[6] struck a final blow to its general relevance by refuting the assertions of Raṅgācārya in favour of the authorship of Śaṅkara. Hacker's remarks tend to be ignored by more recent scholarships that rather shortcut their enquiry by referring to Wilhelm Halbfass's general observations on Sanskrit doxographies, found in *India and Europe* (1988). Therein, one can find three allusions to the SSS under the index entry of 'Ps.-Śaṅkara',[7] including a quotation from the introductory verse[8] of the SSS; a reference to its mention of the 18-fold list of sciences (*vidyā*-s); and two endnotes[9] following the mention of Śaṅkara. However, none of the index entries actually mentions the title of the text. One interested in reviewing the scholarship on the SSS thus finds oneself in a labyrinth of scattered footnotes, some of which suppose a dating that cannot be confirmed by the references. My purpose here is to critically analyse what has been said concerning both the authorship and the possible dates of the SSS, and to contribute my own observations in tune with what we know so far in regard to Śaṅkara's work in particular and the genre of doxography in general. In

(*vaiśeṣika-pakṣa-prakaraṇa*); 6. The thesis of the Naiyāyikas (*naiyāyika-pakṣa-prakaraṇa*); 7. The thesis of Prabhākara (*prabhākara-pakṣa-prakaraṇa*), Mīmāṃsā; 8. The thesis of Bhaṭṭācārya (*bhaṭṭācārya-pakṣa-prakaraṇa*) Mīmāṃsā; 9. The thesis of Sāṅkhya (*sāṅkhya-pakṣa-prakaraṇa*); 10. The thesis of Patañjali (*patañjali-pakṣa-prakaraṇa*) Yoga; 11. The thesis of Vedavyāsa (*vedavyāsa-pakṣa-prakaraṇa*) as expressed in the *Mahābhārata*; 12. The thesis of the Vedānta (*vedānta-pakṣa-prakaraṇa*).

6 See Hacker 1978. The same opinion as Hacker on the authorship of the SSS has also been reproduced in Halbfass 1995: 51–54.

7 Halbfass 1988: 598.

8 Given in Halbfass 1988: 61 n. 26.

9 Halbfass 1988: 535 n. 7, and 60 n. 9.

brief, I suggest that doxography is in keeping with Śaṅkara's pedagogy and that this factor should influence our reception of the SSS.

On the General Authorship of Śaṅkara

However complex the issue of the authorship of Śaṅkara, contemporary scholars tend to consider a relatively limited number of titles as genuine, in comparison to the 400 claimed by the traditional account. To facilitate the presentation of the entire Śaṅkarian library, including works of debatable authorship, S.K. Belvakar gave a threefold division of its numerous titles.[10] The first category regroups the commentaries, consisting of primary interpretation of basic texts such as the *vivaraṇa*-s and *ṭīkā*-s. The second group contains the hymns, the poems, the metric incantations and praises of the gods (*stotra*, *stava* and *stuti*), while the third consists of independent compositions, treatises and compendia. It is in this last category that the SSS is classified, along with other titles such as the *Upadeśasāhasrī*, the *Vivekacūḍāmaṇi*, *Ātmaboddha*, *Aparokṣānubhūti* and *Śatāślokī*. However, other scholars frequently choose not to classify the SSS within any category of Śaṅkara's work.[11] Following the lead of Hacker, Mayeda and Vetter, who applied a complex set of philological criteria to determine Śaṅkara's authorship, the only texts accepted by contemporary scholars as unproblematically coming from the hand of the great Advaitin fall within the first category. They include the famous *Brahmasūtrabhāṣya* (BSB), the commentaries on the main *Upaniṣads*[12] and one commentary on the *Bhagavad-gītā*. The *Pātañjalayogaśāstravivaraṇa* (PYSV)[13] remains a matter of contention, even if valuable arguments have been made to support Śaṅkara's authorship. Of the two other categories delimited by Belvakar, with the exception of the *Upadeśasāhasrī*, all the texts are either rejected as inauthentic or debated.[14]

---

10 Belvalkar (1929: 222).

11 The *Sri Vani Vilas Press* edition (1910), in 20 volumes, does not include the SSS, nor does Karl. H. Potter's *Encyclopedia of Indian Philosophies*, in its volume on *Advaita Vedānta up to Śaṃkara and his Pupils* (1981).

12 Hacker regards as certain the Śaṅkara's authorship of the commentaries on the ten principal *Upaniṣads*: *Īśā*, *Aitareya*, *Kaṭha*, *Kena*, *Chāndogya*, *Taittirīya*, *Praśna*, *Bṛhadāraṇyaka*, *Māṇḍūkya* (traditionally united with Gaudapāda's Kārikā) and *Muṇḍaka*. Śaṅkara's authorship for the *bhāṣya* on the *Śvetāśvatara* is less certain. See Hacker (1978: 48–49).

13 On the *Bhagavadgītā-bhāṣya*, see Mayeda (1965a). On the plausible attribution of the *Pātañjala-yogaśāstra-vivaraṇa* to Śaṅkara, see Harimoto (1999: 36–62). In his more recent book, Harimoto picks up this issue anew with more reserve. See Harimoto (2014: 225–251).

14 On the *Upadeśa-sāhasrī*, see Mayeda 1965b.

On the Authorship of the SSS

Besides the traditional opinion, when it comes to the authorship and dating of the SSS, the present review of literature has met only two early proponents of the authorship of Śaṅkara: M. Raṅgācārya and B. Liebich.[15] Patel Maheshkumar Gokulbhai, in a more recent PhD thesis on the SSS (submitted at the University of Baroda in 2009), attributes the authorship of the SSS to Śaṅkara. However, on the question of authorship, his thesis does not engage with the opinions of previous scholarship and only presents a list of six external and 11 internal pieces of evidence which, by their general weakness, do not add anything significant to the discussion.[16] Hence, although the thesis has other qualities, I will not reproduce its arguments here. First, I am going to summarise the arguments in favour of the authorship of Śaṅkara that have been articulated by scholars prior to the rejection of the said authorship by Hacker, which became authoritative in general scholarship and which I will also summarise subsequently.

Arguments in Favour of the Authorship of Śaṅkara

Raṅgācārya

In the preface to his 1909 critical edition of the SSS,[17] Raṅgācārya acknowledges the debate surrounding the authorship of the text[18] and gives a list of arguments

15 Hacker mentions two German scholars, one against the authorship of Śaṅkara, Hermann Jacobi, and one in favour of it, Bruno Liebich. He refers to the following publications: Jacobi 1921 and Liebich 1923. Liebich argues for the 'possibility' of the text being from the *bhāṣyakāra*. However, Hacker rejects the arguments as inconclusive on the grounds that they do not discuss the Vedānta chapter of the SSS. As for Jacobi, his comments on the SSS are rather succinct, appearing at the end of a book review, and they have been answered in the discussion of Liebich, as I will point out. Therefore, they need not be treated separately in here.

16 Some of the 'pieces of evidence' advanced by Gokulbhai (2009: 1–54) may contribute to locating the SSS in the literary and philosophical context of India. For example, he points out that the SSS does not distinguish between the opinions of the *śvetāmbara* and *digambara* sects of Jainism, which was already distinguished in 1220 CE by Śivabhūti. This might indeed signify that the text reflects an earlier state of affairs, where no distinction was made between these two sects. However, the author simply assumes that this earlier stage in the development of Jainism was the one prevailing in Śaṅkara's time (7th–8th century CE) and that this fact constitutes solid evidence of Śaṅkara's authorship, which is hardly the case. If anything, it can only indicate that the SSS might be earlier than the early 13th century. However, the information provided in each point is not totally devoid of interest in relation to other issues unrelated to the question of authorship.

17 As reprinted in Raṅgācārya (2006: v–xvi).

18 Raṅgācārya alludes to the note of J. Eggeling concerning the description of the SSS manuscript (under no. 2442 in the catalogue of the Sanskrit Manuscripts of the India Office Library in London), where it is stated that the work is '(wrongly) ascribed to Śaṅkarācārya'. See Raṅgācārya (2006: vi).

in favour of Śaṅkara's authorship. For the sake of convenience, I paraphrase and enumerate them here:

1. Argument on method:
    a. Because the style of an author may vary through time and according to the literary context, the evidence based solely on stylistic analysis is insufficient.
2. Arguments of authority:
    a. The reliability of the commentator Śeṣa Govinda, and of his renowned teacher Madhusūdana Sarasvatī, who advocates the authorship of Śaṅkara is undeniable.
    b. The SSS is quoted by Maṇavāḷamāmuni in the *Pramāṇattiraṭṭu* (late 14th–early 15th century), who refers to Śaṅkara as its author in the Sanskrit remark *sarvasiddhāntasaṅgrahe śaṅkareṇa uktaḥ.*[19]
    c. Mādhava,[20] the 14th-century author of the *Sarvadarśanasaṅgraha* (SDS), appears to be familiar with the text, although he does not mention the author by name. There are passages in his Cārvāka and Bauddha sections borrowed from the SSS. Hence, Mādhava regarded the SSS as a reliable source.
    d. All of the five revised manuscripts ascribe the original authorship to Śaṅkara.
3. Arguments of internal consistency:
    a. In the SSS, one finds no mention of the systems of thought that appeared later than the time of Śaṅkara.
    b. The division between the *Vyāsa-mata* and *Vedānta-mata* sections, in the SSS, reflects Śaṅkara's distinction between the doctrine found in the *Mahābhārata* and in the *Vedāntasūtra*, both attributed to Vyāsa. This division was already admitted by Śaṅkara's guru (Govinda Bhagavatpāda).
    c. In the last chapter of the SSS, in the 54th stanza, one finds a mention of the supreme soul under the name of Govinda.[21] Raṅgācārya argues that this name refers to the preceptor of Śaṅkara (Govinda Bhagavatpāda), in tune with a tradition where the guru is deified. Raṅgācārya quotes two similar mentions of Govinda, one in the *Vivekacūḍāmaṇi* and one in *Bhajagovindastotra*, two texts that he also accepts as being authored by Śaṅkara.

Referring to the same manuscript description, Liebich adds that Eggeling gave no reason to support his claim, besides two exclamation marks (!!). See Liebich (1923: 124).

19 The Sanskrit quotation is given in Raṅgācārya (2006: ix).

20 Mādhava is also known as Vidyāraṇya, the 12th Jagadguru of the Śringeri Śarada Pītham.

21 SSS 12.54: *saccidānandagovindaparamātmā vahaty asau | yadā bāhyendriyair ātmā bhuṅkte'rthān svaparāṅmukhān ||*

In brief, Raṅgācārya believes that the authorship of Śaṅkara is supported by a solid set of evidence. In a half-veiled manner, he suggests that those who have doubts might do so out of some general mistrust towards 'Indian tribesmen'.[22] This attitude of suspicion concerning Western Indological scholarship might have contributed to the Indian professor's rejection of evidence based on stylistic analysis and his overall prognosis concerning the authorship of the SSS.

Liebich

Liebich contributes a few more arguments to support the authorship of Śaṅkara, which I will translate and paraphrase by applying the above typology:

1. Arguments of authority:[23]
   a. Mādhava, the 14th-century author of the SDS, borrowed on at least three counts,[24] if not four, from the SSS – depending on whether one verse is borrowed by both texts from an older source. The name of the SDS indicates the deviant character of the text, aiming at a more detailed and vivid representation of each system.
   b. The reliability of both the commentator Śeṣa Govinda and his teacher Madhusūdana Sarasvatī, who attribute the authorship of SSS to Śaṅkara, should be assumed.
2. Arguments of internal consistency:
   a. In the SSS, one finds no account of the systems of thought appearing later than the time of Śaṅkara.
   b. The mention of the three sources of knowledge (*pramāṇa*-s) of the Vaiśeṣika (*pratyakṣa* [immediate perception], *anumāna* [inference] and *āgama* [scripture] – mentioned at v. 33), highlighted by H. Jacobi[25] as a proof of the spurious nature of the SSS,[26] is in fact, according to Liebich, in tune with the desire of the SSS to present the system as 'orthodox', because it mentions the Vedic scriptures (*āgama*) as a valid *pramāṇa*.[27]

22 See Raṅgācārya (2006: x).

23 Liebich does not articulate any argument on method, unlike Raṅgācārya.

24 Liebich mentions the four verses enumerated by Raṅgācārya (Lokāyata-s section (v. 14); Yogācāra section (v. 4 + 7); Mādhyamika section (v. 12)) and focuses his own analysis on the verse taken from the Lokāyata-s section (v. 14).

25 Jacobi (1921: 724).

26 Because the Vaiśeṣika system is usually known to accept only two *pramāṇas*: *pratyakṣa* and *anumāna*.

27 This remark is supported by my general reading of Indian doxographies as essentially dialectical. Rather than being concerned with historical accuracy, doxographies use various rhetorical strategies, such as a precise teleological order in presenting various philosophical views, to promote the worldview of their author against competitors. Here, the author added *āgama* as a valid *pramāna*, for

c. The number of *padārtha*-s (6) and *guṇa*-s (24) attributed to the Vaiśeṣika-s supports the hypothesis that the SSS was written before the tenth-century Bengali scholar Śrīdhara (who taught seven categories in his *Nyāyakandalī*)[28] and thus before the SDS dated to the 14th century. Śaṅkara, in his other discussions against the Vaiśeṣika, also mentions only six categories, which suggests that a further category of non-existence (*abhāva*) was unknown to him.
d. The mention of the *Bhāgavatapurāṇa* suggests a predecessor of the same name. Alternatively, the mention might be a later insertion.
e. The mention of the *rājasa-jana* (the 'rajasic' man)[29] in SSS refers to the *Mahābhārata*. Liebich claims that Jacobi's that it is a 13th-century reference to the Turks is therefore invalid.
f. The low number of *āsana*-s (6) mentioned in the SSS's chapter *Patañjali-pakṣa*, compared to ten in the SDS (*c.* 14th century CE),[30] 15 in the *Svātmarāma* (*Haṭhapradīpikā*) (*c.* 15th century CE), 32 in the *Gheraṇḍasaṃhitā* (*c.* 18th century CE) and 84 in *Gorakṣa (-śataka?)*[31] *(c.* 13th century CE), indicates an early account.

---

the Vaiśeṣika, against historical accuracy, in order to enlist the system in a somewhat coherent set of Brahmanical 'sciences' embracing the Veda-s. The rhetorical effect aims to clearly demarcate the school from the previous non-Vedic systems. Hence, with the Vaiśeṣika begins the presentation of Brahmanical knowledge systems, which are perceived as superior to the previous ones, and come as their progressive refutation, from one system to the other.

28 In a commentary on Praśastapāda's *Compendium of the Characteristics of Categories* (*Padārthadharmasaṃgraha*) from the 6th century CE, Śrīdhara explains that the concept of 'non-existence' was not listed by Praśastapāda as a separate category, because this negative category is dependent on the other six existing positive ontological categories (*bhāva*), and not because it was not considered as an actual or real existing category. See Praśastapāda 1982: 15.

29 In opposition to those characterised by the quality of *sattva* (goodness), the rajasic man is said to be under the influence of passion (*rajas*).

30 The argument of Liebich is unsatisfactory here, since the SSS mentions four *āsana*-s present in the *Vyāsa Bhāṣya*, plus two taken from another source. Laura Von Ostrowski kindly pointed out to me that these two extra *āsana*-s are mentioned much later, in the 13th-century CE *Vasiṣṭha-saṃhitā*. The text is said, by James Mallinson (2017: 87), to be the earliest account, so far, of the *kukkuṭāsana* and *mayurāsana* appearing together. Jason Birch pointed out that the *Marīcisaṃhitā*, a 9th-century Vaiṣṇava *saṃhitā*, in the chapter on *yoga*, lists nine *āsana*-s (*padma*, *bhadra* and *mayurāsana* included) and indicated an earlier reference to *kukkuṭāsana* in the Śaiva *Kubjikāmatatantra*, dated (by Alexis Sanderson (2002) as prior to the 9th century. The 14th-century SDS mentions 10 *āsana*-s already enumerated in the *Vyāsabhāṣya* which, according to the recent estimates by Philip A. Maas (2013), is dated to the period between 325 and 425 CE. Depending on how one understands '*yathā-sukham*' there are already 12 or 13 *āsana*-s in the *Bhāṣya*. Thus, it is possible that at least six centuries before the SSS and 10 centuries before the SDS, a longer authoritative list of *āsana*-s was circulated. Hence, Liebich's suggestion that the number of *āsana*-s just increased with time, starting with the SSS, is an oversimplification.

31 It is not clear which *Gorakṣa* text Liebich is referring to. However, if it is the better-known *Gorakṣaśataka*, Mallinson indicates that it recommends only two *āsana*-s: *padma-āsana* and *vajra-āsana*. For more details, see Mallinson 2012: 258. As for the number of 84 *āsana*-s, one can find more information in Mallinson 2017: 91.

In brief, Liebich agrees that the authorship of Śaṅkara is not definitely proven by his arguments, as it would require a more careful comparison, especially of the Vedānta chapter in the light of Śaṅkara's *Bhāṣya* – a task Hacker undertook almost 60 years later. Yet, his arguments entertain the possibility that the great Indian philosopher Śaṅkara was the author of the text. His most important discussions in this regard, though not conclusive in themselves, are perhaps 1.a) the suggestion that the 14th-century author of the SDS borrowed from the SSS on several occasions; and 2.c) that the number of *padārtha*-s (6) and *guṇa*-s (24) attributed to the Vaiśeṣika-s supports the hypothesis that the SSS was written before the 10th-century Bengali scholar Śrīdhara.

Arguments Against the Authorship of Śaṅkara

Hacker

Concerning the arguments aligned by Raṅgācārya and Liebich, Hacker[32] makes no case for the arguments of authority. He spends no time on the general opinion of Liebich, on the ground that the Vedānta chapter of the SSS was not taken into consideration in his article, while, for Hacker, it is the only one of importance in discussing the alleged authorship of Śaṅkara. He criticises Raṅgācārya's argument of internal consistency 3.c – with reference to the name of Govinda. Otherwise, Hacker indirectly replies to the arguments of authority by politely observing that 'ad hoc interpretations [...] are not seldom met within commentaries'.[33] Hence, Hacker offers only a direct rebuttal of the argument 3.c and provides his own list of observations: notably concerning stanzas 20 to 22 of the first chapter, in support of the thesis that the SSS is not from the same Śaṅkara as the author of the BSB.

Here again, for the sake of convenience, I shall paraphrase the arguments advanced by Hacker:

1. Arguments based on stanzas 20 to 22 of the first chapter of the SSS:[34]

32 Hacker (1978).

33 Hacker (1978: 56).

34 SSS 1.20–22:

bhavaty uttaramīmāṃsā tv aṣṭādhyāyī dvidhā ca sā | devatajñānakāṇḍābhyāṃ vyāsasūtraṃ dvayos samam ||
pūrvādhyāyacatuṣkṣeṇa mantravācyātra devatā | saṅkarṣaṇoditā taddhi devatakāṇḍam ucyate ||
bhāṣyaṃ caturbhir adhyāyair bhagavatpādanirmitam | cakre vivaraṇaṃ tasya tad vedāntaṃ pracakṣate ||

Raṅgācārya gives the following translation:

(v. 20) The *Uttara-Mīmāṃsā* on the other hand consists of eight chapters; and it is also divided into two parts under the head dealing (respectively) with deities and with the wisdom (of true philosophy). Both these divisions of the *Uttara-mīmāṃsā* had their sūtras composed by Vyāsa. (v. 21) In the first

a. If understood in the way suggested by Raṅgācārya's translation, who follows in the footsteps of the commentator Śeṣa Govinda, it would appear that there is a BSB composed by Śaṅkara's teacher. This seems improbable, since Śaṅkara never mentioned it.

b. The title *Bhagavatpāda*, whenever it occurs in Advaitic literature without a name preceding it, refers to Śaṅkara-Bhagavatpāda, the author of the BSB. Hence, from the fact that the SSS mentions the BSB composed by *Bhagavatpāda*, as if it was composed by a third party, it is unlikely that the SSS was written by Śaṅkara the famous theologian, author of the same BSB.

c. The stanzas mention an Uttara-mīmāṃsā consisting of eight chapters (*adhyāya*-s). But we know only of Brahmasūtra-s divided into four chapters, and the same four have been commented upon by Śaṅkara-Bhagavatpāda. '[I]f this Śaṅkara-Bhagavatpāda were identical with the author of the SSS, who enunciated the theory of the eight *adhyāya*-s, in his commentary on the second four *adhyāya*-s (the *Jñānakāṇḍa*) he would very likely have referred to the fact that these constituted only the second part of the system, the first part being the *Devatākāṇḍa*.'[35] This first part is reckoned by Śaṅkara as a distinct work, belonging to the Karma-mīmāṃsā, and not as a part of the Uttara-mīmāṃsā.

2. Arguments based on foreign or missing technical vocabulary in the SSS:

 a. The terms *vivarta* (illusory form – SSS 12, 18) and *sat-cit-ānanda* (existence-knowledge-bliss – SSS 12, 54) are nowhere found within the texts attributed to Śaṅkara.

 b. The theory of *ekajīva-vāda* (advocating the oneness of self – SSS 12, 77–78) points to a later stage of Advaita's development, therefore it was not developed at the time of Śaṅkara.

 c. The juxtaposition of the three theories concerning the *jīva* (self – SSS 12, 77–79) is not in harmony with the phraseology of Śaṅkara's accepted texts.

 d. The theory of *suṣupti* (dreamless sleep – SSS 12, 81) is not in tune with Śaṅkara's doctrine.

 e. The term *nāma-rūpa* (name and form), expected in the exposition on Vedānta, is nowhere found within the chapter of the SSS.

four chapters here (in the *Uttara-mīmāṃsā*) the deities referred to in the *mantras* are (given as) described by Saṅkarṣaṇa. For this reason it is called *Devatā kāṇḍa* (*i.e.*, the part dealing with the deities). (v. 22) A commentary (thereon) in the four chapters has been composed by the venerable teacher. The explanatory commentary which he produced in relation to that (other part of the *Uttara-mīmāṃsā*) is spoken of as *Vedānta*. See Raṅgācārya (2006: 6).

35 Hacker (1978: 56).

f. The *hiraṇyagarbha-pakṣa* (the theory of the cosmic egg) is set forth at the end of the Vedānta chapter. As the conclusion to the whole work, the author declares that it is Kriṣṇa who taught 'the path of those who have renounced all worldly attachments' (*avadhūta-mārga*) and that this can be learned from the *Bhāgavatapurāṇa* (SSS 12, 99) – as if this doctrine of the purāṇa was the highest wisdom, above Advaita. This, in Hacker's view, makes it clear that the Govinda mentioned by the author is no other than Kṛṣṇa, supreme deity of the Vaiṣṇavas, and not Govinda Bhagavatpāda, as claimed by Raṅgācārya. However, Śaṅkara, though a Vaiṣṇava (according to Hacker), is far from teaching the *avadhūta-mārga* and the doctrine of the *Bhāgavatapurāṇa* as superior to 'pure' Advaita.

Among the arguments presented by Hacker, arguments 2.b, 2.c, 2.d and 2.f highlight doctrinal developments known to have emerged after Śaṅkara. Hence, together, they contradict argument 3.a of Raṅgācārya and 1.a of Liebich, stipulating that, within the SSS, one finds no account of thought systems appearing later than the period of Śaṅkara. However, Raṅgācārya and Liebich seem to refer only to the systems of thought used as chapter headings within the SSS. In any case, Hacker's indications point to serious flaws in their judgement. What is more, Hacker limited his criticism to what he knew best, the *Vedānta-pakṣa* chapter. But, looking at the *Patañjali-pakṣa-prakaraṇa*, one can identify another set of anomalies that tend to discredit the hypothesis that the author of the BSB, Śaṅkara-Bhagavatpāda, is the same one who compiled the whole SSS.

New Arguments Against the Authorship of Śaṅkara: Problems of the *Patañjali-Pakṣa*[36]

It has been acknowledged that Śaṅkara was not completely hostile to the *Yoga* presented by Patañjali. His *Pātañjalayogaśāstravivaraṇa* (PYSV), on the assumption that it is indeed from his hand,[37] bears witness to his interest in the system. This is conceivable if we consider that more recent scholars tend to doubt the authorship of Śaṅkara's commentaries on texts other than from the *Prasthānatrayī*,[38] usually

36 Gokulbhai also discusses several elements found in the *Patañjali-pakṣa* of the SSS, noticing that some are not found in the YS but rather related to Haṭha-Yoga. He nevertheless maintains the authorship of Śaṅkara in every respect. See Gokulbhai (2009: 146–147).

37 As suggested by Kengo Harimoto (1999; 2014). However, there are objections to the idea, notably Rukmani 1993.

38 The *Prasthānatrayī*, literally the 'three sources', refers to the three canonical texts of the Vedānta: *Upaniṣad*-s, *Brahmasūtra* and *Bhagavadgītā*.

accepting only 12 of them as authentic.[39] If, indeed, Śaṅkara commented on Patañjali's text, he would have held the *śāstra* in high esteem, as an authoritative source of knowledge. This might serve to explain the high position of the yoga system within the SSS, itself a testimony of its status within the Advaita community.

Hacker even went so far as to suggest that Śaṅkara had been a *yogin* in his early career, [40] before becoming an Advaitin.[41] For his part, Govind Chandra Pande, aligning the work of Śaṅkara with Vācaspati Miśra, argues that the Vedāntic rejection of *yoga* is only partial and concerns mainly the dualistic and realistic elements of Sāṃkhya, whereas yoga's practical method tended to be harmonise with the early Advaita doctrine, *i.e.*, the one present in the BSB.[42] So far, so good. However, I will now show that, on more than one occasion, the *Patañjali-pakṣa-prakaraṇa* of the SSS mentions elements that are not in line with the YS, but rather appear to bear the mark of later developments. The exact ownership of such references will have to be sorted out in a later research. It suffices here to note the problematic mentions that have not been thoroughly examined by scholars yet:

1. The mention of kriyā-yoga: (SSS 10, 15)
   a. The verse defines the practice of *kriyā-yoga* (exertion in [ritual] performances) as: *kriyāyogas tapo mantrajapo bhaktir dṛḍheśvare.* Obviously, *kriyā-yoga* is not absent from the YS. It is mentioned in YS 2, 1: *tapaḥ svādhyāyeśvarapraṇidhānāni kriyāyogaḥ*. One can argue for a correlation between the SSS's trinity of *tapas* (austerity), *mantra-japa* (mantric recitation) and *bhakti* (devotion) and the YS trinity of *tapas*, *svādhyāya* (self-study) and *īśvara-praṇidhāna* (contemplation of the Lord). However, the compound *mantra-japa*[43] is foreign to the YS, as is the term *bhakti.*

39 See Pande (1994: 109).

40 However implausible that lifespan might be, let us observe that, in the case where it would be accurate, one who is supposed to have lived only 32 years, as Śaṅkara, can hardly have had a meaningful 'early' career.

41 Hacker (1968).

42 Pande (1994: 111).

43 The term *mantra* is mentioned only once in the whole YS (4, 1), in a section of the YS which is itself of debated authorship. In this context, it refers to magical formulas which allow one to acquire such powers (*siddhi*-s) as moving about through ether (*ākāśa*) or adopting a minute form (*aṇiman*), as the commentator Vyāsa explains: *mantrair ākāśagamanāṇimādisiddhilābhaḥ*. It has nothing to do with worship nor with the *praṇava* (the *Oṃ* syllable).

The term *japa* ([prayer] recitation) appears in YS 1. 28. It is associated by Vyāsa to the recitation of the *praṇava*, a meaning which might play in favour of reading the compound *mantra-japa* (mantric recitation) as a synonym of *svādhyāya* (self-study). However, this would give only a partial reading of *svādhyāya*, removing the study of treatises on liberation (*mokṣa-śāstra-adhyāyana*), which is an essential source of knowledge for Advaitins. For example, concerning *svādhyāya*, Michel Angot renders Vyāsa's commentary in the following manner: 'Le *svādhyāya* c'est le fait de murmurer des

  b. The SSS verse 10, 15 puts excessive emphasis on devotion to *Īśvara*, in comparison to YS 2, 1. This would be more in tune with a work of Vaiṣṇava leanings, or at least of a *bhakti* nature, but not necessarily in agreement with Śaṅkara's inclinations.

2. The absence of *āsana*-s in the YS and in Vyāsa: (SSS 10, 34)
   a. The SSS mentions six *āsana*-s (sitting postures), as noted already by Liebich: *padma, bhadra, mayūra, vīra, svastika* and *kukkuṭa.* Among them, none are in the YS and four are mentioned in its commentary. *Kukkuṭa* and *mayūra* are not mentioned either by the YS or by its *bhāṣya*, and appear to belong to a later development, popularised by *Haṭhayoga texts.*[44] More research is needed on this issue. It seems unlikely that Śaṅkara would have known or mentioned the two postures while discussing Patañjali's *Yoga.*
3. The absence of *prāṇāyāma*-s in the YS and in Vyāsa: (SSS 10, 37)
   a. The breathing practices of *recaka, pūraka* and *kumbhaka* are not mentioned either by the YS or by its *bhāṣya*, and appear to belong to a later development.
4. The absence of the *nāḍī* theories in the YS and in Vyāsa:
   a. The discussion in the SSS on the several *nāḍī*-s (channels), such as the *suṣumnā* (SSS 10, 50), the *iḍā* and *piṅgaḷā* (SSS 10, 54), the *kuhū, viśva-udarā* and *dhāraṇa* (SSS 10, 55), the *hasti-jihvā, yaśasvinī* and *sarasvatī* (SSS 10, 56), the *śaṅkhinī, payasvinī, gāndhārī* and *pūṣan* (SSS 10, 57), is foreign to the YS and its *bhāṣya.*
5. The absence of the alchemical metaphor in the YS and in Vyāsa: (SSS 10, 52)
   a. The alchemical allusion of the verse *yathā nītā rasendreṇa dhātavaś śātakumbhatām*[45] does not occur in the YS nor within its *bhāṣya.*

[sons] purificateurs comme le *praṇava* 'bourdonnement' (om, o) etc. ou bien c'est l'étude des traités de délivrance' (see YS 2012: 373). Thus, *japa* is only one potential way of doing *svādhyāya.*

As far as Śaṅkara promotes the 'path of knowledge' (*jñāna-mārga*), one wonders why he would replace the study (*svādhyāya*) of *śāstras*, in his description of Patañjali's YS, by mere mantric recitation (*mantra-japa*). To that effect, Natalia Isayeva clearly indicates that, for Śaṅkara, ultimate liberation from *saṃsāra* 'can be revealed not through ritual worship of Īśvara, or personified God, but only owing to a particular kind of knowledge (*jñāna*)' (see Isayeva 1993: 55–56). Another way of looking at the issue would be to see the alteration as intentional and meant to suggest that, because the study of treatises on liberation (*mokṣa-śāstra-adhyāyana*) is missing in Patañjali, this worldview (*darśana*) or insight is lesser, compared to the Advaita.

44 See *supra*, note 25.

45 Raṅgācārya translates as: 'Just as metallic ores, that have been turned into gold by the philosopher's stone ...'

b. The word *rasa* does occur in YS 2, 9, but within a completely different context: *svarasavāhi viduṣo'pi tathārūḍho'bhiniveśaḥ.*[46] Hence, the alchemical allusion of the SSS is not present in the YS.

The five anomalies that I have just outlined suggest that Śaṅkara, who supposedly had a good knowledge of the YS, in the event that the PYSV is his, and who would thus not have attributed to Patañjali ideas that were not his, is not the author of those lines.

The Authorship of Śaṅkara: All or Nothing?

This being said, now ~~that~~ we know for sure that several portions of the text are not from the hand of Śaṅkara, the author of the BSB. Does it refute the hypothesis that Śaṅkara might have composed at least some parts of the SSS? Indeed, is it necessary to adopt the position of all or nothing? Surely, the illustrious Advaita teacher did not compose the whole text. But does it mean that he had absolutely nothing to do with it? Liebich is prone to believe that later insertions within an original core are a possibility. I argue that, based on the composite nature of doxographies, and on the assessment of the function of doxography within the general propaedeutic of the Advaita, which I will present in the next section of this paper, rather than relying strictly on the critical analysis of selected passages of the SSS, as has been done before, it is reasonable to admit the possibility of a text composed in multiple stages, perhaps beginning with Śaṅkara. In fact, when keeping the composite (*saṅgraha*) nature of the SSS in mind, it is awkward to go about demonstrating the authorship of Śaṅkara based on some verses of the text alone, while we know that most of the SSS is not meant to express the author's own ideas. At best, most of the SSS's verses could either be borrowed from competing systems or offer a paraphrasing of their main ideas. Thus, analysing individual verses could help substantiate an approximate dating for example, as Liebich did. But, in the case of the SSS, the method used by Hacker to disqualify the authorship of Śaṅkara is unidirectional. It can disqualify Śaṅkara's authorship of some passages, limited to a single chapter of the SSS, the exposition of the Advaita, but it cannot prove his authorship of any passage, especially not of those unrelated to the Advaita. Hence, it can only disqualify some verses. For, even if Śaṅkara's style and terminology was found in the SSS, nothing can ascertain that it is not a skilful rendition by someone else. Thus, one using Hacker's method alone is left with the only option of disqualifying Śaṅkara's authorship of the SSS altogether, based on selected passages that do not

46 Angot (YS 2012: 398) translates the passage as: 'Persistent spontanément, le vouloir-vivre demeure même chez celui qui sait.' My own free translation of Angot: 'Persisting spontaneously, the will to live remains even in the one who knows.' On *rasāyana* in classical Yoga and Ayurveda, see Maas (2017).

reflect his doctrine and terminology, even if most of the SSS is preoccupied with other doctrines than Śaṅkara's Advaita. As its title explains, the SSS is a mere compilation (*saṅgraha*). It is neither an original work, in the sense that it would formulate new ideas, nor is it a commentary.

Perhaps a new critical edition, considering all the manuscripts available to this day,[47] could help clarify the issue of whether the text was composed in multiple stages or not. Concerning the five manuscripts used by Raṅgācārya, the Indian professor mentions[48] that the two main witnesses used for his edition were full of lacunae.[49] The exact nature of these lacunae is not explained further, but one can see the corrections brought to the texts in the footnotes of Raṅgācārya. The second manuscript from Madras, to which is attached the only available commentary, contains only the first eight chapters. The manuscript from Cochin contains only the last five chapters, whereas the one from Travancore merely contains the chapters on the Vaiśeṣika and the Nyāya systems. From these limited accounts, not having seen the manuscripts, but knowing that most witnesses reviewed by Raṅgācārya contained only some sets of chapters, it is difficult to assess the exact form of the original core text. However, this information needs to be reviewed, since my account of the SSS manuscripts indicates over a dozen 'complete' manuscripts. In any case, the elements that were identified by Hacker and myself as non-Śaṅkarian in origin, or as possible interpolations, appear to be concentrated around specific sections of the text, namely the Patañjali and Vedānta chapters, and their verses more or less follow one another within those sections. This could indicate later additions to a pre-existing set. These suggestions are highly speculative at this stage. Still, one can argue that the doxographical nature of the text could have allowed new elements to be easily aggregated to the core text in the course of time.

Indeed, the doxographical nature of the SSS, being a compendium, a *saṅgraha*, would facilitate aggregation. The *Nāṭyaśāstra* (BhN) attributed to Bharata defines a *saṅgraha* as 'a composition which men of knowledge acknowledge as aggregating with concision a multitude of precise topics taught in the *sūtra*-s and *bhāṣya*-s'.[50] This definition reflects what we know of the genre of doxography. For example, the Classicist André Laks describes how doxographies are either 'fragments' or 'testimonies' dependent on a certain tradition of transmission. The fragment is a literary quotation from an original source, whereas the testimony is rather an abridged version of, a paraphrase, a commentary or an allusion to a source.[51] Hence,

47 See my 'recension of the Manuscripts of the SSS by Region' at the end of this paper.

48 See *supra* note 3.

49 The two are the palm-leaf manuscript from Madras and the one from Mysore.

50 BhN 6.9

vistareṇa upadiṣṭānām arthānāṃ sūtrabhāṣyayoḥ | nibandho yo samāsena saṃgrahaṃ taṃ vidurbudhāḥ ||

The translation is mine. For various editions of the BhN, see Vatsyayan (1996; reprint); Ghosh (1951).

51 See Laks (2007: 27–29).

a doxographical compendium[52] is more or less a collection of topics gathered from here and there and reorganised according to a given strategy. This format can easily afford continuous additions without breaking the unity of the text, especially if the verses are given in a simplified Sanskrit formulation, as is the case for most of the SSS.

Thus, even if the SSS verses had been laid down by Śaṅkara himself, he would have been extracting them from whatever third-party sources he had access to. His authorship, in that case, could only be indirect, as that of a compiler. In other words, the ideas his verses would express would not be his. Only the structural pattern of the SSS and the exposition of Vedānta,[53] the one examined by Hacker, could genuinely be his. And this structural pattern, common among Advaita doxographies, is most significant. It thus remains necessary to wonder if Śaṅkara would have designed it himself or if he would have passed on an already established tradition, in the case where he would have composed the original core of the SSS. Otherwise, had he not conceived of it, would he have approved its method? To probe such queries, one must assess the method and function of doxography within the general propaedeutic of the Advaita.

The SSS in the Light of the Doxographical Propaedeutic of the Advaita

At this point, more needs to be said on the presence of doxography within the Advaita. Generally speaking, although the individual topics discussed within each section of a doxography can be aligned in an *ad hoc* manner, the overall structure of such texts, the sequence of their consecutive sections, betrays a deliberate dialectical strategy. Classicists like Laks, Mansfeld and Runia argued that dialectic is the *Sitz im Leben* of doxography. They were the first to notice how doxographical dialectic is teleological.[54] This is especially obvious in doxographies produced by the Advaitins. To that effect, Halbfass observed: 'the Advaita Vedānta doxographic texts are usually based upon a hierarchical classification at whose apex stands the Vedānta'.[55] What is more, not only is the whole hierarchical pyramid of views dominated by the superior position of the Advaita, but each view (*darśana*)

52 In his notes on a series of conferences on Indian doxography that he gave at *l'École pratique des hautes études*, Gerdi Gerschheimer, beyond the term *saṅgraha*, for 'compendium', also enumerates other Sanskrit words that indicate a doxographical content. He adds *samuccaya* and *saṃkṣepa*, explaining that they designate texts dedicated to exposing in a concise manner views or established doctrines which, in Sanskrit, are designated by the terms *darśana*, *siddhānta* and *mata*. See Gerschheimer (2000–01: 174).

53 I am inclined to believe that, if Śaṅkara had composed the original core of the SSS, for the sake of his students, he would have had no need to summarise his own doctrine. He would simply have explained how it comes as the final word, refuting all others.

54 For a brief overview of the topic, see Laks (1999: 49).

55 Halbfass (1988: 351).

positioned within the text is followed by another that is presented as its logical refutation, what Gokulbhai defines as 'the succeeding refuting the preceding',[56] leaving only the Advaita with no reply. Once this structure is understood, it becomes clear why the author of the SSS did not need to engage in the kind of minute *uttara-pakṣa* (reply to an objection) refutations found in doxographies of the kind of Bhāviveka's *Madhyamakahṛdayakārikā* (MHK), which entertains its own peculiar dialectical structure.

What Halbfass and Gokulbhai failed to notice, however, and what I will now seek to demonstrate, is that this peculiar teleology of Advaita doxographies reproduces a recurring Upaniṣadic pedagogical narrative pattern that Śaṅkara himself commented upon on several occasions and adopted as a teaching device. It is found, for example, in the famous end-story of the *Chāndogya Upaniṣad* (8.7.1–8.12.6), where Indra and Virocana approach their guru, Prajāpati, for instructions about the 'self' (*ātman*). Upon their initial request, they are given a preliminary answer, which happens to please Virocana, the king of demons: the self is like the body that can be seen from a reflection in water. Satisfied with so little, Virocana decidedly leaves his guru in peace and returns home. But, Indra, meditating on the unsatisfactory nature of the answer, comes back to seek further guidance. Several answers are then progressively given to the divine seeker, king among the gods, each time following a preparatory period of purification and contemplation on his part: the self is then said to be like the one who goes happily in a dream; later it becomes like one sleeping a dreamless night. Finally, after a final and shorter interlude, Prajāpati discloses an ever-subtler description of the elusive self, said to be venerated by the gods. Commenting on the story, Jonardon Ganeri made a significant observation worth contemplating while analysing the SSS:

> What is remarkable is the literary device used here, in which progressively more sophisticated accounts of the self are presented as grudging concessions of a recalcitrant god. Indra passes through a sequence of doctrines about the self, each one being an improvement on its predecessor, and perhaps one of the things the story is teaching us is that some such procession is necessary in the quest for self-knowledge. Among two doctrines or propositions, let us say that the first is a 'preparatory condition' for a second if understanding that the first is *false* is required of someone who is to be in a position even to speculate upon the truth or falsity of the second.[57]

Ganeri's remarks about the *Chāndogya* passage is perfectly suited to fathom the dialectic at play in the SSS. It serves to illustrate that the text was not merely meant as 1) a historiographical account of Indian philosophy, nor as 2) a mere introductory debate manual, but rather as 3) a pedagogical device to bring about some philosophical insights, for example inquiry into the nature of the self, using

56 Gokulbhai (2009: 128–131).

57 Ganeri (2012: 18–19).

competing views as many ladders supporting one another and leading towards an ever-subtler understanding of reality.

Angot (NS 2009) observes that the nature of 'truth', and the dialectical process that leads to it, entertained in the myth of Prajāpati, reveals a common Indian understanding of the value of words:

> Ce qui importe ce n'est pas de dire la vérité – celle-ci, au sens où nous l'entendons généralement, n'existe pas au niveau de la parole – que de dire une vérité qui vient élargir celle à laquelle précédemment on avait jusque-là accès.[58]

Similarly, for the Buddhists, Jainas and Advaita Vedāntins who produced doxographical texts, truth (*sat*) lies beyond the realm of words (*śabda*) and established opinions (*siddhānta*). The great Advaita theologian himself relegated the *Veda*-s and related scriptures (*āgama*-s), the very *āpta* (lit. 'authoritative [text]') of his system, to the realm of non-ultimate truth (*aparāvidyā*). This understanding relies on the *Muṇḍaka Upaniṣad* (1.1.4), for example. Accordingly, only Brahman is the ultimate truth (*parāvidyā*). Yet, as pointed out by Ganeri, the words of authorities act as indicators. They offer a guidance that, when carefully followed, effects a widening of views previously assumed, until truth is finally met face to face, without the remedy of words or concepts. This appears to be the Advaitic propaedeutic at play within the SSS.

The *Chāndogya* is not the only *Upaniṣad* to display such a device. Śaṅkara commented on a similar pedagogy in the *Bṛhadāraṇyaka* (Bṛ Up Bh 3.6.1), in a passage where Yājñavalkya responds to Gārgī's cosmological inquiry. Hirst (2005) also noted how this process of 'successively seeing what is more subtle' is found by Śaṅkara in the *Kaṭha Upaniṣad.* Moreover, she added:

> This idea of progressing through stages so that the self beyond all can be realised is shown clearly in Śaṃkara's explanation of what the Upaniṣad means by *saṃkrāmati* ('coming together' or 'going through') in *Tait Up* 2.8.5. [...] Rejecting the views that *saṃkrāmati* means 'attainment' of the self or identification with any one of the five sheaths (of food, breath, mind, understanding, and bliss), Śaṃkara concludes that it means 'realisation alone'. This is the realisation that the self is within yet other than the five sheaths which are simply misidentified with, or superimposed on the self. It is to the realisation of 'brahman (as) reality, consciousness, infinite' (Tait Up 2.1.1), beyond all conceptual construction, that the stages of understanding, through stories of manifestation and interiorisation, lead [...][59]

58 Angot (NS 2009: 115). My free translation: 'What matters is not to tell the truth – it, in the sense that we generally understand it, does not exist at the level of speech – but to tell a truth that extends the one to which we previously had access.'
59 Hirst (2005: 84).

Hirst argues that this 'process of interiorisation' of progressive doctrinal stages is central to Śaṅkara's own pedagogical method.[60] Beginning at his level of understanding,[61] the student must be progressively introduced to higher levels, until the ultimate experience of truth dawns upon him. Hence, it is plausible that the Advaita theologian would have reproduced the same propaedeutic to 'truth' within a short doxographical composition that aims to clarify his understanding of the position of Advaita among the theories of competing groups. If he did not compose the SSS himself, the thinker who did must have been acquainted with Śaṅkara's teaching technic.

What is worth emphasising here is that, just as the teleology at play in Bhāviveka's MHK reproduced the typical dialectic of 'no-view' adopted by Madhyamaka Buddhism, while the teleology of Haribhadra's ṢDS was in tune with the Jaina dialectic of *anekānta-vāda*, the SSS perfectly assimilated the dialectical attitude characteristic of its own Vedic tradition, as found within the *Upaniṣad*-s. Again, the dialectical endeavours found within each of these 'literary technologies'[62] were not solely interested in interreligious debates, but were rather primarily designed to bring about a specific knowledge of significant religious value, while disposing of heterogenous distorting views. In that sense, Indian doxographies in general appear as contemplative guides on the path to liberation, a path essentially resting upon knowledge (*jñāna-mārga*). They somewhat recall Rabbi Moshe ben Maimon's (Maimonides: 1135–1204 CE) famous *Guide for the Perplexed* (מורה נבוכים/ דלאלת אלחאירין) in intent.[63] In any case, one can safely argue that the doxographical

60 For further comments on Śaṅkara's pedagogical method, see also Hirst (2004: 1996).

61 This pedagogy is illustrated in the following Chā Up (7.1.1) quotation: 'Do teach, Venerable', said Nārada as he approached Sanatkumāra. To which he replied: 'come to me with that which you know, I shall explain from that level on.'

62 I am borrowing the expression 'literary technology' from the social studies of scientific knowledge. It was coined by Steven Shapin and Simon Schaffer, two historians of science, in their work *Leviathan and the Air Pump* (Shapin and Schaffer 1985). In a separate publication, Schaffer explains: 'The term "literary technology" indicates how scientists use texts as knowledge-producing tools and connects literary with other scientific work. […] These technologies help fashion the bearer of knowledge as authoritative and competent, and the item of knowledge as independent from the contingencies of human judgment. They make authors and they make facts. In this sense, the array of technologies helps order nature and society' (Schaffer 1998). I argue that doxographies use the epistemological framework of *pramāṇa*-s, in tune with the practice of the *hetu-vidyā* (logical science) to teleologically organise, according to a given propaedeutic, and at times even to examine and secure, claims about reality, so as to both convince and inform the views of their intended audience. In this sense, doxography is a contemplative philosophical literary technology.

63 In his prefatory remarks to the *Guide*, Maimonides stated his intention as follows: 'The object of this treatise is to enlighten a religious man who has been trained to believe in the truth of our holy Law, who conscientiously fulfil his moral and religious duties, and at the same time has been successful in his philosophical studies. Human reason has attracted him to abide within its sphere; and he finds it difficult to accept as correct the teaching based on the literal interpretation of the Law, and especially that which he himself or others derived from those homonymous, metaphorical, or hybrid expressions. Hence he is lost in perplexity and anxiety' (Friedländer 2002 [1st edn 1904]). Similarly, the readership of Indian doxographies, as discussed, is also one conscientiously fulfilling its moral and religious duties and desirous of success in philosophical studies.

presentation of various philosophical hypotheses, within the optic of a teleological dialectic, is an essential component of the propaedeutic methodology of the Advaita promoted by Śaṅkara,[64] itself a hodgepodge of multitudinous doctrines reinterpreted through a Mīmāṃsā-styled exegesis fundamentally resting upon Vedic scriptures. Bhāviveka, writing in the 6th century, already observed this heterogeneous state of affairs happening under the name of 'Vedānta' prior to Śaṅkara,[65] in the *Vedāntatattvaviniścaya* chapter of his MHK, the first written critic of the emerging Hindu system.[66]

In other words, I argue that the communication of the precise understanding of the tenets of Advaita passes through a careful examination and rejection of competing religious positions, and thus that doxographical expositions are no mere coincidences or 'beginners' guides'[67] within the system. Teleological dialectic

64 It has been argued that the Advaitins had extracted their main ideas and dialectics from Buddhism and other competing heterodox teachings, their doctrine consisting essentially in a doctrinal agglomeration. For an overview of the subject, see Isayeva (1993: 10–18). Others have argued that early Advaita doxographies already expressed a desire for sectarian unification (see Nicholson 2010). But the motive of this conglomeration of views might also be religio-philosophical in nature. I suggest considering this attitude towards 'the other' as a dialectical propaedeutic supporting a form of 'spiritual exercise', in addition to the previous readings.

65 Among the Vedānta sources relied on by Bhāviveka can be found the *Gauḍapādiyakārikā* (GK), a text of substantial importance for the doctrinal development of Śaṅkara. On the relation between Bhāviveka and the GK, see King (1995: 35–43).

66 See MHK 8, 86–104. For an English translation of the passages, one is advised to look in Qvarnström (2015: 185–190). Obviously, Bhāviveka's intent is polemical. But he was not the last one to make such observations. It is well known that Rāmānuja, a competing Vedāntin of the Viśiṣṭādvaita filiation, pejoratively labelled Śaṅkara a 'crypto-Buddhist' (*pracchanna-bauddha*), for his apparent adoption of Buddhist ideas and customs. See Isayeva (1993: 14). Modern scholars such as Frank Whaling have even suggested that without Buddhism there would be no Vedānta. See Whaling (1979: 27). Concerning the relation between Mīmāṃsā exegesis and Śaṅkara's system, Johannes Bronkhorst spoke of Śaṅkara's approach as nothing less than a 'palace revolution' within the Mīmāṃsā, meaning that, whereas the prior (*pūrva*) focus of the Mīmāṃsā was on *dharma*, the later (*uttara*) innovation of Śaṅkara is to subordinate the former to his enquiry into *brahman*. See Bronkhorst (2007: 38). Nonetheless, Śaṅkara's exegesis remains strongly influenced by the method of the Mīmāṃsā. Concerning Sāṃkhya, Nicholson (2010: 124–165) summarises the scholarship on the relation between Sāṃkhya's dualism and the Advaita's non-dualism.

67 I argue that the 'soteriological' significance of doxographical expositions, composed in a manner that varies within each religious system, has been overlooked in scholarship, and that this is why many are at pains to explain the relevance of such writings. Although the suggestion seems to betray a serious anachronism, the tendency is to identify Indian doxographical writings with a similar literature available in modern times: the introductory manuals to philosophy. Gokulbhai, for example, suggests: 'The only reason of writing the SSS seems to be the easy grasping of the tenets of all the philosophical systems prevalent, or rather famous in his times in India' (Gokulbhai 2009: 26). Halbfass also presented doxographies as an unimpressive 'by-product' of the Indian philosophical traditions which have unfortunately not 'evolved' to become like the 'Western literature on the history of philosophy' (Halbfass 1988: 355–356). I argue that such opinions betray their holders' inability to understand Indian doxography's method and purpose. They refer instead to a modern understanding of 'doxography' that is foreign to the Indian context.

is made especially important in the exegetical and soteriological context of the Advaita, where ignorance (*avidyā*) is equated with superimposition, *i.e.*, the erroneous attribution (*adhyāropa*) of wrong belief unto an object, and particularly upon the self (*ātman*); and where final beatitude (*apavarga*) consists in gaining the definite knowledge (*jñāna*) of truth, by removing any superimposed attribution. As Hirst mentioned, *adhyāropa-vāda* is the 'method par excellence' of Advaita.[68] By learning about the possible fallacies imputed to the self, through an investigation of non-Advaita positions presented against the background of authoritative scriptures, one becomes acquainted with an ignorance that needs to be identified prior to being neutralised. There is no doubt that *adhyāropa* is especially equated by the Advaitins with the views of their competitors. The 15th-century *Vedānta-Sāra* (VS) of Sadānanda, for example, following the Advaita soteriological propaedeutics, introduces a doxographical account of competing philosophical systems, including various Cārvāka-s, two Buddhists, the Prābhākara-s, the Tārkika-s[69] and the Bhāṭṭa-s within its exposition on *adhyāropa*.[70]

The practice of critically examining competing views is, however, not original to the Advaita, nor to doxography alone, but was already harnessed by Buddhists, among others, appearing under the name of *parīkṣā*, 'investigation', 'examination', an important component of the *Yogācārabhūmiśāstra*'s (YBhŚ) definition of the *hetuvidyā* (lit. 'the science of causes'), 'dialectics', which had a significant impact on later Buddhist philosophers.[71] For our present purposes, let us observe, along with Vincent Eltschinger, that *hetuvidyā* did not only serve apologetic purposes, but was also held to support religious *praxis* as a precondition to the reflective and meditative parts of the path,[72] by removing erroneous views and their corresponding ill-conceived actions. The removal of erroneous attribution (*adhyāropa*) through exegetical methods, as advocated by the Advaitins, thus shares close similarities with its Buddhist elder brother.[73] Similarities between the two worldviews are indeed many.[74] In this light, one better understands how the exposition and refutation of competing views are a significant part of the propaedeutic of the Advaita path.

68 Hirst (2005: 85).

69 Listed together with the Prābhākara-s, it is not clear who are these Tārkika-s referred to in this passage (VS 129), who are supposedly holding that ignorance is the self.

70 The doxographical section begins with the following verse:

'Now will be described the peculiar way so and so imposes this and that upon the individuated self' (*idānīṃ pratyagātmani idam idam ayam ayam āropayati iti viśeṣata ucyate* – VS, 122).

71 For the definition of *parīkṣā* within the YBhŚ, see Eltschinger (2014: 16–19).

72 Eltschinger (2014: 192).

73 On the function of reasoning within Śaṅkara's work, and Advaita in general, see Ram-Prasad 2000; 2001; 2007; Comans 2000; King 1995; Murty 1974.

74 For a historical retrospective of the topic, see Isayeva 1993: 19–30. See also Ram-Prasad 2001; 2007; King 1995; Kaplan 1992; Potter *et al.* 1981; Radhakrishnan 1914; 1929; Whaling 1979.

Coming back to Śaṅkara himself, his own BSB is replete with doxographical materials.[75] The second chapter of the BSB, on *avirodha* (lit. 'non-contradiction'), directly addresses most of the views enumerated in the SSS, namely Sāṃkhya, Yoga, Vaiśeṣika, Buddhist realism and idealism, Jainism and even the Bhāgavata view (absent in the SSS). For the missing Mīmāṃsā (*Prabhākara-pakṣa* + *Bhaṭṭācārya-pakṣa*) and *Vedavyāsa-pakṣa* sections, separately identified in the SSS, one may observe that the whole BSB is more or less an ongoing display of a Mīmāṃsā-styled exegesis of the *Brahmasūtra*, ascertaining the Advaita Vedānta perspective as ultimate. However, within the *Bhāṣya*, clear references to Kumārila or Prabhākara are hard to secure.[76] As for the *Lokāyāta-pakṣa*, meagrely presented in the SSS, it is implicitly refuted by the BSB, especially in the third section of the second chapter, which discusses the origin of the elements, of the mind, of the soul and so on.

Regarding the need for such dialectical discussions within the BSB, one can refer to the passage at 2.2.1, where Śaṅkara answers an opponent who asks, as if vexed that heterodox views were constantly being addressed, whether the views of the Sāṃkhya-s and so on had not already been refuted earlier and what is the need of discussing them all over again. Hence, Śaṅkara replies: 'What we have done so far was just to prove that their interpretations were mere fallacies and not the correct explanations. But here follows a refutation of their reasoning independently of the [Upaniṣadic] texts.'[77] Thus, he explains that his previous evaluation of opposing views refuted fallacious interpretations of scriptures on the ground of 1) a critical examination of authoritative scriptures alone, and that he is providing a second attempt of refutation on the ground of 2) reason, independently of scriptures, by examining the consistency of the views to be refuted. This method recalls the Buddhist definition of *parīkṣā*, provisionally defined by Eltschinger as:

> ... the evaluation, by means of reason(ing) (identified or not to the pramāṇas) and/or scripture (provided the opponent belongs to the same confessional denomination), of an opponents' theoretical and/or practical tenets in order to assess their rationality and, further, the soteriological relevance of the system as a whole [...][78]

There should be little doubt that the insistence of the author of the BSB on the critical examination and refutation of the views of others, as it was for the Buddhists, does not merely serve apologetic purposes, but is also understood as a crucial component of the religious *praxis* he is promoting. Hence, the redaction of a

75 Hugh Nicolson, for example, remarked: 'Even a cursory glance at the text shows that refutations of opposing views compose a large portion of the work' (Nicholson 2007: 530–531).

76 See Halbfass (1983: iii–iv).

77 Translation taken from Gambhirananda (1965: 368).

78 Eltschinger (2014: 18–19).

separate doxographical treatise on his part, dedicated exclusively to this dialectical exercise, would not be impossible.

In brief, the composition of a doxographical treatise is in tune with the general Advaita propaedeutic. I have argued that 1) Advaita doxographies reproduce a recurring Upaniṣadic pedagogic narrative pattern that Śaṅkara himself commented upon on several occasions and adopted as a teaching device; thus 2) the SSS perfectly assimilated the dialectical attitude characteristic of its own Vedic tradition; hence 3) doxographical texts like the SSS were not meant as a) a historiographical account of Indian philosophy, nor as b) mere introductory debate manual, but especially as c) pedagogical devices to bring about some philosophical insights of soteriological concern.

Summary on the Authorship: Unsettled

Now, where are we going with such observations? How do they pertain to the authorship of the SSS? First, I have mentioned that the 'all or nothing' attitude need not be applied to the SSS too strictly. For sure, however, some of its passages are not from the same author as the one of the BSB. Also, since the title of Śaṅkarācārya' was later used by the headteachers of the monastic lineages he is believed to have instigated,[79] it is possible that one or some of them contributed in part or in full to the redaction of the SSS under the same name. This being said, since doxography is not alien to the propaedeutics of the Advaita, but is rather one of its important pedagogical components, both in terms of doctrinal assimilation (for oneself – through self-study) and propagation (for others – through apologetics), it is thus plausible that the great Advaitin teacher himself might have already provided his students with an abridged version of the positions of his opponents in order to train them in recognising and neutralising the many faces of 'ignorance', synonymous with *adhyāropa*.

Would Śaṅkara have put such teachings down in writing by himself or would he have simply communicated it verbally and his disciples later compiled it? Or, did his disciples extract his views on other systems from his many works and compile them with whatever material they had available in relation to their opponents, putting together a kind of teaching device that might have been continuously improved upon and systematised? After all, other traditions, Buddhists and Jainas alike, already had at their disposal such literary technologies and their dialectical

79 The historical role of Śaṅkara in establishing the *maṭha*-s, though claimed by tradition, is not confirmed by inscriptional evidence. Matthew Clark argues that Śaṅkara might be seen as a transitional figure in the shift from Āgamic Śaivism to a new Brahmanical *advaita* institution that was established at Śṛṅgerī (see Clark 2006: 215). Nonetheless, the adoption of the title of 'Śaṅkarācārya', also referred to as *jagadguru* (world guru), by the headteachers of the *maṭha*-s, did eventually become a common practice. See Clark (2006: 79–80).

effectiveness is hardly arguable. None of these possibilities are mutually exclusive, except if one is to insist that the SSS had a single author throughout. Considering the relevance of doxographical lists within the Advaita's religious training, I am inclined to believe that Śaṅkara initiated the Advaita doxographical practice himself, either orally or in writing. A more thorough research could compare the presentations of opponents found in the BSB and in other works of Śaṅkara with the ones in the SSS, along with a general review of all the SSS manuscripts available to date. However, my purpose here was not to bring about the *Urversion* of the SSS, a task that could be considered at a later point.

It is nonetheless significant to observe that a doxographical impetus was present within the Advaita from its very beginnings, in concordance with its pedagogical and soteriological objectives. Thus, aware of how contentious this may sound, as it goes against a line of interpretation established since Hacker, I conclude that no decisive judgement can be made so far on the basis of either the arguments in favour of or against the authorship of Śaṅkara. It remains possible that the authorship of the core of the SSS might be, at best, obliquely attributed to the author of the BSB, through an oral transmission that he would have imparted; or, though less likely, through a basic written template initially forming the core of the SSS – such a basic core would need to be ascertained. This being said, one must keep in mind that, as I pointed out in the initial sections of this paper, the text contains numerous passages and expressions that could not plausibly come from his hand and would consequently have to be seen as later additions, with the unfortunate consequence of breaking the text in parts. On the other hand, rejecting any involvement whatsoever of Śaṅkara in the composition of the SSS had the consequence of discrediting its content and methodology in the eyes of contemporary scholarship. To balance such perceptions, I contend that Śaṅkara would have approved of the SSS structural teleology, which I presented as its dialectical propaedeutic, and that the text is a genuine product of the Advaita, which deserves attention in its own right, regardless of the identity of its author.

It is for this reason that this article began by aligning the several arguments in favour of or against the authorship of Śaṅkara, so as to identify and localise the problematic passages. I argued that these passages are found within precise locations of the text that could potentially be later additions, until proven otherwise. I explained how doxographies are, by nature, composite texts, and new contents can easily be added onto them without breaking their continuity. I then explained that, by adopting another critical perspective, leaving the philological analysis of peculiar passages and rather focusing on the doxographical nature of the text, what may be defined as a structural analysis, we see that doxography is in tune with Śaṅkara's pedagogy and is a logical development of his work as an embattled religious teacher. In this regard, the SSS even appears to support a form of spiritual exercise essential for the soteriological project of the Advaita.

Addendum: On the Dates of the SSS

The question of the dates of the SSS has seen several hypotheses. Of course, if one is to agree that the great theologian is its author, one must consider the possible dates of his life. This happens to be a much-debated issue. Isayeva and Harimoto have convincingly explained how the earliest possible limits for Śaṅkara's lifespan are 650 CE, while the latest are about 800 CE.[80] Hence, for our purpose, one could say that the earliest possible date of composition for some core parts of the SSS, if one is to believe that Śaṅkara is their author, lies somewhere in the second half of the 7th century.

On the other hand, the latest date ever given to the text SSS comes from Andrew Nicholson, who follows Halbfass and Pande, estimating a period between the 14th and 16th centuries.[81] However, Nicholson provides no argument for his claim and this date is nowhere mentioned in the sources he quotes. Pande himself refers all matters related to the SSS to an article in Hindi by Gopinatha Kaviraj, who discussed the text and rejected the authorship of Śaṅkara, among 200 other writings.[82] Concerning Halbfass, the situation is prone to leave one perplexed. Nicholson is, in fact, not the only one to quote Halbfass for dates he never mentioned. On several occasions, while discussing the inclusion of *yoga* among the *darśana*-s, James Mallinson declares the SSS to be from the 12th century.[83] His only supporting proof is a reference to Halbfass, the same provided by Nicholson. Yet, Halbfass never mentioned the 12th century as a possible date of the SSS, even less the 14th, at least not in the book quoted by Nicholson and Mallinson, *India and Europe*. The only mention of a date concerning the SSS found in Halbfass goes as follows:

> Other doxographic works, difficult to date but in any case all written after the first millennium, include: the *Sarvasiddhāntasaṃgraha*, which has been falsely ascribed to Śaṅkara and published a number of times [...][84]

One should note here that Halbfass does not give any reason for his supposed dates and seems to rely on Hacker for his views on the SSS. But Hacker himself did not provide any tentative dates of the SSS. Hence, we can conclude that the dates suggested by Nicholson and Mallinson are unsupported and that Halbfass only

80 Isayeva (1993: 85). Further detailed discussions can be found in Harimoto (2006); Pande (1994).
81 Nicholson (2010: 208, n. 30).
82 Pande (1994: 121). See also note 1.
83 Mallinson (2014: 240; 2017: xvii; 2016: 109). The date of the 12th century is also repeated with reference to Winternitz (1922, see below) in Clayton, Blackburn and Carroll (2006: 50) and in Ranganathan (2007: 330).
84 Halbfass (1988: 350).

provided a vague approximation which he saw as plausible,[85] and in need of no further defence.

In fact, the only scholar I have found who provided an argument for a date located in the 14th century is Hermann Jacobi in 1921.[86] This suggestion has been convincingly dismissed by Liebich,[87] who instead suggests that the text was written before the 10th century Bengali scholar Śrīdhara (*Nyāyakandalī*).[88] In his famous *History of Indian Literature*, Moriz Winternitz supports Liebich's reasoning and suggests that the SSS may thus be taken as a work of the 10th or 11th century, without providing further arguments.[89] Thus far, the only unchallenged latest date remaining, which is substantiated by arguments, is the one of Liebich: before the 10th century.

I would like to observe that, if taken in itself without additional proofs, this dating may appear weak, but could be substantiated by further studies in doxographical literature. If we take into consideration the fact that the SSS presents an extremely simplified and schematic account of competing views, slightly more detailed than the quite similar one provided in Haribhadra's (7th–8th century) *Ṣaḍdarśanasamuccaya* (ṢDS), and also taking into consideration that most early Indian doxographies were composed in verses, this may suggest that the SSS represents an early stage in the composition of philosophical compendia by the Advaitins. Already, by the 14th century, with the SDS of Mādhava, the genre had become more sophisticated and provided more minute details, in prose. This trend of providing more exhaustive accounts of the systems under review, in prose instead of verse, as the centuries pass, can generally be noticed among all the competing doxographical traditions. However, this argument needs to be measured along further proofs, as it provides no certainty. Contrary to Jacobi, who thought that the author of the SSS must have been a young and mediocre writer, I argue that the rudimentary style of similar early doxographies does not diminish the abilities of their authors. One should rather keep in mind the ahistorical and dialectical nature of such texts, in order to better appreciate their teleological structure and overall apologetic and soteriological strategies.

In any case, it would be rather odd to speculate on a date of the SSS coming later than the SDS, especially since the latter borrowed from the former, as mentioned.[90] Taking all these matters into consideration, I suggest that the core of the SSS might have been assembled between the eighth and tenth centuries – the

85 A similar relative datation is also given in Kanazawa (1989: 33, n. 10), and in Lariviere (1981: 185, nn. 32, 3).

86 His argument is based on the mention of the *rājasa jana* (SSS 11, 15–24), which Indian acquaintances of his (?) linked to the 'Mohamedan Turks', indicating that the SSS could only be written after 1311. See Jacobi (1921: 724). However, 14th-century date given to the SSS is also repeated without any argument in Billington (1997: 44).

87 Liebich (1923: 128).

88 Liebich (1923: 127).

89 Winternitz (2008: 506, n. 2, reprint German edn 1920).

90 See *supra*, note 23.

latest date coming at the cost of rejecting Śaṅkara's authorship – still allowing for later additions until the 14th century, when the SDS was composed.

Addendum

Recension of the Manuscripts of the SSS by Region
London:
Biswas 0568, IORL, 1896, under the entry *Sarva-siddhānta-saṅgraha*
No. 2442, Telugu, 2678a.
Madras:
Biswas 0633, GOML, 1940, under the entry *Sarva-darśana-siddhānta-saṅgraha*:
S.N. 23180, palm leaf, complete, D.17159;
S.N. 23181, *with karṇāṭaka-ṭīkā-sahitaḥ*, palm leaf, complete, N 44–2 (Kannaḍa).
Under the entry *Sarva-siddhānta-saṅgraha*:
S.N. 23225, paper, complete, D4760;
S.N. 23226, paper, complete, D.4761;
S.N. 23227, palm leaf, incomplete, D. 4762;
S.N. 23228, palm lead, complete, R. 5112;
S.N. 23229, with commentary of Śeṣagovinda, paper (Telugu), complete, D. 15319.
Mysore:
Biswas 0722, 1884: no entry.
Biswas 9709, GOL, 1967: no entry.
Trivandrum:
Biswas 1008 Trivandrum ORIML, 1986, under the entry *Sarva -siddhānta-saṅgraha*:
S.N. 19489, complete, 1021 B
S.N. 19490, complete, 5379 A
S.N. 19491, complete, 5959 B
S.N. 19492, complete, 8298 A
S.N. 19493, complete, C 2130
S.N. 19494, complete, C 2199 B
S.N. 19495, incomplete, 10538 D 2
S.N. 19496, incomplete, 13263 B
Biswas 1006, Maharajas Library, 1937–38: no entry.
Biswas 1000: no entry.
Undigitised vol. 7, suppl. ra-ha, 2000: no entry.

Abbreviations

BhN	Bharata. *Nāṭyaśāstra* (see Ghosh 1951; Vatsyayan 1996)
BSB	Śri Śaṅkarācārya. *Brahma-Sūtra-Bhāṣya* (see Gambhirananda 2009)
NS	Akṣapāda Gautama. *Nyāya-Sūtra* (see Angot 2009)
Praśastapāda	*Padārthadharmasaṃgraha* (see Ganaganatha 1982)

SSS Śaṅkarācārya *Sarvasiddhāntasaṅgraha* (see Sundar Bose 1929; Sūryanārāyaṇa Śukla 1930; Raṅgācārya 2006)
YS Patañjali. *Yoga-Sūtra* (see Angot 2012)

References

ANGOT, M. (ed. and trans.) (2009) *Le Nyāya-Sūtra De Gautama Akṣapāda, Le Nyāya-Bhāṣya D'akṣapāda Pakṣilasvāmin, L'art De Conduire La Pensée En Inde Ancienne.* Collection Indika. Paris: Les Belles Lettres.

ANGOT, M. (ed. and trans.) (2012) *Le Yoga-Sūtra De Patañjali, Le Yoga-Bhāṣya De Vyāsa, Avec Des Extraits Du Yoga-Vārttika De Vijṇāna-Bhikṣu, La Parole Sur Le Silence.* Collection Indika. Paris: Les Belles Lettres.

BELVALKAR, S.K. (1929) *Sri Gopal Basu Mallik Lectures on Vedānta Philosophy. Part 1.* Poona: Bilvakunja Publishing House.

BILLINGTON, R. (1997) *Understanding Eastern Philosophy.* London & New York: Taylor & Francis.

BRONKHORST, J. (2007) Vedānta as Mīmāṃsā. In Bronkhurst, J. (ed.), *Mīmāṃsā and Vedānta: Interaction and Continuity.* Delhi: Motilal Banarsidass, 1–91.

CLARK, M. (2006) *The Daśanāmī-Saṃnyāsīs, the Integration of Ascetic Lineages into an Order.* Brill's Indological Library 25. Leiden & Boston: Brill.

CLAYTON, J. (2006) *Religions, Reasons and Gods: Essays in cross-cultural philosophy of religion.* Prepared for publication by A.M. Blackburn and T.D. Carroll. Cambridge: Cambridge University Press.

CLOONEY, F.X. (1996) Strategies of Interpretation: Śaṃkara's commentary on Bṛhadāraṇyakopaniṣad. *Journal of the American Oriental Society* 116(1), 58–75.

COMANS, M. (2000) *The Method of Early Advaita Vedānta, a Study of Gauḍapāda, Śaṅkara, Sureśvara and Padmapāda.* Delhi: Motilal Banarsidass.

ELTSCHINGER, V. (2014) *Buddhist Epistemology as Apologetics: Studies on the History, Self-Understanding and Dogmatic Foundations of Late Indian Buddhist Philosophy.* Beiträge Zur Kultur- Und Geistesgeschichte Asiens. Wien: Ôsterreichisch Akademie Der Wissenschaften.

GAMBHIRANANDA, S. (ed.) (2009) *Brahma-Sūtra-Bhāṣya of Śri Śaṅkarācārya.* Delhi: Advaita Ashrama.

GANAGANATHA, J. (ed. and trans.) (1982) *Padārthadharmasaṃgraha of Praśastapāda, with the Nyāyakandalī of Śrīdhara.* Varanasi: Chaukhambha Orientalia.

GANERI, J. (2012) *The Concealed Art of the Soul, Theories of Self and Practices of Truth in Indian Ethics and Epistemology.* Oxford: Oxford University Press.

GERSCHHEIMER, G. (2000–2001) Systèmes « Philosophico-Religieux » (Darśana) Indiens Et Doxographies. *École pratique des hautes études, Section des sciences religieuses. Annuaire.* Tome 109, 173–189.

GHOSH, M. (ed.) (1951) *The Nāṭyaśāstra, a Treatise on Hindu Dramaturgy and Histrionics, Ascribed to Bharata-Muni, vol. I (Chapters I-Xxvii), Completely Translated for the First*

Time from the Original Sanskrit with an Introduction and Various Notes. Bibliotheca Indica Work no. 272. Calcutta, The Royal Asiatic Society of Bengal, 1951.

GOKULBHAI, P. M. (2009) *Sarvasiddhāntasaṅgraha – a Study.* Gujurat: Maharaja Sayajirao University of Baroda.

HACKER, P. (1968) Śaṅkara Der Yogin Und Śaṅkara Der Advaitin, Einige Beobachtungen. *Wiener Zeitschrift für die Kunde Süd-und Ostasiens* 12 3 (Festschrift E. Frauwallner), 119–148.

HACKER, P. (1978) Śaṅkārācarya and Śaṅkarabhagavatpāda, Preliminary Remarks Concerning the Authoriship Problem. In Schmithausen, L. (ed.), *Paul Hacker, Kleine Schriften.* Glasenapp-Stiftung. Wiesbaden: Franz Steiner Verlag, 41–58.

HALBFASS, W. (1983) *Studies in Kumārila and Śaṅkara.* Studien Zur Indologie Und Iranistik. Monographie 9. reinbeck: Dr. Inge Wezler Verlag für Orientalistische Fachpublikationen.

HALBFASS, W. (1988) *India and Europe: An Essay in Understanding.* New York: State University of New York Press.

HALBFASS, W. (1995) *Philology and Confrontation, Paul Hacker on Traditional and Modern Vedānta.* Albany: State University of New York Press.

HARIMOTO, K. (1999) *A Critical Edition of the Pātāñjalayogaśāstravivaraṇa, First Pāda, Samādhipāda, with an Introduction.* Philadelphia: University of Pennsylvania.

HARIMOTO, K. (2006) The Date of Śaṅkara: Between the Cāḷukyas and the Rāṣṭrakūṭas. *Journal of Indological Studies* 18, 85–111.

HARIMOTO, K. (2014) *God, Reason and Yoga, a Critical Edition and Translation of the Commentary Ascribed to Śaṅkara on Pātañjalayogaśāstra 1.23–28.* Indian and Tibetan Studies. Hamburg: Universität Hamburg – AAI-Abt. für Kultur u. Geschichte Indiens und Tibets.

HIRST, J.S. (2004) Images of Śaṃkara: Understanding the Other. *International Journal of Hindu Studies* 8 No. 1/3, 157–181.

HIRST, J.S. (2005) *Śaṃkara's Advaita Vedānta, a Way of Teaching.* Routledge Curzon Hindu Studies Series. London & New York: Routledge Curzon.

ISAYEVA, N. (1993) *Shankara and Indian Philosophy.* Albany: State University of New York Press.

JACOBI, H. (1921) 'Die Bhagavadgītā', Review of Die Bhagavadgītā, by Richard Garbe. *Deutsche Literaturzeitung* 42 50–51, 715–724.

KANAZAWA, A. (1989) Notes on the Sankarsa-Kānda: Under Stimulus from the Article by Lariviere. *Japanese Studies in Indian Philosophy* 57, 31–44.

KAPLAN, S. (1992) The Yogācāra Roots of Advaita Idealism? Noting a Similarity between Vasubhandu and Gauḍapāda. *Journal of Indian Philosophy* 20, 191–218.

KING, R. (1995) *Early Advaita Vedānta and Buddhism, the Mahāyāna Context of the Gauḍapādīya-Kārikā.* Suny Series in Religious Studies. Albany: State University of New York Press.

LAKS, A. (1999) Histoire Critique Et Doxographie, Pour Une Histoire De L'historiographie De La Philosophie. *Presses Universitaires de France, Les Études philosophiques,* La philosophie et ses histoires 4, 465–477.

LAKS, A. (2007) *Histoire, Doxographie, Vérité, Études Sur Aristote, Théophraste Et La Philosophie Présocratique.* Aristote. Traductions Et Études. Louvain-la-Neuve: Éditions Peeters.

LARIVIERE, R. W. (1981) *The Divyatattva of Raghunandana Bhaṭṭācārya: Ordeals in Classical Hindu Law.* New Delhi: Manohar.

LIEBICH, B. (1923) Bemerkungen Zu Śaṅkara's Sarva-Siddhānta-Saṅgraha. *Zeitschrift für Indologie und Iranistik* 2, 124–132.

MAAS, P.A. (2013) A Concise Historiography of Classical Yoga Philosophy. In Franco, E. (ed.), *Periodization and Historiography of Indian Philosophy* 37. Publications of the De Nobili Research Library. Vienna: Sammlung de Nobili, Institut für Südasien-, Tibet- und Buddhismuskunde der Universität Wien, 53–90.

MAAS, P.A. (2017) Rasāyana in Classical Yoga and Ayurveda. *History of Science in South Asia* 5 2, 66–84.

MAIMONIDES, M. (2002) *The Guide for the Perplexed by Moses Maimonides.* Skokie: Varda Books.

MALLINSON, J. (2014) Haṭhayoga's Philosophy: A Fortuitous Union of Non-Dualities. *Journal of Indian Philosophy volume* 42(1), 225–247.

MALLINSON, J. (2012) The Original Gorakṣaśataka. In Gordon White, D. (ed.) *Yoga in Practice.* Oxford: Princeton University Press, 57–72.

MALLINSON, J. (2016) Śāktism and Haṭhayoga. In Wernicke Olesen, B. (ed.) *Goddess Traditions in Tantric Hinduism, History, Practice and Doctrine.* Oxford: Routledge, 109–140.

MALLINSON, J. and SINGLETON, M. (2017) *Roots of Yoga.* London: Penguin Books.

MAYEDA, S. (1965) The Authenticity of the Bhagavadgītābhāṣya Ascribed to Śaṅkara. *Wiener Zeitschrift für die Kunde Süd-und Östasiens* IX, 155–194.

MAYEDA, S. (1965) The Authenticity of the Upadeśasāhasrī Ascribed to Saṅkara. *Journal of the American Oriental Society* 85(2), 178–196.

MURTY, K. S. (1974) *Revelation and Reason in Advaita Vedānta.* Delhi: Motilal Banarsidass.

NICHOLSON, A.J. (2010) *Unifying Hinduism: Philosophy and Identity in Indian Intellectual History.* New York: Columbia University Press.

NICHOLSON, H. (2007) Two Apologetic Moments in Śaṅkara's Concept of Brahman. *The Journal of Religion* 87(4), 528–555.

PANDE, G.C. (1994) *Life and Thought of Śaṅkarācārya.* Delhi: Motilal Banarsidass Publishers.

POTTER, K.H., HARZER, E., SASTRI, S.S., THRASHER, A.W. (1981) Advaita Vedānta up to Śaṃkara and His Pupils. In Potter, K.H. (ed.), *Encyclopedia of Indian Philosophies.* Volume III. Delhi: Motilal Banarsidass.

POUSSIN, L. DE LA V. (1902) Sarvasiddhāntasaṁgraha. *Le Muséon III*, 402–412.

QVARNSTRÖM, O. (2015) *Bhāviveka on Sāṃkhya and Vedānta, the Sāṃkhya and Vedānta Chapters of the Madhyamakahṛdayakārikā and Tarkajvālā.* Harvard Oriental Series, 78. Cambridge: Harvard University Press.

RADHAKRISHNAN, S. (1914) The Vedanta Philosophy and the Doctrine of Maya. *International Journal of Ethics* 24(4), 431–451.

RADHAKRISHNAN, S. (1929) *Indian Philosophy, Volume 2.* London: Harper Collins Publishers.

RAM-PRASAD, C. (2000) Knowledge and Action I: Means to the Human End in Bhāṭṭa Mīmāṃsā and Advaita Vedānta. *Journal of Indian Philosophy* 28, 1–24.

RAM-PRASAD, C. (2001) *Knowledge and Liberation in Classical Indian Thought*. Library of Philosophy and Religion. Hampshire: Palgrave.

RAM-PRASAD, C. (2007) *Indian Philosophy and the Consequences of Knowledge. Themes in Ethics, Metaphysics and Soteriology*. Hampshire: Ashgate.

RAṄGĀCĀRYA, M. (ed.) (2006) *The Sarva Siddhānta Saṅgraha of Śaṅkarācārya: Text with English Translation, Introduction, Notes, Glossary & Index*. Delhi: Eastern Books Linkers

RANGANATHAN, S. (2007) *Ethics and the History of Indian Philosophy*. Delhi: Motilal Banarsidass Publishers.

RUKMANI, T.S. (1993) Śaṅkara's Views on Yoga in the Brahmasūtrabhāṣya in the Light of the Authorship of the Yogasūtrabhāṣya-Vivaraṇa. *Journal of Indian Philosophy* 21, 395–404.

SANDERSON, A. (2002) Remarks on the Text of the Kubjikāmatatantra. *Indo-Iranian Journal* 45, 1–24.

SCHAFFER, S. (1998) The Leviathan of Parsonstown: Literary Technology and Scientific Representation. In Lenoir, T. (ed.), *Inscribing Science: Scientific Texts and the Materiality of Communication, Writing Science*. Palo Alto: Stanford University Press, 182–222.

SHAPIN, S, and SCHAFFER, S. (1985) *Leviathan and the Air-Pump: Hobbes, Boyle, and the Experimental Life. Including a Translation of Thomas Hobbes Dialogus Physicus De Natura Aeris*. Princeton: Princeton University Press.

SŪRYANĀRĀYAṆA ŚUKLA, Ś. (ed.) (1930 (undated print)) *Sarvasiddhāntasaṃgraha, Śrīmacchaṅkarācāryaviracitaḥ*. Kāśī: Kāśī Viśvanātha Press

SUNDAR BOSE, P. (ed.) (1929) *Critically Edited, Translated and Annotated by Prem Sundar Bose*. Calcutta: Navavidhan Press.

VATSYAYAN, K. (ed.) (1996) *Nāṭyaśāstra*. New Delhi: Sahitya Academy.

WHALING, F. (1979) Śaṅkara and Buddhism. *Journal of Indian Philosophy* 7, 1–42.

WINTERNITZ, M. (2008) *History of Indian Literature, Volume III, Part One: Classical Sanskrit Literature, Part Two: Scientific Literature. Translated from German into English by Subhadra Jha*. Delhi: Motilal Banarsidasss.